In Praise of Bureaucracy

D0995434

In Praise of Bureaucracy

Weber • Organization • Ethics

Paul du Gay

SAGE Publications
London • Thousand Oaks • New Delhi

© Paul du Gay 2000

First published 2000

 SAGE Publications Ltd
6 Bonhill Street
London EC2A 4PU

SAGE Publications Inc
2455 Teller Road
Thousand Oaks, California 91320

SAGE Publications India Pvt Ltd
32, M-Block Market
Greater Kailash – I
New Delhi 110 048

British Library Cataloguing in Publication data

A catalogue record for this book is
available from the British Library

ISBN 0-7619-5503-8
ISBN 0-7619-5504-6 (pbk)

Library of Congress catalog card number   00–131348

Typeset by M Rules
Printed and bound in Great Britain by Athenaeum Press,
Gateshead

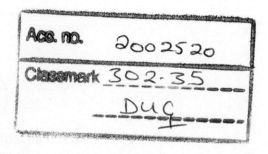

For my parents, Pat and Peter du Gay

Contents

Preface

This is a book about bureaucracy and ethics. More specifically, it is a book about the *ethos* of bureaucratic office. It represents an attempt to recover a certain ethical dignity for a particular form of institution – the bureau – and category of person – the bureaucrat – that have been the target of considerable critical denigration in recent years.

This exercise in recovery is necessary for two reasons. First, because bureaucratic conduct is frequently represented by its critics as inherently unethical. Indeed, talk of 'bureaucratic ethics' is often considered a contradiction in terms. Secondly, because even when bureaucracy is regarded as furnishing an ethos, it is one that is increasingly regarded as outmoded, anachronistic and irrelevant. In an 'external environment' characterized, it is said, by extreme uncertainty, where the capacity to be flexible, innovative and entrepreneurial is at a premium, 'rule-bound' bureaucracy has no future as an organizational form.

The argument of this book is that on both counts, criticism of the bureau is misplaced. In undertaking this exercise in recovery it is important, however, not to imply that bureaucracies are somehow infallible or the best of all possible organizational forms for all circumstances. Adopting such a line would be as ludicrous as suggesting that all bureaux are unethical and inefficient regardless of context. My aims here are more limited. First, to indicate that 'bureaucracies' do not fail in the manner alleged by both their humanist critics in the academy nor in the manner alleged by the advocates of 'entrepreneurial governance' or 'new managerialism' – that is, fail to realize ultimate moral ends, whether these are identified with 'humanity', 'liberty', 'economy', 'community' or any number of other rationales. Secondly, to suggest that while there are undoubted similarities between forms of managerial and other non-manual work in public bureaux and commercial enterprises, there are also significant differences in what we might term their respective 'regime values' – mainly imposed by the constitutional and political environment in which public governmental work is conducted. These significant differences raise a number of important questions concerning the wisdom of attempting to 'reinvent' public bureaux in the image of particular private sector business models. However, this should not be taken to imply that public bureaux are somehow beyond criticism or reform. To the contrary, I suggest that bureaucratic government is a highly contingent affair, dependent upon a quite limited set of ethico-political practices and techniques and on a quite fragile ethical environment.

The point is that these rare, reliable but fragile practices and techniques should not be denigrated for their failure to express a certain morality or to achieve certain 'social objectives' that they are not designed to meet. Instead, they should be respected for their limited but nonetheless important achievements – such as the capacity to divorce the administration of public life from private moral absolutisms – achievements that those of us who are lucky enough to live in pacified socieities should not take so readily for granted. For if we allow radical humanist critique or entrepreneurial discourse to set the terms by which the bureaucratic ethos of office is to be understood and evaluated, then we might expect the job that the public bureau performs for us, among us, to become increasingly inconceivable. Perhaps it is time, once again, to appreciate the ethos of bureaucratic office – albeit in a suitably contextualized manner – as a positive extension of the repertoire of human possibilities rather than merely as a dehumanizing or disempowering subtraction. This book is an attempt to contribute to such a reconsideration.

Acknowledgements

The intellectual and personal debts I have accumulated in writing this book are too numerous to permit each to be acknowledged individually. Nonetheless there are individuals and institutions whose support has been too invaluable to forgo mentioning.

I would like to thank, first, Richard Chapman, Ian Hunter, Jeffrey Minson and David Saunders whose work has motivated this book in ways they are probably not aware of and might well be surprised by. I would also like to acknowledge an intellectual debt to Mark Freedland, Robert Parker and John Rohr; individuals I have never met or corresponded with but whose work I have found myself continually returning to.

Preparatory research for the book was greatly facilitated by a Visiting Research Fellowship at the Australian Key Centre for Cultural and Media Policy at Griffith University. I would like to thank that institution and, in particular, its (then) staff: Tony Bennett, Colin Mercer, Denise Meredyth and Gillian Swanson, for their generous hospitality and support.

A considerable portion of the book was written in the stimulating enviornment of the London School of Economics, where I was a Morris Ginsberg Senior Research Fellow in Sociology during the 1997–98 academic year. I am grateful to the staff of the Sociology Department and especially to Eileen Barker, Stan Cohen, Jacqui Gauntlett, Stephen Hill and Colin Mills for their assistance and encouragement.

A big debt is owed to friends and colleagues who discussed ideas with me, allowed me to steal theirs and generally kept me going. I would like to thank especially: Frances Bonner, John Clarke, Gill Court, Louise Goebel, Stuart Hall, Linda Janes, Liz McFall, Danny Miller, Beverley Mullings, Keith Negus, Sean Nixon, Mike Pryke, Graeme Salaman and Margie Wetherall.

Last but by no means least, I would like to thank Jessica Evans who read through the whole thing and whose acute criticisms, keen editing skills and much else besides cannot be recompensed in a few words, no matter how well chosen.

Introduction: Bureaucratic Morality

These are not the best of days for bureaucracy. Everywhere its demise is reported, demanded and, more often than not, celebrated. The bureau carries a very hefty 'charge sheet', inscribed with multiple offences ranging from the relatively banal – procrastination, obfuscation, circumlocution and other 'typical products' of a 'red tape' mentality – to the truly heinous – genocide, totalitarianism, despotism. Indeed, to judge by some accounts 'bureaucracy', more often than not in conjunction with 'the state', appears to be responsible for most of the troubles of our times.

While anti-bureaucratic sentiment may be pervasive it is not necessarily uniform. There are many variants on the theme in current circulation although three in particular stand out. The first of these is relatively simple to delineate. We might refer to it as the 'popular' conception.

Here, 'bureaucracy' is a term associated with the defects of large organizations applying rules to cases. While such a conception is not peculiar to public sector management, it should be noted that this form of anti-bureaucratic sentiment has been expressed most frequently and vociferously in relation to the activities of state bureaux. Thus, the popular conception often appears to be little more than a long list of what people do not like about their relations with modern, 'positive' government: 'red tape', regimentation, a rising flood of forms, impersonalism and so on and so forth.

Now while these complaints are certainly based on 'facts' of experience it is interesting to note that they often seem to cancel each other out. The citizen who scoffs at the elaborate record keeping undertaken by government offices might well be equally annoyed should an official lose track of her affairs through relying on memory and telephone conversations. Similarly, the common complaint that government departments endlessly follow precedent might well lose its moral force if we find out that we have not received exactly the same treatment as our neighbour, friend or lover did in the same circumstances this time last year.

As Robert Parker (1993: 53–4) has indicated, popular anti-bureaucratic sentiment trades on two dramatic, but rather contradictory representations of the 'typical bureaucrat'. One has this creature endlessly drafting diabolical regulations, 'cunningly contriving new controls over the private citizen' while extending its own, malign influence. The other has bureaucrats positioned as idle loafers, spending their days – as two enthusiastic and influential advocates of contemporary public sector reform have it – 'reading magazines, planning sailing trips, or buying and selling stocks', all at the taxpayers' expense (Osborne and Gaebler, 1992: 127). Both have their heads down, but in rather different postures!

At the very least these somewhat contradictory representations suggest that bureaucracy is not a simple phenomenon, and that 'popular' conceptions of it are confused and paradoxical.[1] More positively though, they also suggest that while we may sometimes experience a sense of personal frustration in our dealings with state bureaux, we might learn to see such frustration as a largely inevitable by-product of the achievement of other objectives that we also value very highly: such as the desire to ensure fairness, justice and equality in the treatment of citizens – a crucial qualitative feature of modern government that we largely take for granted. Peter Blau (1956) long ago argued that detailed information that offends or irritates the individual from whom it is requested is exactly the requirement of efficient and effective administration. And as Parker (1993: 62) suggests, 'the bureaucratic revolution', in the sense of an office-ridden, form-ridden, regulation-ridden existence is largely inevitable as long as we want modern, democratic, positive government. We may be able to get along with fewer forms and simpler forms and thinner files, but forms and files will always be with us, and the sensible, if not always emotionally satisfying, thing is to learn to live with them.

This in turn suggests, as John Rohr (1989: 185–6) has eloquently argued, that it is not altogether wise for citizens to apply to state bureaux the sorts of moral or ethical analyses they routinely apply to matters of individual conscience. Rather, it is important for citizens to recognize that state bureaucracy might possess its own ethical and moral legitimacy – its own independent 'bureaucratic morality' (Dwivedi and Olowu, 1988; Rohr, 1988).

The idea that bureaucracy might be a substantive ethical domain in its own right not only flies in the face of 'popular' reasoning about state bureaux, it also offends certain influential social theoretical and philosophical conceptions of bureaucracy that also regard this form of organization as inherently unethical. In this second variant of anti-bureaucratic sentiment, the bureau is routinely conceived of as the one-sided expression of an 'instrumental rationality' which can sustain its identity only through repressing and marginalizing its 'other' – the emotional, the personal, the sexual and so forth. From this perspective, 'bureaucratic culture' is assumed to be based upon a series of 'foundational separations and exclusions' – between reason and emotion, pleasure and duty, public and private and so on – whose 'absent presence' erupts on to the organizational surface in the form of cumulatively disabling dysfunctions. It is further assumed that these separations and exclusions are coterminous and historically invariant and that, as a result, the rational conduct of bureaucratic office is both ethically and emotionally vacuous.

In the field of organizational analysis (broadly defined), for example, this particular form of reasoning has emerged in recent years as something akin to a 'nodal point' connecting a number of diverse strands of critique – from the overtly populist bureaucracy-bashing prescriptions of the management gurus through the 'epochal' theorizing of contemporary postmodernist and post-stucturalist organizational sociology to radical feminist analyses of the gendered nature of bureaucratic rationality.[2] Whether the critic of bureaucratic culture in question is Tom Peters (1987, 1992, 1994), Zygmunt Bauman (1989; 1993) or Rosemary Pringle (1989), certain shared assumptions are discernible. Chief amongst these is a thoroughly romantic belief that the principle of a full and free exercise of personal capacities is akin to a moral absolute for human conduct.

This principle represents something of a benchmark against which the general inadequacy of bureaucratic norms and procedures is to be registered. The specializations of function and conduct attendant upon bureaucratic organization are represented as introducing a violent 'split' into individual subjective and social being. The instrumental 'spirit of bureaucracy' makes fragmented and anomic that which should be organic and 'whole'. It is because bureaucracy fosters only rational and instrumental human faculties, to the exclusion of an individual's sexual, emotional, or other substantive dispositions, that it must be seen as a fatally flawed vehicle for the realization of moral personality.

Common to this form of critique is the treatment of instrumental and value-oriented action as two sides of a single moral and political whole. What might rather be thought of as a distinction, in the manner Rohr (1989) suggests, between different socio-ethical comportments – the distinction between the pursuit of ethical goals as absolute imperatives, in the field of religion, for example, and their pursuit within the limits of a procedurally organized environment, in the bureau, say – is thus treated as a normative (philosophical) distinction between the ethical as such and something else entirely: the technical, the amoral and so on. Once this normative hierarchy is in place, it can be used to frame a general discrimination between 'citizenly' commitments and 'official' duties, for instance, as if this were a distinction between the ethical as such and its 'other': the instrumental, the prudential, the technical. In this understanding of the matter, 'morality' can only be returned to 'public service' once the 'wound' or 'split' is healed, when official and citizenly commitments, for example, are once again aligned, and hence the human personality is again morally and ethically integrated.

This form of bureau critique relies for its effectiveness upon a theoretical lexicon that is self-consciously Weberian. Taking over some of Weber's chief theoretical categories, such as the distinctions between 'formal' and 'substantive' rationality, it marries these to a reading of his analysis of

bureaucracy to produce a scathing romantic critique of bureaucratic governance. The reading of Weber that these critics prefer is a remarkably
familar one. Weber is positioned as the grand theorist of modernity, whose
analysis of the rationalization of existence highlights the interrelated
material and cultural transformations that implanted formal or instrumental rationality as the dominant regulative principle in the
development of modern societies. Bureaucracy plays a crucial role here,
we are told, because it is the primary institutional carrier of 'formal
rationalization'.

In this reading then, Weber's central theme is assumed to be the increasing instrumental rationalization of all spheres of human conduct, the
crucial role played by bureaucracy in this, and the ethical and emotional
disfigurements this produces. 'Rational bureaucracy' is continually associated here with the Weberian metaphor of the 'iron cage'. Similarly,
bureaucrats are rendered inhuman through their representation as specialists without soul and 'automata of the paragraphs'.

While this reading of Weber has achieved a near axiomatic status, certainly within the social sciences, the conclusions drawn concerning the
ethical and moral defects of the bureau appear to be the very antithesis of
those posited by Weber himself (see Hennis, 1988, 1996; Turner, 1992). In
his classic account of the profession and vocation of bureaucratic 'office-
holding', Weber (1978: 958ff.) refuses to treat the impersonal, expert,
procedural and hierarchical character of bureaucratic reason and action as
unethical or morally bankrupt. Instead, he makes it quite clear that the
bureau comprises a particular ethos, or *Lebensführung* – not only an ensemble of purposes and ideals within a given code of conduct but also ways
and means of conducting oneself within a given 'life-order'. In other
words, and in a move almost identical to that made more recently by Rohr
(1989), Weber insists that the bureau must be assessed in its own right as a
particular moral institution and that the ethical attributes of the bureaucrat
be viewed as the contingent and often fragile achievements of that socially
organized sphere of moral existence.

The ethical attributes of the 'good' bureaucrat – adherence to procedure,
acceptance of sub- and superordination, commitment to the purposes of
the office and so forth – do not therefore represent an incompetent subtraction from a 'complete' or 'all-round' conception of personhood. Rather
they should be regarded as a positive moral and ethical achievement in
their own right. They represent the product of particular ethical techniques
and practices through which individuals develop the disposition and
capacity to conduct themselves according to the ethos of bureaucratic office
(Weber, 1978; Hunter, 1991; Minson, 1993).

Weber's argument that bureaucracy constitutes a substantive ethical
domain in its own right poses a significant challenge to the key assumption
underpinning this second strand of bureau critique: that the principle of a
full and free exercise of personal capacities can be made to function as an
'ultimate' ethical comportment for human beings. As Weber makes clear,

modern, highly differentiated societies are comprised of many discrete ethical domains and these neither represent different versions of some single homogeneous good nor fall into any natural hierarchy. The temptation to treat the ethical persona of the bureaucrat as a partial realization of the principle of 'complete' personal development is thus one that should be avoided.

The third and final strand of contemporary anti-bureaucratic sentiment is seemingly less abstract and philosophical than the second. Indeed, significant changes in the working practices of millions of public officials have been, and continue to be, conducted under its auspices. This variant of bureau critique derives from two distinct discursive locales – public choice theory and contemporary managerialism (Campbell, 1993; du Gay, 1995; Self, 1993). There are obvious differences between the two – with public choice casting the problem of the public bureau as one of 'control' and seeking measures through which elected representatives might tame the autonomy of the bureau by putting it under tighter political control, and managerialists problematizing the defects of the public bureau in terms of its failure to work more like a commercial enterprise. However, they can nonetheless be seen to work together to constitute a particular discursive formation. For example, public choice theorists have advocated many managerialist measures to achieve tighter political control of public bureaux while managerialists have frequently cited public choice axioms concerning the budget-maximizing propensities of unelected bureaucrats as evidence when arguing that public service bureaucracies need to be structured more like private enterprises (Campbell, 1993: 123).

The problematizations of public bureaux, and the main ingredients for their reform, emerging from this discursive formation have come to be known collectively as 'the new public management' and, more recently, as 'entrepreneurial governance'. According to the authors commonly charged with formulating the latter term, 'entrepreneurial governance' consists of ten 'essential principles' which link together to 'reinvent' public sector organizations:

> Entrepreneurial governments promote *competition* between service providers. They *empower* citizens by pushing control out of the bureaucracy, into the community. They measure the performance of their agencies, focusing not on inputs but on *outcomes*. They are driven by their goals – their *missions* – not by their rules and regulations. They redefine their clients as *customers* and offer them choices – between schools, between training programs, between housing options. They *prevent* problems before they emerge, rather than simply offering services afterward. They put their energies into *earning* money, not simply spending it. They *decentralize* authority, embracing participatory management. They prefer *market* mechanisms to bureaucratic mechanisms. And they focus not simply on providing public services but on *catalyzing* all sectors – public, private and voluntary – into action to solve their community's problems. (Osborne and Gaebler, 1992: 19–20)

These ten elements or principles comprise something like a 'shopping list' for those seeking to modernize state bureaux in OECD countries. Even when allowing for real and significant differences between countries, most modernization efforts have involved the simultaneous deployment of a number of these key elements. At the very least, it is obvious that the principles articulated by Osborne and Gaebler and the mechanisms used to operationalize them do interact quite strongly. So, for example, the separation of purchasing from provision is a prerequisite for the introduction of market-type mechanisms, which are, in turn, a crucial means of disaggregating traditional bureaucracies. Similarly, the setting of performance targets is a useful precursor to moving the terms of employment for bureaucrats towards fixed-term contracts and performance- related pay schemes (Pollitt, 1995). In other words, there do seem to be good reasons for regarding these ten elements or principles as something like an interacting set or system, as Osborne and Gaebler suggest they are, rather than evaluating each as if it were a single and distinct project or programme. As the Australian Department of Finance indicated: 'the various strands of reform are no accident of history. They are mutually supportive and their integrated nature is crucial to the overall success of the reforms' (quoted in Pollitt, 1995).

If the new public management or 'entrepreneurial governance' has one overarching target – that which it most explicitly defines itself in opposition to – then it is the impersonal, procedural, hierarchical and technical organization of the Weberian bureau. Put simply, bureaucratic government is represented as the 'paradigm that failed' in large part because the forms of organizational and personal conduct it gave rise to and fostered – adherence to procedure and precedent, abnegation of personal moral enthusiasms and so forth – are regarded as fundamentally unsuited to the exigencies of contemporary economic, social, political and cultural environments. In an era of constant and profound change, a new paradigm is required for the public sector if that sector is to survive at all. Entrepreneurial governance is represented as just such a paradigm.

Quite obviously, a key feature of entrepreneurial governance is the crucial role it allocates to a particular conception of the commercial enterprise as the preferred model for any form of institutional organization of goods and services. However, in keeping with its own ethico-cultural concerns, of equal importance is the way in which the term refers to capacities and comportments that display or express enterprising qualities on the part of individuals and collectivities, characteristics such as responsiveness to users' desires and needs, keener personal ownership of one's work and the wider goals and objectives it contributes to and the ability to accept greater responsibility for securing certain outcomes efficiently.

Refracted through the gaze of entrepreneurial governance, bureaucratic culture appears inimical to the development of these capacities and dispositions and hence to the production of enterprising persons. The bureaucratic commitment to (local and specific) norms of impersonality, neutrality, objectivity and so forth is regarded as antithetical to the cultivation of the sorts of entrepreneurial competences which alone are held to guarantee a manageable and hence sustainable future. Thus, entrepreneurial governance not only provides a critique of bureaucratic culture, it also offers a solution to the problems posed by continuous and unrelenting change through delineating certain principles which, when taken together, constitute a 'total' method for governing organizational and personal conduct in the present.

Because this approach presupposes that no organizational context is immune from the winds of change, it naturally assumes that all organizations – whether hospitals, charities, banks or government departments – will need to develop similar norms and techniques of conduct, for without so doing they will lack the capacity to pursue their preferred projects. As Kanter (1990: 356) forcefully argues, all organizations – public, private and voluntary – 'must either move away from bureaucratic guarantees to post-entrepreneurial flexibility or . . . stagnate – thereby cancelling any commitments they have made'.

While such insistent singularity has obvious attractions – offering as it does an easily graspable and communicable worldview that can act as a catalyst of transformation – it does tend towards a 'one best way' or 'universal science' approach to the conduct of management that has proven, historically, at best questionable (Elcock, 1995; Self, 1997). Even if one accepts that there may be some generic management principles that are 'universally' applicable (and that requires a considerable leap of faith) they are always applied in a specific context, including a value context. The nature of the management task, and the appropriateness of the management method deployed, can be defined only in relation to the objectives of the organization being managed, the values to be upheld by its managers as determined by its governors and the status of its relationships with its users, whether citizens, clients, consumers or customers. In this sense, as Rohr (1988: 167) indicates, management is best understood as a 'function of regime and not as a universal science'.

While there are undoubted similarities between forms of managerial and other non-manual work in public bureaux and commercial enterprises, there are also significant differences in regime values – mainly imposed by the political environment within which public governmental work is conducted – which may make it highly undesirable for public officials to model their conduct too closely on that of their private or commercial management counterparts. As Ivor Jennings (1971: 26) rather quaintly, yet also pertinently, put it, 'allegations of procrastination, lack of imagination and "red tape"' levelled against state bureaux by those who would have them act more like commercial enterprises 'are not entirely justified':

> It is true that a decision on an important issue may take time. A business man may be able to gamble on his "hunch" because he makes profits on the swings

when he suffers losses on the roundabouts. A civil servant must not make a mistake because he is acting on behalf of his Minister, and neither a minister nor a civil servant can balance his successes against his failures. It is usually necessary, therefore, for two or more civil servants to be consulted, and this process takes time. 'Red tape' is commonly associated with financial control. The business man can risk losses provided he makes a sufficient profit over the year. The public and the House of Commons rightly insist that there shall be no losses of public funds. Financial 'red tape' has been laid down not so much by the Treasury as by the Public Accounts Committee of the House of Commons, a body...which has developed a whole volume of rules and precautions which it expects the Treasury and the Comptroller and Auditor general to enforce against the departments . . . These restrictions affect the speed and efficiency of administration, not through defects in the civil servants but through the very nature of public administration. (1971: 26)

This once again focuses attention on the issue of the milieu-specificity of particular norms of conduct and comportments of the person. It also returns us once more to the work of Max Weber. After all, wasn't it Weber (1978: 1404) who suggested that the ethos governing the conduct of the state bureaucrat and that governing the conduct of the business leader were non-transferable? Indeed, in addressing the kinds of responsibilities these 'persons' have for their actions Weber insisted on the irreducibility of different spheres of ethical life and on the consequent necessity of applying different ethical protocols to them. For him, any attempt 'to establish commandments of identical content' across 'life orders', whether philosophically or managerially motivated, was a distinctly 'unworldly' endeavour .

What all three forms of bureau critique outlined above share is just such a tendency towards this sort of 'unworldliness'. In their different ways, they evaluate the ethos of bureaucratic office in relation to its failure to register a certain sort of morality. For the populist and philosophical variants, the failure is registered in terms of a distinction between personal and collective morality. Because the ethos of bureaucratic office is antithetical to the consistency and interactive unity of heart and mind which both of these variants appear to expect of an 'authentic' moral personality, it is interpreted as a symptom of moral failure.

For the entrepreneurial managerialists, the ethico-moral demands are rather different. Here, the (public) bureau 'fails' because it is seen to be incapable of fostering the forms of conduct and habits of action – entrepreneurial morality – that are deemed essential for organizational survival and flourishing in the dislocated external environments of the present. Unless public bureaux learn to become more entrepreneurial, it is argued, they will lack the capacity to pursue their goals and objectives.

This raises some important questions. For example if, as Weber suggested, the ethos governing the conduct of the state official and that governing the conduct of the entrepreneur are indeed non-transferable, what exactly are the gains to be derived from making public bureaux function more like business enterprises? If public bureaux do take up the entrepreneurial challenge and reinvent themselves in the manner suggested, might this not serve to incapacitate their ability to pursue certain of their goals and objectives by redefining the very nature of their organizational project? If management is a function of regime, then might not the 'regime values' embedded in the British (or American, Australian, etc.) constitutional tradition provide a more apposite basis for normative reflection on appropriate attitudes and conduct for British (American, Australian, etc.) public sector bureaucrats than the very different values governing the conduct of private enterprise? As Peter Self (1997: 17) puts it, 'because of the different tasks and conditions of bureaucracy, the introduction of market-style tests of incentives, competition and rapid turnover can produce perverse results'. The dangers posed are again those consequent upon attempting to 'establish commandments of identical content' across different life orders (Weber, 1994b: 357).

Personae and life orders: from Max Weber

This book aims to recover a certain ethical dignity for the mundane routines of bureaucratic administration in the face of these persistent populist, philosophical and entrepreneurial critiques. It is at once an attempt to better understand and to defend the ethos of bureaucratic office. In advancing this objective it draws heavily upon the work of the premier theorist of bureaucratic culture, Max Weber. However, this is not the Weber of general theories of rationalization, modernity or domination but the one reconstructed by Wilhelm Hennis (1988, 1996): a Weber whose 'central theme' is the formation of 'personalities' fitted to existence within distinct 'life orders' (*Lebensordungen*), especially the methodical orderings of professional life. The problematic for this Weber is the match between the properties of personae and the properties of specific cultural settings (see Saunders, 1997). Investigation of a persona in an order of living – Weber's 'special sociologies' – entails attending to the practical techniques or tools for living a given 'conduct of life' (*Lebensführung*).

According to Hennis (1988: 24) 'it is not so much the complexity, but rather the simplicity of Weber's problematic – confronting us in our modernity, poised upon our intellectual heights – that is an obstacle to its comprehension'. Asking what this image of Weber implies, Hennis (1988: 104) answers that to a high theory-oriented social science which, in Weber's words, sought to 'shift its location and change its conceptual apparatus so that it might regard the stream of events from the heights of reflective thought', 'special sociologies' of personae and their life orders would have little interest. However, if we managed to descend from these 'heights of reflective thought', they might become very important indeed.

The milieu-specificity of personae figures largely in Weber's (1994b: 357) famous lecture on 'The profession and vocation of politics' (and, of course, in the equally famous 'Science as a vocation'). There he addresses this question to his audience:

> But is it in fact true that any ethic in the world could establish substantially identical commandments applicable to all relationships, whether erotic, business, family or official, to one's relations with one's wife, greengrocer, son, competitor, with a friend or an accused man?

Only by being not of this world could an ethic claim such universality. Weber drew the following lesson for his audience: 'We are placed in various orders of life, each of which is subject to different laws'. No ultimate moral or philosophical justification for a given form of life is therefore possible 'because the different value systems of the world stand in conflict with one another' (Weber, 1989: 22). Between these value systems there is in fact a battle between gods of different religions: '[D]estiny not "science" prevails over these gods and their struggles. One can only understand what the divine is for one system or another, or in one system or another' (Weber, 1989: 23).

In the absence of such a universal moral norm, Weber asks, how then are we to develop 'character' or 'personality'?[3] His answer is clear and direct: 'Ladies and gentlemen! Personality is only possessed in the realm of science by the man who serves only the *needs of his subject*, and this is true not only in science' (1989: 11) (original emphasis). Hence, he encouraged his audience to be 'polytheistic' and to take on the persona specific to the 'life order' in which they were engaged.[4] As for those who would attempt to follow one god despite the plurality of 'life orders', this monotheistic attitude was delusory as long as the battle of the gods remained inconclusive. (For a full discussion of these issues see Saunders, 1997: Chapter 9.)

When Weber addresses the issue of our differentiated personae, he is not therefore engaging in the familiar moral chorus against what are said to be the 'fractured' lives of 'we moderns'. These personae are not an indication of fundamental existential fragmentation (Saunders, 1997: 110). Instead, the plurality of modern personae is simply a historical fact that needs to be faced. Thus, he cautions against the idea of an ultimate, supra-regional persona – whether cast in philosophical or managerial terms – that could function as the normative measure of all others, bureaucratic personality included (in Hennis, 1988: 35).

In keeping with the spirit of Weber's argument, this book can be read as an attempt to defend the ethos of bureaucratic office from 'unworldly' philosophical and managerial bids to 'establish commandments of identical content' across plural life orders.

The book is divided into two parts. I am concerned in Part I predominantly with exploring the religious and romantic genealogy of the contemporary philosophical variant of bureau critique. Through an engagement with the work of three influential, but very different, contemporary 'anti-bureaucrats', Alasdair MacIntyre (Chapter 1), Zygmunt Bauman (Chapter 2) and Tom Peters (Chapter 3), I trace the presence of an abiding philosophical assumption: that ultimately there must be a single source of moral value and that this source is to be found in the ideal of the fully developed person – the principle of complete, all-round human development. Whether this ultimate ethical comportment for human beings is articulated in terms of an Augustinian Christian-theological frame of reference (MacIntyre), in relation to the inner conviction of the person of conscience (Bauman) or the libertarian romanticism of the maximally 'businessed' person (Peters), it nonetheless functions as a moral absolute against which the general inadequacy of bureaucratic norms and procedures is to be registered.

In their very different ways, these three critics demand that all areas of life should be united, and that the individual overcome the alienating distinction between the different social roles she is forced to inhabit. They seem unable to abide the idea that what is relevant in one domain of existence need not be so in another. It is this religious and romantic ideal of a whole expressed in each of its parts that shapes their respective anti-bureaucratic visions.

As I make clear throughout Part I, this is quite the opposite view to that expressed by Max Weber, who insisted upon the irreducible plurality of 'value spheres'. Refusing to accept that there was a unified moral personality underpinning and unifying human action, Weber consistently indicated that the different life orders do not constitute the anomic fragments of some denied totality. Instead, he argued that there are many discrete ethical domains and these neither represent different versions of some single, homogeneous good nor fall into any natural hierarchy.

Following Weber, I argue that if the bureau is seen in this light – as a distinctive life order with its own particular ethos of existence – then it cannot be open to problematization for its failure to realise ends it was not designed to meet. The religious and romantic temptation to treat the ethical persona of the bureaucrat as a partial realization of a 'fuller' mode of being is one that should be avoided. The urge to unity in this regard, as Weber indicated, is a potential fanaticism.

In Part II the main themes introduced in Part I are developed in relation to a rather different object of analysis: the restructuring of public service bureaux in the name of 'the new public management' or 'entrepreneurial governance'. Attention here is focused on the new norms and techniques of organizational and personal conduct being instituted within state bureaux in Britain and other OECD countries and the priority they accord to specific forms of market-oriented managerial ethics.

Through a detailed examination of various of these changes – the disaggregation of traditional bureaucracies into semi-autonomous 'executive agencies', the development of market and quasi-market-type mechanisms, the introduction of performance targets, indicators and output objectives –

I raise a number of concerns about the implications of too enthusiastically harnessing individual enterprise to the achievement of public goals and the pursuit of public interests. In particular, I suggest that such an approach pays insufficient attention to the different 'regime values' governing the conduct of business management and public administration. I argue that whilst state bureaucrats bear a real responsibility for the efficient and economic use of resources at their disposal[5] – and to this end should be ready and able to use such methods of management as will offer the best prospect of optimal performance – their function cannot be exhaustively defined in such terms. Because a system of representative government requires officials to act as the custodians of the constitutional values it embodies, it cannot frame the role of bureaucrats solely in terms of efficient management, performance, reponsiveness and securing results. The pursuit of better management in government, no matter how important it is in and of itself, has to recognize the political limits to which it is subject. In failing to do this contemporary programmes of organizational reform in the public sector sail perilously close to the 'unifying' strategy criticized so acutely by Weber; in this instance by making particular market-oriented managerial ethics function as the normative organizational measure of all others – public bureaucratic personality included – regardless of regime values.

In the concluding chapter I summarize the main themes developed in the book and offer some parting comments regarding the relationship between the bureaucratic ethos of office and the requirements of good government today. Representative democracy, I suggest, still needs the bureaucratic ethos.

Notes

1. In *The Case for Bureaucracy* (1985) Charles Goodsell presents a large body of survey data indicating that satisfaction with government services is far higher than popular representations of the 'diabolical' bureaucracy allow for or appreciate. He argues that the cases that appear in the press and are generalized into an image of an unacceptable whole are there precisely because they are unusual, rather than the norm.
2. For classic examples of guru-style 'bureau-bashing' see Peters and Waterman, 1982; Peters, 1987, 1992, 1994. For postmodernist variants: Bauman, 1989, 1993; Burrell, 1997. And for 'radical' feminist critiques: Ferguson, 1984; Pringle, 1989 and various chapters in Savage and Witz, 1994.
3. Weber's use of the term 'personality' is very different from its contemporary 'personalist' psychological and moral philosophical deployments. He indicates, for example, that 'personality' in the fields of science and politics is conferred only upon those who have effectively escaped the 'self' and who devote themselves exclusively to the work at hand (Turner, 1992: Chapter 6). For Weber, individuals can and do find a (personal) focus for moral life in types of ethos that derive from impersonal ethical institutions, rather than from their own

individual moral relections. It is in this sense that 'bureaucrats', for example, can and should be 'personally' committed to the ethos of their office even though that ethos lies outside of their personal moral predilections or principles. For Weber, it is just such commitment that confers 'personality' upon the official.

4. Honigsheim gives testimony to this 'polytheism' in Weber's own conduct. Rarely, he wrote, has a man of this kind 'presented himself to the world as fragmented, and at each opportunity declared himself to belong to a particular sphere rather than presenting himself as a totality'. 'You cannot make a lively tune out of that,' he concluded (Honigsheim, quoted in Hennis, 1988: 187).

5. Taken as these are from the people that state bureaucrats serve and returned to them in the form of benefits and entitlements legitimized by the system of government.

PART I

The Religious and Romantic Origins of 'Bureau Critique'

Alasdair MacIntyre and the Christian Genealogy of 'Bureau Critique'

As 'managerial' values have spread ever wider, encompassing objects and domains previously considered beyond their reach, critical understandings of the meaning and function of management have undergone a significant transmutation too. In contrast to the rather shadowy role as functionaries of capital that managers were allocated in the cruder formulations of labour process theory, for example, all forms of contemporary organizational critique allocate a much more important role to the conduct of 'managing' than has generally been the case before. Agreement amongst practitioners of the critical enterprise may not always extend much beyond this but the influential role of 'management' in the reproduction and transformation of organizational life is now taken for granted.

This acknowledgement that 'management matters' has had some distinctly destabilizing effects for more determinist forms of critical organizational analysis, particularly, but not exclusively, those of a Marxist bent. However, proponents of 'radical' management critique have been remarkably inventive in plundering ostensibly 'alien' theoretical sources in order to bolster their flagging sense of mission. Communitarian political and moral philosophy, post-structuralist cultural theory and postmodern social theory, to name some of the more obvious recruits, have all received their joining instructions in the battle to problematize the conduct of management (Hassard and Parker, 1993; Willmott, 1993; Burrell, 1997).

Foremost amongst the moral philosophers whose work has provided a constant source of inspiration for critical theorists of management in recent years is Alasdair MacIntyre. MacIntyre's (1981) arguments about the 'character' of the Manager have commanded considerable support within critical organizational circles and have regularly been cited by critical intellectuals keen to unmask an ethical vacuum at the heart of the managerial enterprise (Anthony, 1986; Deetz, 1995; Mangham, 1995; McMylor, 1994)[1].

Although both MacIntyre and his admirers are united by their criticism of management in general, it is interesting to note that the object of MacIntyre's critique is in fact quite specific. It is none other than Max Weber's 'ideal typical' bureaucrat. A detailed analysis of MacIntyre's critique of the manager offers a very useful entrée to the philosophical variant of bureau critique outlined in the Introduction to this book. In particular, it provides valuable insights concerning the ethos of this form of critique and the persona of the critical intellectual who practises it.

The chapter begins by delineating and examining the central arguments of MacIntyre's *After Virtue* and indicating the crucial role allocated to the bureaucratic 'manager' as an agent of moral decay. In particular, attention is focused upon the ways in which MacIntyre attempts to hold the character of the manager accountable to a particular ideal of the person, one that derives many of its characteristics from Christian theology.

I then compare MacIntyre's conception of the bureaucrat with Max Weber's. I argue that although MacIntyre deploys a distinctively Weberian theoretical lexicon in formulating his case against both Weber and his 'ideal typical' bureaucratic manager his conclusions concerning the ethical vacuity of bureaucratic conduct are the very antithesis of Weber's own. While Weber is concerned to offer a positive description of the bureaucrat as a bureaucrat, MacIntyre attempts to hold the bureaucrat accountable to an 'ideal' of the person derived from a very different ethical milieu. However, because the person of the bureaucrat does not attempt to approximate to this 'ideal' it cannot be criticized for failing to meet its demands.

The predicament

Alasdair MacIntyre's widely praised text, *After Virtue* (1981), is a work of moral philosophy which offers a critique of something called 'management' as part of an attempt to diagnose the presumed disintegration of moral relationships in modern liberal societies. MacIntyre claims that modern morality is in a grim state. Indeed, he paints Western history as an unremitting process of impoverishment and decay. Past societies, we are told, were orderly and healthy while ours is sick and chaotic. People who were once firmly located in harmonious communities are now rootless and

soullless. Social relations have been torn assunder by atmostic individualism. A solidaristic communal order has given way to an egotistical and
morally hollow one. Normative consensus has been supplanted by endless
disagreement. Deep pre-modern forms of social identity have been dislocated by thinner and more universal ones. As a result, modern humanity is
clueless about how to live the moral life. (For a detailed discussion of
MacIntyre's thesis see Holmes, 1993.)

For MacIntyre, the diagnosis is so bleak because the decline of a *telos* or
objective purpose to human existence has stripped us modern souls of any
objective conception of the end or goal of human life, any idea of the
good life that morality can subserve. According to him, the shift from an
Aristotelian language of morality (in which a thoroughgoing hierarchy
exists among conceptions of the good life) to a contemporary emotivist
doctrine, in which morality is purely and simply a matter of personal
preference, has led to rationally interminable moral disputes (1981: 11).
Without a shared view of our moral purpose we seem incapable of decid-
ing between rival claims, for we continually invoke competing moral
rules.

The absence of a fixed, monistic view of human morality to which our
individual choices must be subordinated has, in turn, effectively removed
all limits to the scope of individual choice. All associations and life-plans
have become voluntary. Because moral discourse has become the expression of individual preferences, incapable of rational consensus, practical
reason has come to be equated with the instrumental reason of bureaucratic institutions, the choice of efficient means to arbitrarily chosen ends.
Whatever the mutual antagonism of individualism and bureaucratic
impersonality, MacIntyre argues, they are dialectical opposites that thrive
on one another (1981: 35). And they do so to most telling effect in what
MacIntyre refers to as the 'character' of the 'manager'.

Emotivist culture and the 'character' of the 'manager'

According to MacIntyre:

> A moral philosophy . . . characteristically presupposes a sociology. For every
> moral philosophy offers explicitly or implicitly at least a partial conceptual
> analysis of the relationship of an agent to his or her reasons, motives, intentions
> and actions, and in so doing generally presupposes some claim that these con-
> cepts are embodied or at least can be in the real social world. (1981: 23)

So what might the social embodiment of emotivism actually entail?
MacIntyre (1981: 23) argues that its primary requirement is 'the obliteration
of any genuine distinction between manipulative and non-manipulative
social relations'. According to him, emotivist moral philosophy regards
moral discussion as nothing more than an attempt by one party to alter the
preferences and opinions of another party so that they accord with their

own, regardless of the means deployed to effect this change. No distinction is made between reasons that will influence the other party in the desired manner and ones that the party in question will judge to be good; 'there is no such thing as appeal to genuinely impersonal criteria whose validity the person must judge for herself regardless of her relationship to the speaker' (Mulhall and Swift, 1992: 75).

By collapsing the distinction between personal and impersonal reasons, emotivism undermines the possibility of treating persons as ends. 'To treat someone as an end is to offer them what I take to be good reasons for acting in one way rather than another, but to leave it to them to evaluate those reasons' (MacIntyre, 1981: 23). For emotivism, though, no moral debate can be anything other than an attempt by one party to make another party an instrument of their own purposes, 'by adducing whatever influences or considerations will in fact be effective on this or that occasion' (MacIntyre, 1981: 24).

If emotivist moral discourse regards all moral debate as involving manipulative interpersonal relations then, MacIntyre suggests, emotivist sociology will hold the same view of social relationships *per se*. In order to show what the world looks like through emotivist eyes, MacIntyre proceeds to describe three central 'characters' of modern culture each of whom embodies the obliteration of manipulative and non-manipulative relations in a particular way. MacIntyre uses the term 'character' to refer to the fusion of a specific role with a specific personality type in a way 'that emblematizes certain moral and metaphysical ideas embedded in a culture' (Mulhall and Swift, 1992: 75). The three central characters of 'our' emotivist culture are the Aesthete, the Therapist and the Manager (MacIntyre, 1981: 23–35). The Aesthete regards the social world as an arena for the satisfaction of his or her own desires, and social relations as occasions for contriving behaviour in others that will be responsive to his or her wishes. The Therapist is similarly disinclined to treat people as ends in themselves, concentrating rather on techniques through which neurotic symptoms can be effectively transformed into 'directed energy' and 'maladjusted individuals into well adjusted ones'. The Manager represents the obliteration of the distinction between manipulative and non-manipulative relations in the socio-economic field in much the same way that the Therapist represents this obliteration in the sphere of personal life. The Manager treats ends as given, as outside his or her scope; his or her concern also is with technique, with directing human and non-human resources in order to achieve these pre-determined goals with maximum efficiency and effectiveness.

For my purposes, of course, it is the character of the Manager which is of most interest. Indeed, MacIntyre (1981: 74) himself describes the Manager as the 'dominant figure of the contemporary scene', laying at the door of this creation considerable responsibility for the degeneration of morality alluded to earlier.

Managerial moral fictions

So what is it about the Manager that makes this character quite so culpable in MacIntyre's eyes? Well, while he regards each of his three characters as traders in 'moral fictions' – concepts which purport to provide us with an objective and impersonal criterion but which singly fail so do – he does not believe the Aesthete or the Therapist have any fictions 'which are peculiarly their own, which belong to the very definiton of their role'. By contrast, the Manager is a character with a moral fiction all of its own. MacIntyre (1981: 74) argues that 'among the central moral fictions of the age we have to place the peculiarly managerial fiction embodied in the claim to possess systematic effectiveness in controlling certain aspects of social reality'.

Moreover, while the Manager's claim to effectiveness is represented in morally neutral terms, MacIntyre (1981: 74) argues that this claim is actually a morally loaded one because it is inseperable from 'a mode of human existence in which the contrivance of means is in central part the manipulation of human beings into compliant patterns of behaviour; and it is by appeal to his own effectiveness in this respect that the manager claims authority within the manipulative mode'. In other words, it is this character's possession of its own unique – and to the philosopher's mind 'most culturally powerful' – moral fiction, within which is embedded a particular claim to authority, which leads MacIntyre to describe the Manager as *the* 'central character of the modern social drama' (1981: 104). And, as should now be obvious, when MacIntyre allocates someone a crucial role in modern society he is not paying them a compliment. Because the Manager is so central to the 'contemporary scene', MacIntyre argues that if he can show this character's claims to expert effectiveness to be largely groundless then 'to a disturbing extent our morality will be disclosed as a theatre of illusions' (1981: 77). Having already written off modernity as a catastrophe and having positioned the Manager as a key character in this catastrophe, it will come as no surprise to learn that MacIntyre also concludes that the Manager's claims to effectiveness are totally unsupportable and that, as a result, our morality is indeed a 'theatre of illusions'. But how exactly does the philosopher reach this conclusion?

MacIntyre believes that the Manager's assumed authority rests upon the claim to possess systematic effectiveness in controlling certain aspects of social reality. He argues that in order to vindicate this claim, managerial expertise requires a stock of law-like generalizations which would enable 'the manager to predict that, if an event or state of affairs of a certain type were to occur or to be brought about, some other event or state of affairs of some specific kind would result' (1981: 77). This claim, he argues, and its related presumption concerning the existence of a domain of morally neutral 'fact' in which the manager can be 'expert', parallels the claims made by natural scientists.

Civil servants and managers alike justify themselves and their claims to authority, power and money by invoking their own competence as scientific managers of social change. Thus, there emerges an ideology which finds its classical form in a pre-existing sociological theory, Weber's theory of bureaucracy . . . [I]n his insistence that the rationality of adjusting means to ends in the most economical and efficient way is the central task of the bureaucrat and that therefore the appropriate mode of justification of his activity by the bureaucrat lies in the appeal to his (or later her) ability to deploy a body of scientific and above all social scientific knowledge organized and understood as comprising a set of universal law-like generalizations, Weber provided the key to much of the modern age. (1981: 86)

MacIntyre regards modern science as profoundly immoral. This is in large part due to the role of science in destroying theism, in discrediting those religious worldviews on which, he claims, morality itself depends. A society where science is revered, he argues, is a society adrift. The crux of his argument against the Manager therefore appears to be that this character derives its claims to expertise from science and that science cannot tell us how to live.

According to MacIntyre, the apple of scientific knowledge is a poisoned fruit because it disputes the reality of chance. It does so, by claiming, purportedly, that the human species can somehow replace God. Social science, in particular, hubristically denies 'the permanence of *Fortuna*', Machiavelli's 'bitch goddess of unpredictability' (1981: 93). It was and remains, he argues, terribly naive for Enlightenment thinkers and their heirs to assume that 'fragility and vulnerability could be overcome in some progressive future'. But that is what science and those – such as the Manager – who act in its name continue to claim.

MacIntyre's rebuttal of science in general, and social science in particular, leads him to conclude that the claims of 'bureaucratic managerial expertise' are illusory. The manager's claim to authority, he asserts

is fatally undermined when we recognize that he possesses no sound stock of law-like generalizations and when we realize how weak the predictive power avaialable to him is . . . The dominance of the manipulative mode in our culture is not and cannot be accompanied by very much actual success in manipulation . . . [T]he notion of social control embodied in the notion of expertise is indeed a masquerade. Our social order is in a very literal sense out of our, and indeed, anyone's, control. No one is or could be in charge. (1981: 106–7)

Belief in managerial expertise is thus disastrously misplaced.

The Manager as *character* is other than he at first sight seems to be; the social world of everyday hard-headed practical pragmatic no-nonense realism which is the environment of management is one which depends for its sustained existence on the systematic perpetuation of misunderstanding and of belief in fictions. (1981: 107)

According to MacIntyre, the Manager's 'objectively grounded' claims are in essence nothing more than expressions of his own arbitrary, but disguised, will and preference. The effects of Enlightenment scientific prophecy, MacIntyre claims, 'have been to produce not scientifically managed social control, but a skillful dramatic imitation of such control. It is histrionic success which gives power and authority in our culture. The most effective bureaucrat is the best actor' (1981: 107).

In sum, then, MacIntyre conjures up for us a world in which moral discourse is impossible. And the most important agent in the destruction of morality may be management, a characteristic modern activity that, in its conduct and in its intentions, exemplifies all the worst aspects of emotivist culture.

The solution

Having diagnosed the moral ills of modern liberal societies and unpacked the contribution of the Manager to the contemporary malaise, MacIntyre sets out to recover what he considers to be the most distinctive feature of Aristotelian ethics – the idea that there is a single answer to the question 'What is human life lived at its best?' For MacIntyre, our success as moral beings – as 'good' teachers, parents, games players, etc. – depends upon our understanding this answer.

The gravest error of modern ethics, as far as MacIntyre is concerned, lies in having surrendered Aristotle's view that human life has a *telos* or objective purpose. Nowhere does MacIntyre find a clearer expression of the rejection of Aristotelianism than in what he understands as the Enlightenment project of providing an autonomous foundation for morality. This project was the attempt to give the moral rules inherited from the preceding culture a systematic justification that would not appeal to any extramoral (metaphysical or theological) views about the end or purpose of human existence. In other words, the hope of the Enlightenment was to develop a conception of morality independently of a religious worldview (Larmore, 1987). From this development has arisen the modern doctrine of pluralism, the view that the idea of the good life can be variously interpreted by reasonable people, and morality itself has become the site of rationally interminable disagreements. MacIntyre's attacks upon modern liberal societies indicate his unambiguous opposition to these developments. For him, the price of giving up Aristotle's conception of the good life is ultimately nihilism.

In seeking to provide a distinctive answer to the question 'What is human life lived at its best?' MacIntyre attempts to rehabilitate Aristotelian concepts such as virtue and the good life by linking them with the ideas of a practice and of the narrative unity of human life.

For MacIntyre a 'practice' can be defined as a co-operative human activity with shared standards of excellence that determine a form of success which is intrinsically related to the activity involved (1981: 175). Such 'internal goods' (success in game-playing, for example) cannot be characretized except in relationship to the activities that constitute the practice in question; and it is these activities that are to be understood as the exercise of a particular 'virtue'. As MacIntyre indicates: 'A virtue is an acquired human quality the possession and exercise of which tends to enable us to achieve those goods which are internal to practices and the lack of which effectively prevents us from achieving any such goods' (1981: 178). Practices are to be distinguished from 'institutions' because the latter are forms of activity directed towards external goods such as money, power and status. External goods constitute resources, whose value lies not in how we acquired them but rather in what we can do with them. For MacIntyre, then, the possession and exercise of the virtues is inextricably linked to participation in practices and that participation requires accept-ance of the authority of the standards, rules and regulations operative within the practice at any given time. The idea of 'given time' is important here as it indicates the way in which MacIntyre conceives of practices as historical phenomena.

While entry into a practice demands the subjection of an individual's personal predispositions and preferences to the standards prevailing in the practice, it does not entail, subsequent to that individual's insertion into it, that s/he automatically accept every judgement made by the commu-nity of practitioners. As MacIntyre indicates, such judgements will often be disputed; for any given practice will have a history within which its par-ticipants' perceptions of its standards and regulations will change, and such disputes are the motor of that change.

For MacIntyre, the main point to note is that such disputes will be subject to certain constraints. They cannot be regarded as purely subjec-tive or arbitrary (i.e. emotivist). The standards of the practice provide a framework within which reasoned argument may be conducted and while that framework may be subject to change, it cannot be completely problematized, for the framework constitutes the practice and its total rejection would obliterate the practice rather than simply change its parameters.

At one level, participation in practices can be seen to socialize an indi-vidual into forms of life in which human judgements of worth are immune to the threat of emotivism. Practices so defined, however, can often turn out to be at odds with one another. MacIntyre himself acknowl-edges that there can be and often are conflicts between different conceptions of the good life, embodied in different practices; the demands of being a good parent may well come into conflict with the demands of being a good teacher and so on. In order to avoid, what he considers to be the disaster of pluralism, MacIntyre therefore falls back upon the idea that human beings have a *telos* to their existence that *transcends* specific practices, an overarching purpose that consists in the narrative unity of a good life.

[W]ithout an overriding conception of the *telos* of a whole human life, conceived of as a unity, our conception of certain individual virtues has to remain partial and incomplete . . . unless there is a *telos* which transcends the limited goods of practices by constituting the good of a whole human life, the good of a human life conceived of as a unity, it will *both* be the case that a certain subversive arbitrariness will invade the moral life *and* that we shall be unable to specify the context of certain virtues adequately. (1981: 202–3) (original emphasis)

It is interesting to note the subtle shift in MacIntyre's vocabulary here, with talk of practices and goods gradually being supplanted with notions of *the* good and the discussion moving from human beings who inhabit specific social roles to 'man' as such. We can see MacIntyre turning away from a broadly social constructionist account of human practices and virtues – where becoming a moral agent is defined in relationship to social conditions of training and practice – to a decontextualized teleological concern with the realization of essences.

From the many to the one

According to MacIntyre (1981: 52ff.), traditional theories of the virtues included three components: untutored human nature as it happens to be, human nature as it could be if it realized its *telos*, and the precepts of rational ethics as the means for the transition from one to the other. What this presupposed, he argues, is a distinction between potentiality and its fulfilment in reality and an account of what the true end or fulfilment of human nature might be. Enlightenment culture, he claims, jettisoned a conception of the human *telos*; but its effort to derive moral rules simply from human nature 'as it happens to be' was bound to fail because human beings are so diverse and anyway disinclined to obey those rules (1981: 53). Thus moral claims lack the means to achieve objectivity in Enlightenment culture, where by objectivity is meant that moral statements 'can be called true or false in precisely the way in which all other factual statements can be so called' (1981: 59).

MacIntyre views the concept of *telos* as crucial to securing the objectivity of moral belief because its reactivation alone can enable the immediate transition of statements of fact to statements of value. He argues that we can move immediately from factual premises such as 'This watch does not keep the time accurately' to the evaluative conclusion that what we have on our hands is a bad watch, because we know that a watch has a distinct purpose or function (a *telos*) – to keep time accurately. 'To call a watch good is to say that it is the kind of watch which someone would choose who wanted to keep time accurately (rather than, say, to throw at the cat)' (1981: 59). According to MacIntyre this presupposition concerning use of the term 'good' is that everything that it is appropriate to label 'good' and 'bad' – including persons and actions – has, as a matter of fact, a *telos* or objective purpose. Thinking of human beings as in possession of a *telos* means we can make immediate transitions from 'is' to 'ought', since our understanding of the fulfilled or final state of human nature allows us to distinguish between actions and traits that do, and those that do not, contribute to the development and realization of that *telos*, and thus to judge the former 'good' and the latter 'bad'. With human life conceived of in essentialist terms, MacIntyre argues, it once again becomes possible to treat moral judgements as factual statements (1981: 59).

But how do we know what the human *telos* consists of? What is man's true end? What is a good man apart from any social context providing obligations for this person to discharge? According to MacIntyre (1981: 219), 'the good life for man is the life spent in seeking for the good life for man'. When forced to give some content to this tautologous statement, MacIntyre argues that man's overarching purpose consists in the unity of a narrative quest embodied in a single life. This quest exhibits two distinct features. The first is that without some notion of a final *telos* there could not be any beginning to a quest. Some conception of the good for man is necessary to the functioning of the quest. So where does such a conception spring from? According to MacIntyre (1981: 219), it is in 'looking for a conception of *the* good which will enable us to order other goods, for a conception of *the* good which will enable us to understand the place of integrity and constancy in life, that we initially define the kind of life which is a quest for the good'. So far, not so good in the explanatory reach stakes.

The second feature of the quest appears to take us in a radically different direction: back down the route of anti-essentialism in that the search for the good does not presuppose looking for 'something already adequately characterized, as miners search for gold or geologists for oil' (1981: 219). Rather, 'it is in the course of the quest and only through encountering and coping with the various particular harms, dangers, temptations and distractions which provide any quest with its episodes and incidents that the goal of the quest is finally to be understood'. This odd brew of predestination and individual agency leads him to redefine the nature of virtue. In addition to a socially acquired human capacity (1981: 78) virtue is reconfigured as a quality necessary for human flourishing in the abstract. Virtue, MacIntyre argues, is now to be understood as something which not only sustains practices and enables 'us to achieve the goods internal to practices', but also as something which will 'sustain us in the relevant kind of quest for the good, by enabling us to overcome the harms, dangers, temptations and distractions which we encounter, and which will furnish us with increasing self-knowledge and increasing knowledge of the good' (1981: 219).

But what exactly are we to make of all this? If virtue is contextual, how can it also be a-contextual? If the gravest intellectual sin of 'liberalism' is to conceive of human beings apart from their social roles, why does MacIntyre, critic of this liberalism, end up doing exactly the same thing? The answer to this conundrum resides in the theoretical strategy deployed in *After Virtue* and so it is to the character of that strategy that I now turn my attention.

MacIntyre's dialectical catechism

'Shuttling back and forth between the Church and the left', as Stephen Holmes (1993: 116) puts it, 'MacIntyre has never been able to decide for long which to eulogize: reverence or impertinence; obedience or rebellion'. The appeal of *After Virtue* lies, perhaps, in its simultaneous commitment to both. It is this Janus-faced quality of MacIntyre's theoretical strategy that enables him, for example, both to deploy broadly social constructionist arguments to spank liberal individualism for its presumed 'atomism' and to utilize theological essentialisms to represent the good for 'man' outside of all social context. However, if this Janus face is the secret of MacIntyre's success it is also the source of *After Virtue*'s central theoretical limitations.

So what is the main problem with the central theoretical strategy of *After Virtue*? Well, its one that the text shares with dialectical theory more generally: critique cannot escape the orbit of the binary oppositions it seeks to problematize because critique itself is nothing more than a theoretical oscillation between these concepts. Thus we have seen that MacIntyre calls into question the notion of the self-formative subject by subordinating this figure to the influence of social conditions and relations. But he then problematizes the social side of this equation by insisting that it is possible to talk of 'man' in the abstract outside of all social context because human beings have a *telos* to their existence that transcends specific practices. Thus each term is temporarily held in suspension, while its oppositional partner is affirmed, then reaffirmed as the pendulum of critique reverses its swing. The result of this theoretical movement is that neither side of the binarism – that of the asocial subject and that of the socially determined human person – is decisively criticized or permanently renounced. On the contrary, 'the problematization of a concept in dialectical critique is always a prelude to its reaffirmation as, with the reversal in the axis of critique, the dubious concept takes its turn as the self-evident ground for another round of problematization' (Hunter, 1992: 126) .

Thus in *After Virtue* we find two rather different MacIntyres endlessly battling with one another. One defends an over-socialized conception of man. The other wishes to safeguard Christianity's idea of the immortal soul. One dresses down liberals for the myth of the pre-social individual, and the other accepts original sin, a trait which as Holmer (1993: 120) has shown, is clearly imposed 'apart from and prior to any particular social and political order'. About the cosmopolitanism of the Enlightenment, the first MacIntyre argues that the 'wider the audience to whom we aspire to speak, the less we shall speak to anyone in particular'. But the second MacIntyre refuses to level the same charge against Jesus. Sometimes he argues that people's worth depends upon their contribution to their community. At other times, he praises Augustine's counsel to cast off traditional social roles, and to disentangle oneself from Roman society. As Stephen Holmes concludes:

the tradition-loving MacIntyre elevates the member/non-member distinction into the centre-piece of his moral theory, while the tradition-spurning MacIntyre praises *caritas* for inducing a healthy indifference toward group membership. The former urges you to adore your rich local tradition, while the latter assures you that it will mean absolutely nothing when you meet your Maker. (1993: 119–20)

In *After Virtue*, then, as in dialectical critique more generally, radical doubt and programmatic adherence are curiously interdependent. This practice of mutual modification, in which each side is successively played off against the other as a means of synthesizing the moral fragmentation and divisions brought about by 'modernity', has at its core a vision of the ideally integrated moral world and of the completely developed moral personality inhabiting it.

Common to many variations on this dialectical theme is a whole/part model of social, cultural and moral existence in which that which does not form an organic whole must be fragmented and anomic. It is this ideal of a whole expressed in each of its parts that shapes MacIntyre's vision of both society and individual in *After Virtue*. It moves him to demand that a substantial notion of the 'good' unite all areas of social life and that the individual overcome the alienating distinctions between roles that modern forms of social differentiation have produced. The difficulty with this view of wholeness and the repudiation of social spheres it entails is, amongst other things, its inability to furnish any practical norms for cultural, social or political conduct (Walzer, 1984; Hunter, 1987, 1993; Larmore, 1987: Chapter 5; Walzer, 1984).

As Carl Schmitt (1986: 17) indicated long ago, this form of critique involves the suspension of belief in all institutional specializations, every operative distinction, institutional norm or procedure, time-frame and binding decision. To speak of 'the total point of view' or of 'wholeness' in this context simply means that one has mastered the technique of denigrating as 'utilitarian', 'instrumental' or 'reformist' any particular norm of cultural, moral or social conduct (Saunders, 1991, 1997; Hunter, 1994). It does not mean that one has developed some new all-encompassing set of norms for such conduct, for such summational or holistic norms are simply not available. After all, how can one demand from a contextualized, situated human being a mode of action or thought that is free from the entanglements of actual situations and the lines of demarcations they declare? What dialectical critique therefore provides, it seems, is 'a technique for withdrawing from the discursive and institutional spheres in which cultural, moral and social attributes are actually specified and formulated' (Hunter, 1987: 110).

If cultural, social and moral interests and attributes can only be described and assessed in relation to particular delimited norms and techniques of conduct – that is those made available by the actual array of historical institutions in which such attributes and interests are formed – then conceptions of the human *telos*, the homogeneity of morals and so forth that underlie *After Virtue*, are unintelligible in the forms in which they are presented (Larmore, 1987: 131).

One of MacIntyre's master arguments in *After Virtue* is that the contextual justification of moral beliefs cannot secure their objectivity. Instead, he assumes that the objectivity of morals can be ensured only if we can show how they can be justified as a whole and that this justitifcation *en masse* is possible only if they are seen to promote some purpose that is ours, whether or not we know it, and that such a *telos* can be ours only if there is a God who has created us to that end.

By why should objectivity entail homogeneity? MacIntyre himself argues in his more pluralist moments that contextualism does inded entail objectivity. In his discussion of practices MacIntyre argues convincingly that 'internal goods' (success in game-playing, intellectual endeavours or other forms of conduct) can only be characterized in relationship to the activities constituting the practice in question. To the extent that moral beliefs are thus contextually justifiable (or 'immanent') they can quite legitimately lay claim to objectivity, as their evident truth or falsity is practice specific (Weinrib, 1988).

However, MacIntyre cannot live with the consequences of adopting this stance because to do so entails giving credence to the idea of pluralism: the notion that there are 'many versions of the good life that neither represent different versions of some single, homogeneous good, nor fall into any discernible hierarchy' (Larmore, 1987: 23). In order to avoid the 'fact' of pluralism MacIntyre is forced to resort to the idea that we have an objective purpose or *telos* that trancends specific practices. Unsurprisingly, this *telos* is singularly devoid of content for, as I argued earlier, cultural, social and moral interests and attributes can be described and assessed only in relation to particular delimited norms and techniques of conduct and it is precisely such contextualism that the notion of *telos* (as well as that of the homogeneity of morals) is designed to avoid.

Persons and contexts

MacIntyre is keen to stress that becoming a moral agent is dependent upon social conditions of training and practice that we do not ourselves control. He also admits that these social conditions and the persons they constitute are, in fact, quite diverse. However, in order to avoid what he considers to be the disaster of pluralism, he argues that this diversity of personhood is in fact a chimera. For underlying it is an essential unity waiting to be revealed and realized. Despite surface appearances to the contrary, MacIntyre argues, persons are basically unified agents, because they have a *telos* or objective purpose that transcends the practices within which their differing capacities and attributes are constituted, even if they do not know it yet themselves.

However, attempts to define the human *telos* apart from the actual social institutions and practices with which specific categories of person emerge are destined to end disappointingly. If particular practices give rise to specific forms of personhood then these can be seen to represent autonomous ethical comportments which are irreducible to common underlying moral principles.

According to Amélie Rorty, attempts such as MacIntyre's to rescue the concept of the person from the array of institutions and practices in which many different forms of personhood are constituted derive many of their characteristics from an Augustinian Christian-theological frame of reference:

> Augustine held that our basic activities are directed toward integrating the divided and corrupt psyche of the natural, fallen condition, so that we can freely consent to being the agents of God's purposes. Augustine used his analysis of the doctine of the Trinity – his account of how the three persons of the divinity form a single substantial unity – to explain how persons can be simple unified agents despite the diversity, and sometimes the conflicts, among their faculties and powers. (Rorty, 1988: 7)

No one reading this passage could fail to recognize the imprint of this Christian model of the person in MacIntyre's conception of the human *telos*, specifically in its desire to restore unity to a 'divided and corrupt psyche' so that it might 'freely consent to being the agent of God's purposes'.

As Rorty also argues, this Christian integrationist or 'monopersonalist' conception of the person is highly contentious, its claims about the true form of persons giving rise to arguments that have proven extremely intractable. Her advice on how to deal with such arguments is very instructive:

> Some of the appparently intractable debates about persons occur when the concerns of one context are imported to another, in the premature interest of constructing a unified theory, or as a rhetorical move in a political polemic. The appearance of forced options often arises from a misguided attempt to derive decisions from 'the' (illicitly decontextualized) concept of a person. When there are repetitive irresolvable debates about the primacy of competing concepts of the person . . . the first move should be to formulate the issues that lie behind the dispute, specifying the distinctive sources and contexts of conflicting intuitions. (Rorty, 1988: 7)

If MacIntyre's concept of 'the' person is derived from a theological context, at what cost is that conception imported to other domains or milieux, where quite different conceptions and comportments of the person have arisen? We can begin to answer this question by focussing once again upon MacIntyre's conceptualization of the manager as a particular sort of person.

MacIntyre's managerial chimera

MacIntyre's Janus face is nowhere more evident than in his critique of the manager. At one and the same time he allocates to this creation both extraordinary social power and total impotence. As Laura Nash (1995: 227) has indicated, MacIntyre's manager

> is accorded a truncated, superhuman personality whose sheer hyper rationalism and amorality can be made to account for all that is bad in our lives . . . [T]he manager looms larger than life, a stock character in the drama of efficient functionalism, frighteningly devoid of all feeling or conscience (Hey! Whatever works!). Or no, the manager looms *smaller* than life, a shallow, gray flannel wimp, brainwashed by the 'organization' to do whatever is necessary despite the pitiful lack of any meaningful rewards for his or her service. Either way, the managers are our demi-demons . . . Thus to the degree that managerial thinking asserts itself in our lives, the demon prevails and morality is undermined.

At the heart of MacIntyre's representation of management and the manager as demi-demonic lies a particular interpretation of the work of Max Weber. According to MacIntyre, 'Weber's thought embodies just those dichotomies which emotivism embodies, and obliterates just those distinctions to which emotivism has to be blind . . . Weber then . . . is an emotivist and his portrait of bureaucratic authority is an emotivist portrait' (MacIntyre, 1981: 26).

MacIntyre's representation of Weber's 'theory of bureaucracy' as both descriptive and expressive of emotivism has a great deal in common with the interpretation of Weber's work that has achieved near axiomatic status within the field of critical organizational studies in recent years. Contemporary readings of Weber within the latter field place enormous emphasis on bureaucracy as the primary institutional carrier of 'formal rationalization' in modern societies: 'bureaucratic organization . . . was the most pervasive institutional expression of formal or instrumental rationality; it established an objective decision-making mechanism, based on impersonal rules and specialist knowledge, which excluded all . . . moral . . . considerations' (Reed, 1992: 40).

What this approach shares with that of MacIntyre is an appropriation of Weber's chief theoretical categories – the distinctions between instrumental and value-oriented social action, formal and substantive rationality – married to a particular reading of his analysis of bureaucracy to produce a distinctly dialectical critique of bureaucratic government. At the centre of this critique lies the figure of the bureaucrat: an amoral technical expert who treats ends as given and whose primary concern is therefore with the rational direction of human and non-human resources in order to achieve these pre-established goals with maximum efficiency.

This way of depicting the persona of the bureaucratic manager allows it to appear as one side of a full moral personality, the other side of which is represented by the 'critical intellectual'. Unsurprisingly, this latter figure is portrayed as possessing moral attributes opposed and complementary to those of the bureaucrat: namely, a commitment to substantive values and a lack of a technical means of realizing them.[2] Central to this dialectical theme is the treatment of bureaucratic and critical intellectual rationality as the two sides of a single moral and political whole. The contemporary dominance of the former and hence marginalization of the latter thus signifies the fragmentation of an ideally integrated moral personality. While this critical discourse on Weber and the bureau relies upon a theoretical lexicon that is self-consciously Weberian, it's conclusions concerning the ethical and moral vacuity of bureaucratic norms and practice are the very antithesis of Weber's own.

For Weber the 'managerial' character of bureaucratic administration is not the result of the disintegration of morally unified personhood. Weber refused to accept that there was a unfied moral personality underpinning human action. Indeed, he consistently indicated that different spheres of existence or different life orders (*Lebensordnungen*) do not constitute the anomic fragments of some denied totality. For Weber, there are many discrete ethical domains and these neither represent different versions of some single homogeneous good nor fall into any natural hierarchy.

Far from being a sphere of existence from which moral or ethical concerns have been evacuated by the onslaught of 'instrumental rationality', bureaucracy is itself what Weber terms a *Lebensführung* – 'not only an ensemble of purposes and ideals within a code of conduct but also ways and means of conducting oneself within a given "life-order"' (Minson, 1991: 13). In Weber's account the impersonal, expert, procedural and hierarchical character of bureaucratic reason and action is not treated as a symptom of moral deficiency; instead the bureau is represented as having its own distinct ethic of existence. The ethical attributes of the 'good bureaucrat' – strict adherence to procedure, acceptance of hierarchical sub- and superordination, abnegation of personal moral enthusiasms, commitment to the purposes of the office – are the product of definite ethical practices and techniques through which individuals acquire the predisposition and capacity to conduct themselves according to certain norms.

In contrast to MacIntyre, Weber makes it very clear that the 'rationality' and 'objectivity' entailed by the bureaucratic ethos cannot be interpreted as embodying a claim to objectivity in an *epistemological* sense. The cultivation of an objective, rational demeanour should not be seen – as MacIntyre would have us view it – as a colossally immodest attempt to cultivate a God's-eye view, a general capacity for impartiality which operates through a normative exclusion of the value-laden dimensions of human existence. For instance, Weber insists upon the historical specificity of the 'rational' imperatives of bureaucracy in the following terms: '. . . decisive is that this "freely" creative administration. . . would not constitute a realm of *free* arbitrary action and discretion, of *personally* motivated favour and valuation such as we shall find to be the cause among pre-bureaucratic forms'

(Weber, 1978: 979). The objectivity and rationality required of the bureaucrat in this case entails the capacity to set aside pre-bureaucratic forms of
patronage. What is to be excluded as irrational by this form of conduct is
not value-laden action *per se* but those forms of 'private' group preroga-
tives and interests which, 'governed as they were by a completely different
ethos, it was at other times deemed quite legitimate and "reasonable" to
pursue' (Minson, 1991: 15).

Weber proceeds to indicate that bureaucratic rationality does not require
the eradication of all personal feelings and their replacement by soulless
instrumentalism. Such stereotypes ignore the fact that bureaucratic culture
does not necessitate the dissolution of emotional relationships within the
boundaries of the organization but only engenders a general antipathy
towards those relations that open up the possibility of corruption, through,
for example, the improper exercise of personal patronage, the indulgence
of incompetence or through the betrayal of confidentiality. As Minson
(1991: 15) argues,

> the supposition of an essential antipathy between bureaucracy and informal
> relations such as friendship – at least at the level of official norms – hinges on a
> romantic identification of such relations with freedom form normative compul-
> sion, spontaneous attraction, intimacy, free choice etc.

From these very brief examples it is possible to see that the demands for
objectivity, impartiality and rationality inscribed within the bureaucratic
ethos cannot be interpreted as embodying a claim to 'universal objectivity',
as MacIntyre suggests they are.

Similarly, MacIntyre's representation of Weber and the bureaucratic
manager as 'emotivist' depends for its effectiveness upon a wholly unre-
alizable conception of instrumental reason, where what counts as rational
is restricted to formal calculations about means, to the exclusion of 'substantive' goals and commitments. According to MacIntyre, the
development of formal bureaucratic rationality is premised upon the cultivation of an attitude of moral neutrality by managers. Because the
manager treats ends as given, as outside his or her scope, questions about
the means of managerial effectiveness are divorced from questions of the
morality of the ends which his or her effectiveness serves or fails to serve.

As Charles Larmore (1987: xiii–xiv) has noted, however, MacIntyre is
entirely wrong to represent Weber's concept of 'formal rationality' as being
narrowly instrumental and dependent upon arbitrarily given ends. Unlike
those pursuing a dialectical critique of bureaucratic governance, Weber
does not maintain a general theoretical distinction between formal and
substantive rationality by relating them as means to ends inside a single
moral sphere. According to Larmore, Weber's distinction between formal
and substantive rationality has to be interpreted in the light of the very different but equally *ethical* perspectives informing them. In 'The profession
and vocation of politics' (1994b), Weber characterized the ethos appropri-

ate to forms of substantive rationality as an 'ethics of ultimate ends' or the 'ethics of conviction'. This ethos consists in a set of fundamental beliefs which persons commit themselves to put into practice regardless of the consequences of so doing. For Weber, however, ethical interests and capacities are not the expression of a universal moral personality; rather they are the plural creation of historically specific ethics or *Lebensführungen*. The ends of value-rational action are therefore multiple and specific to particular spheres of life: religious, economic, political, aesthetic and so forth. Hence the ultimate character of such action merely refers to the zeal with which a particular end is adhered to in one of these domains of existence.

The ethos associated with the development of formal rationality is certainly premised upon the cultivation of indifference to certain ulitmate moral ends. However, this indifference is predicated upon an awareness of the irreducible plurality of and frequent incommensurability between passionately held 'ultimate' moral ends and thus of the possible heavy cost of pursuing one of them at the expense of the others. Seen in this light, formal rationality is not associated with the development of an amoral instrumentalism, as MacIntyre would have it, but with a liberal-pluralist 'ethics of responsibility' which does take account of the consequence of attempting to realize esssentially contestable values that frequently come into conflict with other values (Minson, 1991: 17).

It is a mistake therefore to treat the bureau as the merely instrumental side of an integrated moral personality, as MacIntyre is wont to do. For the bureau comprises the social and, in Weberian terms, 'spiritual' conditions of a distinctive and independent organization of the person. Among the most important of these conditions are first, 'that access to office is dependent upon lengthy training in a technical expertise, usually certified by public examination; and second, that the office itself constitutes a vocation (*Beruf*), a focus of ethical commitment and duty, autonomous of and superior to the holder's extra-official ties to kith, kin, class, or for that matter, conscience' (Hunter, 1994: 156). In Weber's account these conditions mark out the bureau as a particular sort of life-order, and they provide the bureaucrat with a certain ethical demeanour and status-conduct. Unlike office-holding in the pre-modern worlds so loved by MacIntyre, the privileges of modern bureaucratic office are not personal possessions:

> Rather, entrance into an office . . . is considered an acceptance of a specific duty of fealty to the purpose of the office (*Amstreue*) in return for the grant of a secure existence. It is decisive for the modern loyalty to an office that, in the pure type, it does not establish a relationship to a person, like the vassal's or disciple's faith under feudal or patrimonial authority, but rather is devoted to *impersonal* or *functional* purposes. (Weber, 1978: 959, original emphasis)

The procedural, technical and hierarchical organization of the bureau thus provides the ethical conditions for a particular comportment of the person.

The ethical attributes of the good bureaucrat – strict adherence to procedure, commitment to the purposes of the office and so forth – are not an incompetent subtraction from the 'complete' (self-realizing) comportment of the person. On the contrary, as Ian Hunter (1994: 157) has indicated,

> they are a positive moral achievement requiring the mastery of a difficult ethical milieu and practice. They are the product of definite ethical techniques and routines – 'declaring' one's personal interest, developing professional relations with one's colleagues, subordinating one's ego to procedural decision-making – through which individuals develop the disposition and ability to conduct themselves according to the ethos of bureaucratic office.

If Weber is right then it is futile to attempt to judge and govern the conduct of bureaucrats according to criteria deriving from other departments of ethical life. This is particularly the case where the proposed standards are derived from the ethics of traditional religious and modern humanist intellectual life, as they are in MacIntyre's critique of the bureaucrat. It is precisely the overly 'principled' and hence 'other-worldly' character of these ethics that makes them incapable of comprehending the specific character of the bureaucratic ethos and its radical independence of religious or humanist moral absolutes (du Gay, 1995; Hunter, 1994; Minson, 1993).[3]

Concluding comments: critic of management as heir of religion

Instead of offering a positive description of the ethos of office – as Weber is at pains to do – MacIntyre attempts to hold the bureaucratic manager accountable to a specific ideal of the person. The ideal in question – that of the fully developed or complete human being – has its own particular genealogy, deriving many of its characteristics from Christian theology. MacIntyre's 'ideal' of the person as an agent directed towards integration (and hence salvation) has next to nothing in common with Weber's account of the person of the bureaucrat, and for good reason. These very different personae represent independent moral comportments formed in specific ethical milieux through the transmission of definite ethical disciplines and routines. As such they are irreducible to common underlying moral principles.

The problem is that MacIntyre insists on treating his own status persona – that of the 'complete' person – as 'ultimate' for all comportments of the person, the bureaucrat included. Because the person of the bureaucratic manager cannot meet the criteria for existence that MacIntyre sets for it, though, it must in his eyes forever remain a partial or failed version of the complete or integrated persona it should ideally be. Thus, in criticizing the impersonal bearing of the bureaucratic manager as 'one sided' or 'instrumental' in relation to the complete development of the Christian integrationist person, MacIntyre is doing no more than attempting to sub-ordinate one comportment of the person to another by sheer exercise of ethical force. If bureaucratic managers actually attempted to become that which MacIntyre suggests they ought – and that is a cosmic 'if' – one thing is certain: they would no longer be managers in any recognisable sense of the term. They might be well be critical intellectuals or even priests but bureaucrats they most certainly would not be.

One could imagine such a status shift on the part of bureaucrats appeal-ing to MacIntyre's nostalgic, communitarian yearnings. After all, as Charles Larmore (1987: 41) has indicated, political systems lacking a highly developed bureaucratic apparatus, such as the Greek polis – which MacIntyre continually insists on using as a large paddle for spanking modern man – have perhaps proven to be arenas for a broader and more subtle exercise of virtue than anything we can witness in modern Western political life. However, it is also worth bearing in mind the price to be paid for these more 'virtuous' arrangements; for example, far less free-dom to pursue other activities independently of political control and far less predictability in state decision-making.

Life in a virtuous polis may not suit modern souls. For while citizens of MacIntyre's anti-bureaucratic polis might well have the satisfaction of knowing that whatever decision their government makes it will be morally correct, they might also be somewhat worried about when their garbage will be collected or how their taxes will be calculated. Without the mana-gerial mentality and administrative ethic of the bureau many of the mundane governmental tasks we take for granted would not be carried out and, as a consequence, the everyday ordering of our existence could be put under unbearable strain.

Attending to the mundane daily consequences of life organized accord-ing to the vivid and imaginative scenarios of critical intellectuals such as MacIntyre is a useful way of highlighting the extent to which such critical thinking is characterized by an exemplary withdrawal from the institu-tional realities of managing.

That the prestige accorded to MacIntyre's critique of the character of the bureaucratic manager within critical organizational circles seems directly proportional to its implausibility and other-worldliness should alert us to an important point: that some real social authority flows from the cultiva-tion of a world-fleeing moral persona. As Ian Hunter (1994: 167) argues, to criticize the dominant organization of social life by undertaking an exemplary withdrawal from it – an abstention that claims transcendence through access to a more elevated or 'truer' mode of being – is something like a practice of 'secular holiness'.[4] It is also 'the mark of a spiritually exalted and morally venerated social type'.

That some real social prestige *is* accorded to the critical world-fleeing moral persona may well account for its continued reproduction. It may also explain why there is likely to be no early dissolution of what we might term the 'permanent structure' of this form of anti-bureaucratic thought.

Notes

1. However, contemporary forms of organizational critique have considerably more in common with the predecessors their advocates seek to distance them from than the latter seem to realize. It is interesting to note, for example, that underlying both Marx's critique of liberal economic and political ideals and that espoused by MacIntyre is a belief that that which does not form an organic whole must be fragmented and anomic. It is this romantic ideal of a whole expressed in each of its parts that shapes their respective visions. In their rather different ways both Marx and MacIntyre argue that all areas of social life should be united, and that the individual overcome the alienating distinction between the different social roles he or she is forced to inhabit. Neither appears to be able to abide the idea that what is relevant in one domain of existence need not be so in another. To the extent that they assume that a theoretical shift from Marx to MacIntyre represents something of a step forward in the battle to problematize management, practitioners of contemporary organizational critique would do well to explore the basic elements of political romanticism which informs the work of both thinkers. (See for example, Gaukroger, 1986 and Larmore, 1987, Chapter 5.)
2. The humanist and the bureaucrat are not the only possible protagonists for this exemplary play of dialectical virtues. For some commentators (Ferguson, 1984; Pringle, 1989) the technical rationality of the bureau is identified with masculinity and it falls to women to redeem politics morally through their feminine moral identities.
3. It needs to be remembered that at the time of its historical emergence – in the European religious civil wars of the early modern period – it was precisely the bureau's capacity to divorce public administration from private moral absolutisms that made it the privileged instrument of a novel pragmatic statecraft. This bureaucratic capacity to divorce politics from absolute principles is a contingent historical achievement that those of us lucky enough to live in pacified societies should not take for granted. Rather than berating the bureau for its presumed 'amoral technicism' we need to learn to exercise our historical imaginations a little more and appreciate this rare, delicate and reliable human invention in its own terms.
4. It was, perhaps, MacIntyre's remarkable capacities as a practitioner of the art of 'secular holiness' that Ernest Gellner was referring to when he teased him for his ability 'to get on a soapbox and sound like a bishop' (Gellner, quoted in Holmes, 1993: 116).

2

Bauman's Bureau: 'Modernity', Identity, Ethics

Towards the end of an otherwise very supportive review of MacIntyre's critique of 'the Manager', Iain Mangham (1995: 202) begins to worry about the Christian integrationism that pervades MacIntyre's discourse. While he believes that MacIntyre's criticisms of the modernist manager are pretty much correct, Mangham is nonetheless concerned that MacIntyre's search for universal principles of morality is both a philosophically fruitless endeavour and a potentially deleterious one. He indicates that attempts to found human conduct on universal principles and organic notions of social relations are destined to end in tears because they fail to acknowledge the heterogeneity of morality.

In contrast to MacIntyre's demand that a common notion of the good unite all areas of social life, Mangham (1995: 202) highlights Zygmunt Bauman's belief that there can be no 'universal and unshakeable' foundation for morality and that ambiguity, ambivalence, confusion and uncertainty are part and parcel of the human condition and hence something we have to learn to get along with. Rather than looking to MacIntyre's pre-liberal world of moral certainty for a new ideal of managerial conduct, Mangham (1995: 202) commends Bauman's postmodern vision of a world in which 'the mistrust of needs, desires and whims is to be replaced by a mistrust of unemotional, calculating reason'. In contrast to the rational, 'technicist' character of the modern bureaucrat, Mangham argues that the manager as postmodern character would be a great respecter of ambiguity, feel enormous regard for human emotions and appreciate actions without purpose and calculable rewards.

As Mangham suggests, while MacIntyre and Bauman look in rather different directions for their ideals of moral conduct, their respective scenarios are framed in relationship to a common foe: something called 'modernity'.

MacIntyre regards modern society as a 'moral calamity', and attaches much of the blame for this state of grave disorder on the instrumental, rationalist attitudes fostered within those central institutions of modernity: science and rational-legal bureaucracy.

Bauman's critique of modernity similarly focuses on the role of science and rational-legal bureaucracy in undermining the capacity for individual 'moral' action and responsibility. Like MacIntyre, Bauman (1989: 17–18) regards 'the culture of instrumental rationality', which he assumes governs the conduct of both scientists and bureaucrats, as an insidious development because it undermines what he considers to be the essence of moral relationships – responsibility for the Other born of proximity to the Other. For Bauman, responsibility (and hence morality) is silenced once proximity is eroded, and scientific and bureaucratic practice precisely enable such a seperation to take place because they 'extend the distance at which human action is able to bring effects' (1989: 193).

Both MacIntyre and Bauman draw stark, indeed startling, attention to what they consider to be the moral impoverishment of modernity. They also share a similar set of assumptions concerning the causes, if not the remedies, of this moral malaise. For both critics, chief amongst the culprits is the managerial mentality of rational-legal bureaucracy where 'the "objective" discharge of business takes place 'according to calculable rules and without regard to persons' (Weber quoted in Bauman, 1989: 14). Now, if Bauman's analysis of the bureau and the bureaucrat shares much in common with that of MacIntyre, as Mangham claims that it does, and if MacIntyre's critique of the character of the bureau and the bureaucrat is largely erroneous, as I argued it was in Chapter 1, then what precisely is to be gained by switching from one to the other? Why prefer Bauman to MacIntyre, as Mangham encourages us to do, when these authors share similarly problematic assumptions about the conduct of bureaucratic management? Once again, a certain critical ethos seems to have an important role to play here.

So Mangham is willing to endorse MacIntyre's critique of the character of the 'modernist' manager but not what he considers to be the underlying conservatism of MacIntyre's vision of a new managerial character. The problem with both the modernist manager and MacIntyre's pre-modern alternative, as far as Mangham is concerned, is their shared fixation with controlling the conduct of human beings, with establishing and regulating 'effective standards of universal behaviour' (1995: 202). Despite his perceptive criticisms of modernity, in Mangham's eyes MacIntyre's critical credentials – his radicalism – are undermined by his apparent (conservative) theism.

Bauman's postmodern character is conceived of by Mangham as 'radically different' – and hence as possessing more critical potential or reach – in that it eschews this desire for rationality and control and respects ambiguity, emotion and non-rationality (1995: 201–3). This character is the product of a self that is now thought to be not stable but multiple, mutable and continually in the process of becoming. It is a creation that rejects the exclusionary discourses that have delimited its perceptions and abrogated its freedom of action in favour of a more flexible, deregulated and multi-directional mode of being (Deetz, 1995: 223). The capacity for being permanently unsettled is therefore constitutive of this character's radical potential in Mangham's eyes and appears to be the primary reason for his preferring Bauman to MacIntyre.

But what precisely does embracing this 'radical' sort of multiplicity and provisionality entail? What practical norms for cultural, social, economic or political conduct does it furnish? These are important questions, ones that Mangham signally fails to provide any answers to. In the light of his silence, one is left wondering exactly what the relationship might be between this radical character and the institutional realities of managing.

In what follows I attempt to shed some light on the status of this post-modern character and its relationship to the conduct of bureaucratic management by focussing on selected elements of the work of the theorist Mangham commends to our attention: Zygmunt Bauman. In particular, I concentrate on the problematization of bureaucratic management con-tained within Bauman's *Modernity and the Holocaust* (1989) and argue that on both sociological and historical grounds Bauman's critique of bureau-cracy (and modernity) is fundamentally misguided.

As his critique of the bureau and the bureaucrat plays an important (if implicit) role in strengthening the appeal of something called 'postmoder-nity', disputing the explanatory power and reach of that critique may also, I argue, serve to qualify enthusiasm for the aforementioned radical post-modern character. Indeed, it may also strongly recommend some very ordinary and common attributes of modernity.

Modernity, bureaucracy and the Holocaust

Modernity has faced many criticisms in recent years, as Chapter 1 made evident. Few of these have been quite as vociferous and disturbing as those levelled by Zygmunt Bauman in *Modernity and the Holocaust*. In essence, Bauman's chief claim is that the potential for a Holocaust exists in all modern societies. The Holocaust, he argues, is 'an outcome of a unique encounter between factors by themselves quite ordinary and common' (Bauman, 1989: xiii), ordinary and common, that is, in every modern society. Among these common and ordinary factors Bauman includes the existence of a modern rational bureaucracy, the availability of modern sci-ence and technology, the rational, logical approach to problem-solving which, bound up as it is with these phenomena, permeates the whole of modern society, and lastly the state's centralization of the means of coercion and violence. The importance of these conditions for Bauman's argument is that they combine to undermine the possibility of individuals exercising what he considers to be their innate capacity for moral action. For him, the presence of these factors effectively removes from the modern person the burden of individual moral responsibility (1989: 28). And these conditions, common to all modern societies, make each and every one of those societies capable in principle of modern genocide (see also O'Kane, 1997).

For my purposes, it is Bauman's analysis of bureaucracy which is of most interest. Indeed, Bauman himself allocates a particularly important role to 'bureaucratic culture' in the development of the Holocaust.

> the bureaucratic culture which prompts us to view society as an object of admin-
> istration, as a collection of so many 'problems' to be solved, as 'nature' to be
> 'controlled', 'mastered' and 'improved' or 'remade', as a legitimate target for
> 'social engineering', and in general a garden to be designed and kept in the
> planned shape by force (the gardening posture divides vegetation into 'cultured
> plants' to be taken care of, and weeds to be exterminated) was the very atmos-
> phere in which the idea of the Holocaust could be conceived, slowly, yet
> consistently developed, and brought to its conclusion. (1989: 18)

Bauman's bureau

As the above quotation makes clear, Bauman views bureaucracy as the prime institutional carrier of what he terms 'the civilizing process' of modernity. This phrase refers to the structured ways in which 'the desiderata of rationality' are emancipated from 'interference by ethical norms or moral inhibitions' (1989: 28). For Bauman, then, bureaucracy is the primary organizational vehicle through which instrumental rationality is promoted to a predominant position within modern society to the detriment or exclusion of alternative (moral) criteria of action.

Re-reading Weber, Bauman argues, enables us to see the vital role bureaucracy plays in advancing the rationalization of conduct in a variety of domains. According to Bauman (1989: 28–9), Weber's work reveals the ways in which the bureaucratic organization of economic life, for example, privileges 'end oriented, rational action' over 'processes ruled by other (by definition irrational) norms, thus rendering it immune to the constraining impact of the postulates of mutual assistance, solidarity, reciprocal respect etc.' which are held to hold sway in non-business, unbureaucratized, formations. For Bauman, the key feature of Weberian bureaucracy is its demoralizing tendencies. 'The fundamental condition' of bureaucracy's success 'as an instrument of rational coordination of action' is its 'silencing of morality' (Bauman, 1989: 29).

So how precisely does modern bureaucracy function as 'a moral sleeping pill' (Bauman, 1989: 26)? For Bauman, 'the essence of bureaucratic structure and process' is the dissociation of 'instrumental rational criteria' from 'moral evaluations' of the ends they serve. However, this dissociation is itself premised upon two parallel processes: 'the meticulous functional division of labour' on the one hand, and 'the substitution of technical for moral responsibility' on the other (Bauman, 1989: 98).

According to Bauman (1989: 98–9) 'all division of labour (also such division as results from the mere hierarchy of command) creates a distance
between most of the contributors to the final outcome of a collective activity, and the outcome itself'. Unlike a pre-modern unit of work, in which all
members 'share in the same occupational skills, and the practical knowledge of working operations actually grows towards the top of the ladder',
persons 'occupying successive rungs of modern bureaucracy' have no
total picture but instead are simply cogs in a machine whose entirety they
can never fully grasp. 'What such practical and mental distance from the
final product means is that most functionaries of the bureaucratic hierarchy may give commands without full knowledge of their effects' (1989:
99).

Because he conceptualizes the essence of moral relationships in terms of
proximity, it is unsurprising that Bauman views the separation and distance characteristic of the bureaucratic division of labour (as opposed to
the presumed 'organic' nature of pre-modern arrangements) as crucial elements in the 'silencing of morality'. This tendency towards distanciation is
exacerbated once that bureaucratic division becomes functional because
now 'it is not just the lack of direct personal experience of the actual execution of a task to which successive commands contribute their share, but
also the lack of similarity between the task at hand and the task of the office
as a whole (one is not a miniature version, or an icon, of the other), which
distances the contributor from the job performed by the bureaucracy of
which he is a part' (1989: 99–100).

For Bauman, the functional division of labour undermines the possibility of individual cogs in the bureaucratic machine comprehending even at
an abstract, purely notional level the final outcome to which their own discrete, specialized efforts are ultimately contributing. Moral awareness and
responsibility are dissolved, he argues, when a complete 'process' is split
into minute functional tasks and those tasks are in turn separated from
each other. By concentrating on their own individual tasks, each bureaucrat
is able to avoid overall moral responsibility for the outcome to which their
own efforts ultimately contribute.

The second process responsible for 'silencing morality' through separation and distanciation is closely related to the first. According to Bauman
(1989: 100), the substitution of technical for moral responsibility would
not have been possible without 'the meticulous functional dissection and
separation of tasks'. Technical responsibility differs from moral responsibility, he argues, because it 'forgets' that the action to which it is oriented
is a means to a goal over and above itself. This forgetting is intimately connected to location within a functional division of labour 'where outer
connections of action are effectively removed from the field of vision'
(1989: 101). Because the bureaucrat's actions appear to her/him as ends in
themselves, the only forms of judgement appropriate to those actions are
ones intrinsic to it.

Hand-in-hand with the vaunted relative autonomy of the official conditioned by his functional specialization, comes his remoteness from the overall effects of divided yet co-ordinated labour of the organization as a whole. Once isolated from their distant consequences, most functionally specialized acts either pass moral tests easily or are morally indifferent. When unencumbered by moral worries, the act can be judged on unambiguously rational grounds. What matters then is whether the act has been performed according to the best available technical know-how, and whether its output has been cost-effective. Criteria are clear-cut and easy to operate . . . To put it bluntly, *the result is the irrelevance of moral standards for the technical success of the bureaucratic operation.* (Bauman, 1989: 101; italics in original)

Once inserted within a complex functional differentation of labour, and hence distanced from the ultimate outcomes to which their conduct contributes, bureaucrats are free to concentrate on the 'good' – ie technically proficient – performance of the job at hand. Morality is thus reduced to 'the commandment to be a good, efficient, diligent expert and worker' (Bauman, 1989: 102).

Associated with this privileging of technical over moral responsibility within the bureau is what Bauman (1989: 102; italics in original) describes as '*the dehumanization of the objects of bureaucratic operation*: the possibility to express these objects in purely technical, ethically neutral terms'. According to Bauman, dehumanization is an inescapable aspect of the functioning of all bureaucracies as, he suggests, Weber was well aware. Because the bureau discharges its business, as Weber has it, 'objectively' and without 'regard to persons', it must by its very nature disregard the essential humanity of its human objects and instead approach them as 'a set of quantitative measures' (1989: 102).

Through its inherent distanciating effects, bureaucratic procedures reduce human objects to 'pure, quality free, measurements' and thus rob them of that which makes them distinctive.

Dehumanization is inextricably related to the most essential, rationalizing tendency of modern bureaucracy. As all bureaucracies affect in some measure some human objects, the adverse impact of dehumanization is much more common than the habit to identify it almost totally with its genocidal effects would suggest. Soldiers are told to shoot targets, which fall, when they are hit. Employees of big companies are encouraged to destroy competition. Officers of welfare agencies operate discretionary awards at one time, personal credits at another. Their objects are supplementary benefit recipients. It is difficult to perceive and remember the humans behind all such technical terms. The point is that as far as bureaucratic goals go, they are better not perceived and not remembered . . . once effectively dehumanized, and hence cancelled as potential subjects of moral demands, human objects of bureaucratic task-performance are viewed with ethical indifference. (Bauman, 1989: 103)

For Bauman (1989: 163), modern legal rational bureaucracy 'is an instrument to obliterate responsibility'. This effect is achieved through the everyday operation of the most mundane components of bureaucratic organization: the minute separation of tasks; the pursuit of rational calculation; the dispassionate, 'objective' conduct of business; and the application of calculable rules to human objects without regard to them as persons. Such a concatenation of elements makes the bureau, in Bauman's eyes, 'intrinsically capable of genocidal action' (1989: 106).

Modern legal rational bureaucracy: Weber *contra* Bauman

Weber's conception of modern legal rational bureaucracy holds the key to Bauman's argument, much as it does to MacIntyre's. While he does not suggest that modern bureaucracy *must* result in Holocaust-style phenomena, it is obvious that Bauman regards bureaucratic culture as fostering forms of human conduct that exclude moral considerations and that, as a result, Holocaust-style solutions can easily flow from the instrumental atmosphere that bureaucracy induces. In this regard, his position is remarkably similar to that of MacIntyre. Both critics of modern bureaucracy highlight the rationalizing, instrumentalizing logic of bureaucratic conduct and point to its role in undermining what they – somewhat differently – conceive of as the essence of moral relationships.

While Bauman's critical discourse on the bureau, like MacIntyre's, draws upon a theoretical lexicon that is self-consciously Weberian, its conclusions concerning the ethical and moral emptiness of bureaucratic conduct are the very antithesis of Weber's own. Indeed, both sociologically and historically, Bauman's analysis of the bureau diverges from Weber's in crucial respects, despite Bauman's (1989: 28–9) claim effectively to be following in Weber's footsteps.

In Bauman's re-reading of Weber on bureaucracy, Weber's central theme is assumed to be the increasing instrumental rationalization of spheres of life that bureaucratization engenders, and the ethical and moral disfigurements this produces. Unfortunately, as Hennis (1988, 1996), for example, has indicated, Weber is innocent of the so-called Weberianism that adopts a uniform conception of rationalization. Instead, Weber precisely warned against viewing rationalization as a unilinear, monolithic process that colonizes everything in its path to similar effect. Rather than imputing to rationalism some singular, ceaseless logic, meaning or direction, Weber (1930: 77–8) argued that

> The history of rationalism shows a development which by no means follows parallel lines in the various departments of life . . . In fact, one may – this simple proposition, which is often forgotten, should be placed at the beginnings of every study which essays to deal with rationalism – rationalize life from fundamentally different basic points and in very different directions. Rationalism is a historical concept which covers a whole world of different things.

As I argued in Chapter 1, rather than being both the vanguard and organizational epitome of some generalized, modern process of 'instrumental
rationalization', bureaucratic conduct is rational in very particular ways.
Weber makes it quite clear, for example, that bureaucratic forms of rationality and objectivity do not entail epistemological claims to possess 'the
point of view of the universe', that general capacity for 'impartiality' and
'distanciation' which Bauman views as integral to the 'civilizing process'
and which, he argues, operates through the exclusion of the value-laden
aspects of human existence.

Similarly, Bauman's scathing attack on bureaucratic conduct as entailing
an ' "objective" discharge of business . . . without regard to persons' is
based on assumptions about personhood that are totally devoid of historical specificity. Rather than a general disposition to dehumanize objects of
administration, the phrase 'without regard to persons' has to be located
within a specific historical context. What Weber has in mind here is an
early modern conception of the person – as a notable personage, a bundle
of prestigious statuses. The 'objectivity' required of bureaucrats and
bureaucratic decision-making therefore entails a trained capacity to treat
people as 'individual' cases, i.e. apart from status and ascription, so that
the partialities of patronage and the dangers of corruption might be
avoided. Only by sleight of hand can the historically specific senses in
which Weber speaks of bureaucratic culture precluding 'personally motivated' actions be extended from their intended reference to signifying a
general process of dehumanization.

For Bauman the essence of bureaucratic structure and process is the dissociation of instrumental rational criteria from moral evaluations of the
ends they serve. And it is this 'dissociation process' that makes the bureau
such a powerful 'moral sleeping pill' in his eyes. The problem with this
argument is that it relies upon a wholly fantastical conception of 'instrumental rationality', where what counts as rational is restricted to formal
calculations about means to the detriment of 'substantive' goals and commitments. As the example of discharging business 'without regard to
persons' indicates, the formal rationality of bureaucratic conduct itself
gives rise to substantive ethical goals and is rooted in its own particular
life-order: that of the bureau.

Weber regards the 'formalistic impersonality' of bureaucratic administration – its instituted blindness to inherited differences in status and
prestige – as a source of democratic equalization. As he puts it, 'the
dominant norms are concepts of straightforward duty without regard to
personal considerations. Everyone is subject to formal equality of
treatment' (1978, I: 225). In a similar vein he indicates that officials have a
tendency to treat their official function from 'what is substantively a
utilitarian point of view in the interest of the welfare of those under their
authority' (1978, I: 225–6).

Conversely, the substantively rational pursuit of moral ends is not
always in itself ethically desirable. Weber's prime example of a

substantively rationalized legal system is one that is theocratically oriented. The moral zeal that Bauman finds lacking in 'formally rational' institutional settings is certainly much in evidence in such a system. Here, decisions made based on the ultimate imperatives of religion are allowed to hold sway over the formal rationality produced by strict adherence to 'positive' legal technique and procedure. Is Bauman really suggesting that such moral absolutism is to be preferred to legal formalism, simply because it is 'substantively' and not 'formally' rational? Surely not. Especially given the fact that legal formalism is itself capable of promoting 'substantive ethical goals' because of its procedural imperviousness to ultimate, overriding moral imperatives. As Weber argued:

> Formal justice is thus repugnant to all authoritarian powers, theocratic as well as patriarchic, because it diminishes the dependency of the individual upon the grace and power of the authorities. To democracy, however, it has been repugnant because it decreases the dependency of the legal practice and therewith of the individuals upon the decisions of their fellow citizens . . . In all these cases formal justice, due to its necessarily abstract character, infringes upon the ideals of substantive justice. It is precisely this abstract character which constitutes the decisive merit of formal justice to those who wield the economic power at any given time and who are therefore interested in its unhampered operation, but also those who on ideological grounds attempt to break down authoritarian control or to restrain irrational mass emotions for the purpose of opening up individual opportunities and liberating capacities. (Weber, 1978, II: 812–13)

Unlike Bauman, then, Weber does not deploy the categorical distinctions betwen formal and substantive, instrumental and value-oriented rationality to support a general normative analysis of social and political life. As the above examples make clear, there are two basic reasons for this. First, value-oriented and substantive forms of rationality do not constitute what Ian Hunter (1994: 150–1) has described as 'a single universal Kantian moral imperative capable of functioning as a moral yardstick for all other forms of rationality'. On the contrary, they represent a 'range of uncompromising, absolute ethical comportments' whose civic consequences may on occasion be highly undesirable. Secondly, Weber's examples are too firmly located in the particularities of historical and political circumstance for them to support the general 'means versus ends' moral discrimination that Bauman (and, as we have seen, MacIntyre) utilizes them for.

If it is this generalized opposition between means and ends that allows Bauman to categorize bureaucratic conduct as profoundly amoral, then indicating the artificiality of this division also calls into question Bauman's characterization of the bureau as ethically and morally deficient.

For Weber bureaucracy is a particular instituted style of ethical life, or *Lebensführung*, it is not treated as a symptom of moral deficiency. Instead, the bureau is represented as a specific 'order of life' subject to its own laws. Chief among these as we have seen, are that access to office is dependent upon lengthy training in a technical expertise, usually certifiable by public examination, and that the office itself is a 'vocation' (*Beruf*), a focus of individual moral commitment and ethical action which is separate from and privileged over the bureaucrat's extra-official ties to kith, kin, class and individual inner conscience (Weber, 1978, II: 958–9; du Gay, 1994a: 667–9; Hunter, 1994: 156).

The procedural, technical and hierarchical organization of the bureau provides the ethical conditions for a particular comportment of the person. The ethical attributes of the 'good bureaucrat' – strict adherence to procedure, commitment to the purposes of the office, abnegation of personal moral enthusiasms, acceptance of sub- and super-ordination, *esprit de corps* and so forth – represent a moral achievement having to reach a level of competence in a difficult ethical milieu and practice. They are the outcome of a specific organizational *habitus* – declaring one's personal interest, subordinating one's own deeply held convictions to the diktats of procedural decision-making, etc. – through which individuals learn to comport themselves in a manner befitting the vocation of office-holding.

To judge the moral tendency of bureaucracy *tout court*, as Bauman presumes to do, is a pointless exercise, one that Weber himself refuses to indulge in. Such an exercise seems all the more sterile when the conception of bureaucracy deployed is abstracted from the historical and political conditions in which it is to be found. As Weber (1978, II: 990–1) argues, the mere fact of bureaucratization does not unambiguously tell us about the concrete direction in which it leads in any given social formation. 'Hence one must in every individual historical case analyze in which . . . directions bureaucratization has there developed'. Embedding bureaucracy (properly understood *contra* Bauman's chimera) in a specific historico-political context is a crucial first step towards delineating its 'concrete directions'.

From administration without government . . .

As with so much of his work, Weber's political writings possess a dual character. They were occasioned by his concern with contemporary events and problems, and yet they always seem to point beyond their immediate context towards much wider considerations. Concern with the political fate of Germany, for example, is always high on Weber's agenda, yet his discussion of the fate of politics in Germany, 'however intense its immediate engagement, always has implications for our fundamental understanding of the politics of the modern western state' (Lassman and Speirs, 1994: xi).

Writing during and after the First World War, Weber's primary consideration was with the very survival of the German state. Returning to a theme that had pervaded his earlier work, Weber stressed that Germany was a nation lacking political education and political will. The policies of the wartime government had made this only too obvious. For Weber

(1994a: 270), the Wilhelmine political system exhibited a pronounced 'will to powerlessness'. Parliament, he argued, offered a poor training ground for real politicians, those who 'lived for politics' rather than simply living 'off politics'. Government ministers were mostly appointed from the state bureaucracy with responsibility to the Kaiser and not to Parliament (O'Kane, 1997). The resultant 'rule by officials' had produced a government that was rule-following and lacked the personal initiative characteristic of a system where ministers were dependent upon an electorate for their continued tenure in office and where they had to defend their policies against an organized opposition. For Weber, this all-important form of personal responsibility was signally lacking in the German system of government.

> Precisely those who are officials by nature and who, in this regard, are of high moral stature, are bad and, particularly in the political meaning of the word, irre-sponsible politicians, and thus of low moral stature in this sense – men of the kind we Germans, to our cost have had in positions of leadership time after time. This is what we call 'rule by officials'. Let me make it clear that I imply no stain on the honour of our officials by exposing the political deficiency of this system, when evaluated from the standpoint of success. (Weber, 1994b: 331)

In Weber's account, the Wilhelmine state did not offer the conditions for fostering strong parliamentary leaders – those for whom politics was a vocation, who obtained office through victory in popular elections and who had learnt the skills necessary for the conduct of political office, such as oratory, through public debate and advocacy – and so persons of this sort were not available to serve the Weimar Republic.[1] This meant that the central issue that needed to be addressed as far as he was concerned was how to prevent the bureaucratic elimination of genuine political activity and, thus, how to nurture the conditions under which professional politi-cians could emerge to save the state from the 'negative politics' of 'rule by officials'.

In the modern state this placed the question of the nature and role of Parliament at the top of the governmental agenda: 'How is Parliament to be made capable of assuming power? Anything else is a side-issue' (Weber, 1994a: 190; italics in original). Weber advocated a strong Parliament as the proper arena for the conduct of national politics, for two main reasons. First, Parliament was important because it provided the venue in which genuine political leaders could be selected. Secondly, political activity for and within a parliament – which for Weber meant universal suffrage, compet-ing mass parties, and charismatic leaders appealing directly to the electorate for support for policies initiated by the parties and their leaders (and certainly not by the masses in themselves) – was a crucial counter-balance to what he saw as the 'inescapable power . . . of the bureaucracy in the state' (Weber, 1994a: 159).

These points are important for Weber because he recognizes a close affinity between bureaucracy and democracy (1978, II: 983–5). The political demands typically arising within democratic states can only be met by large-scale bureaucratic administration (1978, II: 972). This in turn, will often lead to the bureaucracy usurping a political leadership role if left (politically) ineffectively controlled and scrutinized. As Weber (1994a: 177–8; 1994b: 330–3) was continually at pains to point out, the politician and the bureaucrat occupy different orders of life which are subject to different laws. In addressing the different kinds of responsibility that bureaucrats and politicians have for their actions, Weber insisted on the irreducibility of different spheres of ethical life and on the consequent necessity of applying different ethical protocols to them.

> In terms of what he is really called upon to do (*Beruf*), the true official – and this is crucial for any judgement of the previous regime here in Germany – should not engage in politics . . . The official should carry out the duties of his office *sine ira et studio*, 'without anger and prejudice'. Thus he should not do the very thing which politicians, both the leaders and their following do, which is to fight. Partisanship, fighting, passion – *ira et studium* – all this is the very element in which the politician, and above all, the political *leader*, thrives. *His* actions are subject to a quite different principle of *responsibility*, one diametrically opposed to that of the official. When, despite the arguments advanced by an official, his superior insists on the execution of an instruction which the official regards as mistaken, the official's honour consists in being able to carry out that instruction, on the *responsibility* of the man issuing it, conscientiously and precisely in the same way as if it corresponded to his own convictions. Without this supremely ethical discipline and self-denial the whole apparatus would disintegrate. By contrast, the honour of the political leader, that is, of the leading statesman, consists precisely in taking exclusive, *personal* responsibility for what he does, responsibility which he cannot and may not refuse or unload onto others. (1994b: 330–1; original emphasis)

By distinguishing their components and indicating how they belong to and only make sense within the boundaries of their own respective spheres of life, Weber indicated the limits to both bureaucratic and political conduct.

The limits to bureaucracy and bureaucratic action that Weber describes and advocates are expressed primarily in relation to his specific (historically and politically particular) fears about the damage being done to the worldly interests of the early twentieth-century German state by 'rule by officials'.[2] These are not, however, the general and principled limits envisaged by Bauman, who demands that the bureaucrat take personal moral responsibility for otherwise 'technicist' decision-making and who imagines bureaucratic expertise as an incomplete fragment of an integrated moral personality.

For Weber, a crucial feature of modern society is the fact of pluralization or social differentiation (1994b: 362–3). Refusing to accept that there was a unified moral personality underpinning and unifying human action,

Weber instead argued that there are many discrete ethical domains and these neither represent versions of some single homogeneous good nor fall into any natural hierarchy. Rather than seeking to transcend the inescapable differences between these spheres, Weber argued that we have to learn to regionalize or compartmentalize their respective dominance (1994a: 157; see also Rorty, 1988: 7).

For Weber, then, it is fruitless, vain and indeed potentially dangerous to attempt to govern one sphere of life according to criteria derived from other departments of life. As he makes clear in 'Parliament and government in Germany' and 'The profession and vocation of politics', the monopolistic tendencies of state bureaucracy in early twentieth century Germany posed a constant menace to the autonomy of other social spheres. Weber indicates that the bureaucratic de-differentiation of life orders demanded, for example, by the romantic socialism of 'naive littérateurs' and already evidenced in the practice of 'rule by officials', was 'in the process of manufacturing the housing of future serfdom, to which, perhaps, men will have to submit powerlessly . . . *if they consider that the ultimate and only value by which the conduct of their affairs is to be decided is good administration and provison of their needs by officials (that is 'good' in the purely technical sense of rational administration)* ' (1994a: 158; my italics).

With bureaucrats themselves being allowed or encouraged to take direct political responsibility for the actions of the state, it appeared to Weber that an ethic of administration was fast freeing itself from its proper moorings and was set to efface government as a political process.

> Officialdom has passed every test brilliantly wherever it was required to demonstrate its sense of duty, its objectivity and its ability to master organizational problems in relation to strictly circumscribed, official tasks of a specialized nature . . . But what concerns us here are political achievements rather than those of 'service', and the facts themselves proclaim loudly something which no lover of truth can conceal, namely that rule by officials has failed utterly whenever it dealt with political questions. This has not happened by chance. Indeed, to put it the other way round, it would be quite astonishing if abilities which are inwardly so disparate were to coincide within one and the same political formation. As we have said, it is not the task of an official to join in political conflict on the basis of his own convictions, and thus, in this sense of the word, 'engage in politics', which always means fighting. On the contrary, he takes pride in preserving his impartiality, overcoming his own inclinations and opinions, so as to execute in a conscientious and meaningful way what is required of him by the general definition of his duties, even – and particularly – when they do not coincide with his own political views. Conversely, the leadership which assigns tasks to the officials must of course constantly solve political problems, both of power-politics and of cultural politics (*Kulturpolitik*). Keeping this under control is the first and fundamental task of parliament. Not only the tasks assigned to the highest central authorities, but each individual question, no matter how technical, at the lowest levels of authority can become politically important, so that political considerations then determine the way it is resolved. It is politicians who must provide a counterbalance to the rule of officialdom. The power

interests of those occupying the leading positions in a system ruled purely by officials are opposed to this, and they will always follow their inclination to enjoy as much uncontrolled freedom as possible, and above all to maintain a monopoly over ministerial posts for the promotion of officials. (Weber, 1994a: 177–8)

Forged in the party system and tempered by the organized adversarialism of the Parliament, the politician belongs to an order of life quite unlike that of the bureaucrat. The party leader possesses the political abilities and ethical demeanour required by the unremitting struggle to gain and retain power. This, and not the trained expertise and impersonal dedication of the official, is what equips the politician to pursue the worldly interests of the state in the face of a hostile and unpredictable economic and political environment.

For Weber, claims to embody a representational totality made by and on behalf of the state bureaucracy in early twentieth-century Germany were politically dangerous precisely because they required bureaucrats to assume a role they were signally ill-equipped so to do: to become professional politicians. The political stability and social dynamism that rested upon the separation of these two distinct life orders were threatened by a process of bureaucratic de-differentiation that seemed destined to produce a system of administration without government.

. . . to government without administration

So Weber's concerns about the growth of bureaucratic power are very different from those of Bauman. Whereas the former's pessimistic analysis is rooted in the specificities of the German political system of the late nineteenth and early twentieth centuries, the latter's is abstracted from any particular historico-political context. For Weber, the problems with state bureaucracy in Germany arose not from its overarching embodiment of some cultural spirit of 'instrumental reason' but from an illegitimate extension of its administrative ethos into the sphere of political leadership. In this the state bureau was acting beyond the limits of its competence. For Bauman the issue is very different. Bureaucracy *tout court* is an object of critique because it signally fails to realize ultimate moral ends identified with humanity. Unfortunately for Bauman, as something that the bureau does not attempt this is a mission it cannot be accused of failing.

The limitations of Bauman's ahistoric critique of bureaucracy become even more evident when attention is focused on the relationship between the Nazi regime and the Civil Service in Germany. As Jane Caplan (1988: 337), for example, has indicated, rather than being the technical-administrative handmaiden of Nazism, the German state bureau was itself subjected to continuous assault by the National Socialists in the latter's attempt to realize its promise of a political new order.

No one who has studied the intricacies and contradictions of policy in the Third Reich can doubt that this was a period of profound assault on the personnel and principles of the German administration . . . the fragmentation of the apparatus of government, the chronic conflicts in policy-making and execution, and the persistent violation of procedural norms resulted from the destructive impact of National Socialist rule on the standards of administrative practice previously developed in Germany. (Caplan, 1988: 322)

The image of Nazi Germany as an efficient, bureaucratic machine w lich Bauman endorses has been superseded in historical researches by a picture of the Third Reich as a system of semi-institutionalized conflict whose exponents wanted 'the power of government without the ballast of administration' (Caplan, 1988: vii). By parasitically and progressively dissolving the institutional apparatuses it had inherited, the Nazi regime effectively undermined the administrative structures on which its own stabilization and reproduction depended.

Even before they seized power, the Nazis had expressed considerable antipathy towards state officials. *Mein Kampf* indicates Hitler's despair at the capacity of the state and its officials to perform its essential protective function in relation to the *Volk*. As Caplan (1988: 103) points out, this fear could be precisely located by Hitler. Purporting to explain how the Jews had contrived to evade the natural watchfulness of the German people and pass themselves off as Germans, he railed against the state's inability to realize that, whatever the disguise deployed, 'he is always the same Jew':

That so obvious a fact is not recognized by the average head-clerk in a German government department . . . is also a self-evident and natural fact; since it would be difficult to find another class of people who are so lacking in instincts and intelligence as the civil servants employed by our modern German State authorities. (Hitler, quoted in Caplan, 1988: 103)

This loathing of state officialdom powered the visible antagonism between the Nazi Party as *Kampfbund* and the bureaucracy as a rule-bound system, epitomized in National Socialists contrast between the action-oriented, street-fighting storm-trooper and the cosseted, apathetic, pen-pushing clerk.

By the early 1930s, evidence was accumulating that the Nazis would not allow bureaucratic practice to stand in the way of their political agenda. The experience of Nazi rule at regional level before 1933 caused considerable disquiet amongst civil servants. In Oldenburg, for example, where the Nazis unexpectedly took power after the May 1932 elections, there was considerable political interference in administrative personnel policies. A freeze on most Civil Service promotions and appointments was imposed and a number of officials were forcibly retired and party members were substituted (Caplan, 1988: 114). After the seizure of power in 1933, the politicization of the organs of state by the Party proceeded in earnest. This was accompanied by the destruction of political and social opposition.

In a process parallel to the subjugation of the democratically elected assemblies, Nazi activists moved to gain control over the apparatuses of national, regional and local administration by expelling known opponents and other unsympathetic civil servants from office, and by securing the appointment of politically reliable alternatives. Mixed in with this, and mocking the party's own virulent critique of alleged Weimar standards, was a spoils system for 'deserving' party members . . . These pressures frequently met resistance from civil servants dismayed at the violation of normal procedures, whatever their own political proclivities. (Caplan, 1988: 138)

The purge of appointed civil servants (on the grounds of their ethnicity, gender, political beliefs, religious beliefs, etc.) and their replacement with unqualified party activists, the bypassing of procedural norms, the blatant disregard for the rule of law and so on and so forth all point, *contra* Bauman's argument, to a process of de-bureaucratization rather than to a natural affinity between the Nazi Party and the state bureaucracy. For the Nazis the ultimate goal was to 'train a civil-service corps that was no longer distinguishable from the party leadership corps' (Sommer, quoted in Caplan, 1988: 183).

This blurring of political leadership and state administrative apparatus represents exactly the sort of de-differentiation that Weber railed against in his political writings. However, rather than representing a takeover bid for the polity by the state bureau, as Weber described the situation earlier in the century, the Nazis moved from the opposite direction, instigating a takeover bid for the state bureau by the political leadership. Either way, the political freedom and flexibility predicated on the separation of these two spheres were undermined by a totalizing logic antithetical to the borders, boundaries and compartments of a modern liberal-democratic polity.

Because the Nazis refused to draw any distinctions between party and state, activist and citizen, they demanded that state officials saw themselves as the Führer's vassals. In so doing, they sought to turn bureaucrats into something else entirely: a cross between pre-modern serfs and political activists.

The presiding image of the New Order was the substitution of an *organic* community of co-operation for the corruption and bureaucratism of the Weimar Republic, a substitution which was to enable the official to become truly the servant of 'the people' instead of an abstract state. Thus, 'nomination to civil-servant status is a mark of faith on the part of the Führer . . . and thus . . . of the people themselves'. The civil servant should see himself as the 'mediator between the will of Adolf Hitler as Führer of the Reich, and the German people as nation', whose task was not just to 'discharge his duties without professional error or reproach, but [to] dedicate his life to the national community' (H. Neef, quoted in Caplan, 1988: 193–4).

This organic theme was developed in Nazi propaganda which drew on the imagery of feudalism to describe the status of the civil servant and, especially, his relationship to the Führer. Placing the Civil Service and

National Socialism in an imaginary historical lineage, the Nazis claimed that the feudal duties owed by civil servants were core Germanic values which had been buried by centuries of racial impurity and national weakness, apart from a brief resurgence in eighteenth-century Prussia. Since that time, the state had been degraded to the level of an economic enterprise, empty of moral worth. The advent of the Third Reich was now set to heal this fractured history and restore a real continuity with the Germanic and Prussian order (Caplan, 1988). The civil servant was invited to see himself as the Führer's vassal; his oath of allegiance being not simply a commitment to the competent performance of his official duties, but representing the establishment of a liege relationship that was to last until death. In a complete reversal of the ethos of office, the Nazis stressed that the relationship between official and political leader

> is not simply a constitutional or legal one, but is like that of the Germanic vassal, who for life and death in all circumstances and at all times knows and feels he is bound to his leader. Through his personal bond with the leader the civil servant receives a proof of trust, in the same way that members of the National Socialist movement and its formations are also bound by oath of loyalty to the Führer. (Neef, quoted in Caplan, 1988: 195)

While Bauman argues that the Nazi bureaucracy was the very epitome of 'modernity', the Nazis themselves looked not to modernity but back to pre-modern times to characterize the conduct they required of state officials. As Friedrich and Brzezinski (1965: 206, quoted in O'Kane, 1997: 50) argued, 'what we find under totalitarian dictatorships is . . . a marked deviation and retrogression where previously a higher degree of bureaucratization existed'.

The political discourse of Nazism was cast in the mould of a (pre-modern) organic theory of society in which each part expresses the essence of the whole. Such a commitment to organic wholeness could not accommodate separated spheres of life and autonomous institutions. The Nazis could not allow the state bureaucracy to function as its own life order, for example, as this went against their own claims to represent the totality of the state and the nation. However, by undermining the bureaucratic character of the institutional apparatuses of government that they had inherited in pursuit of this impossible ideal of totality – through extreme politicization, through 'personalizing' the relationship between official and political leadership, through disregarding procedural norms and overriding the rule of law – the Nazi regime effectively consumed the sources of its own survival as a functioning political system. In other words, by seeking to operationalize a fantasy of government without modern administration, the regime proved incapable of generating the conditions for its own stabilization and reproduction, in terms either of institutions or of policy-making procedures.

Postmodern ethics – who needs 'em?

On both sociological and historical grounds, Bauman's critique of bureaucracy and modernity is extremely problematic. Given that this critique
plays an important role in strengthening the appeal of something Bauman
calls 'postmodernity', exposing the weaknesses of his case against the
bureau and, indeed, against other institutions of modern society more generally may also call into question the wisdom of embracing the
'postmodern' as he conceives of it.

Because Bauman represents modernity and bureaucracy in such fantastical, and wholly negative, terms, it is unsurprising that they seem
indefensible. After all, what rational person would freely consent to defend
modern society if its relationship to morality conformed to the following
basic description?

> From the perspective of 'the rational order', morality is and is bound to remain
> *irrational*. For every social totality bent on uniformity and the soliciting of the dis-
> ciplined, co-ordinated action, the stubborn and resilient autonomy of the moral
> self is a scandal. From the control desk of society, it is viewed as the germ of
> chaos and anarchy inside order; as the outer limit of what reason (or its self-
> appointed spokesmen and agents) can do to design and implement whatever
> has been proclaimed as the 'perfect' arrangement of human cohabitation.
> (Bauman, 1993: 13)

Luckily, no rational person need worry about defending this monstrous
creation for it does not bear any relationship to any actually existing –
democratic, plural, differentiated – modern societies. Rather, in a manner
reminiscent of MacIntyre and, perhaps more obviously, of the Frankfurt
School, it seems set on equating modernity with totalitarianism.[3] Such a
move is remarkably specious, for it overlooks the extent to which totalitarianism involves the tyrannical violation of crucial 'constitutive' features
of modernity, such as social and political pluralism.

As Niklas Luhmann (1980: xx) has indicated, the sort of perspective
deployed by Bauman, and the moral opprobrium that accompanies it,
results from an unthinking application of (obsolete) descriptive categories
derived from classical thought rather than a realistic appraisal of the
(modern) situation. As the previous chapter made clear, in modern, highly
differentiated societies individuals cannot be located exclusively inside
any single social system or 'sphere of life'. According to Luhmann (1980:
xx), in modern social formations, 'subsystems and organizations, including
the poltical system, must be conceptualized as excluding men as concrete
psycho-organic units. No man is completely contained inside them.' By
casting modern societies in the mould of totalitarianism, Bauman fundamentally misconceives such aspects of modernity. Viewed historically, such
modern phenomena as 'impersonal' bureaucratic administration, which
Bauman treats as symptomatic of a general totalitarian will to dehumanize,

have had a number of profoundly anti-totalitarian consequences. Through treating people as individual cases – i.e. apart from status and ascription – bureaucratic forms of depersonalization have had the effect of breaking down chains of personal dependency and surveillance rather than intensifying them, as Bauman would have it.

And as we saw with respect to administrative policy in Nazi Germany, totalitarian regimes have a tendency to personalize and politicize that which modern societies have sought to depersonalize and depoliticize. Refusing to work with modern distinctions between party and state, the Nazis characterized the relationship between Führer and civil servant – in pre-modern terms – as one of vassalage. Rather than accepting modern forms of compartmentalization wherein individuals are not exclusively located within any one life order, the Nazis were committed to a vision of organic wholeness whereby the Nazi polity must express 'the whole man'. In this as in so much else, rather than epitomizing the 'essence' of modernity, as Bauman insists they did, the Nazis looked back to pre-modern times.

If not modernity, then what?

It is hardly surprising then that Bauman's (mis)representation of modernity as totalitarianism should implicitly strengthen the appeal of something called postmodernity. For if modern society functions according to the logic of a 'total institution', as Bauman (1989: 165; 1993: 122) suggests it does, then the 'democratic society' and 'social pluralism' he associates with postmodernity will naturally seem more appealing to liberty-loving folk.

The problematic nature of this tactic can be seen more clearly when we examine the role Bauman attributes to pluralist political democracy as a countervailing factor in the relationship between modernity and Nazi genocide. According to Bauman (1989: 165), the very best antidote to those totalitarian tendencies dwelling at the heart of all modern, rational societies – and manifest so visibly in Hitler's Germany – is the presence of political and social pluralism. While modern societies, he argues, sought to 'overcome variety' in the pursuit of order by extending the scope and reach of 'a given institutional power, political and cultural', with predictably disastrous consquences, the postmodern perspective pierces through this myth of rationality and universality by indicating that '*pluralism is the best preventive medicine against morally normal people engaging in morally abnormal acts*' (1989: 165; original emphasis).

There are a number of problems with this argument but one stands out. Political democracy of the pluralist variant is itself a crucial aspect of modernity. Pluralist democracy is a product of modern times, and part of the reason for this, as Weber indicated, is that modern democracy is constitutively linked to the development of a rational-legal bureaucracy. Only by (illicitly) making modernity and bureaucracy synonymous with totalitarianism can social and political pluralism be assigned a postmodern pedigree.[4]

It might be tempting to think that Bauman's espoused pluralism makes him something of a modernist despite his own intentions. After all, he describes 'postmodernity' as 'modernity without illusions'. As the illusions in question – which basically boil down to 'the belief that the "messiness" of the human world is but a temporary and repairable state, sooner or later to be replaced by the orderly and systematic rule of reason' (1993: 32) – appear to be little more than the product of Bauman's own imagination, perhaps his much vaunted postmodernity is in fact just 'modernity' *minus Bauman's own illusions*? If we look at one of the very few examples of 'postmodern ethics' that Bauman sees fit to offer, such an interpretation appears to possess some plausibility. While he argues that 'morality' as proximity is a pre-modern phenomenon but nonetheless 'the only morality we have' (1993: 217), Bauman remains just enough of a realist to acknowledge that such a morality is 'woefully inadequate' in a (modern) society in which much important action is action at a distance.

In probably his only discussion of management that comes close to assuming that this activity is not irrevocably immoral, Bauman argues that whereas modern management practice pretended to possess 'the kind of certainty which the experts with their scientific knowledge' always claim to offer, postmodern management ethics deals with 'what-has-not-happened-yet, with a future that is endemically the realm of uncertainty and the playfield of conflicting scenarios' (1993: 221). This postmodern management ethics involves 'visualizing' the long range effects of action.

> The duty to visualize the future impact of action (undertaken or not undertaken) means acting under the pressure of acute uncertainty. The moral stance consists precisely in seeing that this uncertainty is neither dismissed nor suppressed. (1993: 221)

The idea that 'visualization' is 'the first duty' of any future ethics would strike many senior managers in both public and private sector organizations as odd, given that assessing the likely impact of a range of potential courses of action in an environment of some uncertainty is a crucial aspect of the work they perform. Only by making 'modern' management ethics conform to a fantastical notion of 'instrumental rationality' can Bauman offer such a formulation as 'postmodern' revelation.

We need only remember that Weber's concept of 'formal bureaucratic rationality' in no sense conforms to the narrow conception of instrumentalism that Bauman projects on to modern forms of management. As I argued in Chapter 1, modern forms of bureaucratic ethics associated with the development of formal rationality are certainly premised upon the cultivation of indifference towards certain ultimate moral ends. However, this indifference is founded upon an awareness of the irreducible plurality of and frequent incommensurability between passionately held, 'ultimate' moral ends and thus on the possible consequences and costs (read 'long range effects') of pursuing one of them at the expense of the others. Seen in this light, rather than in Bauman's totalitarian terms, 'formal bureaucratic rationality' is not associated with the development of amoral instrumentalism but with a liberal-pluralist ethics of responsibility which does take account of the effects of attempting to realize certain essentially contestable values that frequently come into conflict with other values.

Once again, that which Bauman attributes to postmodern ethics is in fact the very epitome of modern ethics, properly understood.

So, to what extent can Bauman be described as a modernist *malgré lui*? Well, on the one hand, as the above examples suggest, Bauman's 'postmodernity' is something like 'modernity without illusions': Bauman's own illusions, that is. In undercutting – unintentionally – the very indictments of modernity he seems most concerned to stand by, Bauman comes close to being a modernist despite himself. However, and regrettably, this is only half the story. For, on the other hand, Bauman's postmodernity also embraces certain pre-modern attributes which are antithetical in the extreme to some of the most important constitutive features of modernity, including those, such as social and political pluralism, that Bauman himself appears to cherish. Once again, it is Bauman's misconceptions of 'modernity' that lead him down this unfortunate path.

Religion and romance in Bauman's postmodernity

In addition to charging modernity with furthering the illusion that 'the messiness of the human world' is repairable, Bauman also claims that modernity is engaged in an ongoing project to 'disenchant' and 'depersonalize' (or 'dehumanize') the world in an attempt to create a uniform, rational order. According to him, in the light of the postmodern turn these forms of 'rational madness' are also, thankfully, being reversed (1993: 33–5).

Two questions immediately come to mind. First, does 'modernity' seek to disenchant and depersonalize in the manner Bauman suggests? And, secondly, what are the potential costs of reversing these processes?

Because Bauman so rarely steps down from the dizzy heights of theory to address the banal practical contexts within which cultural, social and moral attributes are formed, his description of disenchantment and depersonalization is always somewhat abstract. So, we learn, for example, that modernity *tout court*, is characterized by a generalized 'mistrust of human sponteneity, of drives, impulses and inclinations resistant to prediction and rational justification'. This general disposition to 'disenchant' is contrasted with the postmodern world, where 'mystery is no more a barely tolerated alien awaiting a deportation order. In that world, things may happen that have no cause which made them necessary; and people do things which would hardly pass the test of an accountable, let alone "reasonable" purpose.' Here the mistrust of emotion, drives, pulses and so forth characteristic of modernity is replaced with a 'mistrust of unemotional, calculating reason' (1993: 33).

Once 'modernity' is disaggregated and its highly specialized 'spheres of life' attended to in their own terms, this generalized portrait of disenchantment soon loses whatever descriptive power and critical purchase it is assumed to possess. As we saw in Chapter 1 in relation to the life order of the bureau, the objectivity and rationality required of the bureaucrat is not achieved at the cost of obliterating emotion, friendship and morality from the organizational universe, as Bauman would have us believe. Rather than requiring the eradication of all personal feelings and their replacement with 'soulless instrumentalism', bureaucratic conduct only engenders a specific antipathy towards those relations that open up the possibility of corruption, through, for example, the improper exercise of personal patronage – 'jobs for the boys' etc. – indulging incompetence or by betraying confidences.

The demands for objectivity, impartiality and rationality inscribed within the bureaucratic ethos cannot therefore be seen to embody a total disregard for human emotions. The supposition of just such an antipathy between 'bureaucratic reason' and 'human emotions' on the part of Bauman is premised upon a romantic identification of such relations with freedom from normative compulsion, spontaneous attraction, intimacy and so forth. Once again, categorical distinctions between formal and substantive, instrumental and value-oriented rationality are used by Bauman to support a general normative analysis of social and moral existence. And, as we saw earlier, such a generalized opposition between means and ends has little in the way of explanatory power.

Similar problems beset Bauman's discussion of modern processes of 'depersonalization'. Modernity, he argues, has been in the business of defaming and degrading all 'human acts that have only "passions" and spontaneous inclinations for their cause'.

> The modern mind is appalled by the 'de-regulation' of human conduct, of living without a strict and comprehensive ethical code, of making a wager on human moral intuition and ability to negotiate the art and usages of living together – rather than seeking the support of the law-like, depersonalized rules. (1993: 33)

This 'modern' generalized degradation of 'personal morality' is contrasted with the postmodern concern with entrusting the fate of human coexistence to the innate pre-social, moral capacities of human beings. According to Bauman, postmodern processes of moral re-personalization represent a rediscovery of an 'essential' fact: that ultimately, nothing can replace the 'intimate consent of the whole soul' (1993: 35).

Bauman's concern with the 'whole person' registers his inability to come to terms with the plural, differentiated nature of personhood in modern societies. For, as I argued earlier, the highly specialized spheres of life characteristic of modern societies involve an abstraction from and indeed, indifference to, multiple aspects of the lives of concrete individuals. Thankfully, we do not depend upon the personal moral propensities of our postmen and women to ensure that our mail is delivered, but rather on what Luhmann (1980: xx) terms a set of abstract 'membership rules' that link wage remuneration with a codified set of professional obligations. It is the pre-eminence of just such a set of anonymous or depersonalized forms of social organization (based on codified 'entrance/exit' rules) that has signalled a substantial breakdown of chains of personal dependency. A couple of brief examples should suffice.

Consider the case of judicial impartiality. Equality before the law is a form of depersonalization. It refers to a series of filtering mechanisms that have been inscribed into the legal sphere which work to make such factors as political party, religious belief and economic status irrelevant to an individual's position as a legal person. Obviously, there are leakages, but the point to hold on to is that almost without noticing it we define discriminatory justice in terms of failure in the filtering mechanisms rather than by appealing to any human 'essence' which is the exact same in all citizens (Holmes and Larmore, 1980: xxiv). The idea of 'one person one vote' has similar institutional connotations. It means that voting booths in modern democracies (and the secret ballot is obviously relevant here) are 'depersonalized' to every facet of an individual's life apart from their role as a voter. In each context, formal mechanisms of depersonalization can be associated with freedom.

If it can be shown, as I have argued it can, that *contra* Bauman, modern processes of 'disenchantment' and 'depersonalization' do not have wholly negative consequences, what then are the likely effects of attempting to throw these into reverse?

Logics of de-differentiation

At one point in his critique of the bureau, Bauman (1989: 165) argues that a fundamental feature of the totalitarian state is its attempt to transform 'all its agencies into mirror reflections of each other'. This form of de-differentiation, he continues, undermines pluralism and poses a threat to individual freedom.

Such a logic of de-differentiation could be seen at work in the political discourse of Nazism, where a commitment to organic wholeness was unable to accommodate the existence of specialized, separate spheres of life and autonomous institutions. As we saw earlier, the Nazis developed their organic theme in relationship to the conduct of bureaucratic administration by demanding that civil servants develop a *personal* bond of allegiance to the Führer rather than an impersonal devotion to their office, and by representing themselves as engaged in a moral crusade to *re-enchant* a state that had been degraded to the level of a formal organization. Such logics of re-enchantment and re-personalization were, and indeed are, fundamentally opposed to the legal-rational conduct of administration and the liberal-pluralist ethics of responsibility it embodies.

By insisting that bureaucrats stop being bureaucrats and become enthusiastic Nazis, by demanding that they did not treat people as individual cases but subject them to absolutely unequal treatment, depending upon their ethnicity, religious beliefs, sexual orientation, political persuasion and so forth, national socialism destroyed an important modern technique of depersonalization and undermined the crucial contribution that such a technique makes to the maintenance and protection of social pluralism and individual liberty.

While espousing a strong belief in pluralism, Bauman seems unable to see that his equally fervent desire for re-enchantment and re-personalization represents a tyrannical threat to such pluralism precisely because it leads to the de-differentiation of spheres of existence. Bauman is led to such an absurd position because he insists on representing 'modernity' as if it were totalitarianism and hence is unable to offer a positive sociological, political or historical account of its plural life orders.

This error occurs because Bauman, unlike Weber, deploys the categorical distinctions between formal and substantive, instrumental and value-oriented rationality to support a general normative analysis of social and political life. In other words, he attempts to sustain a general theoretical distinction between formal and substantive rationality by relating them as means to ends inside a single moral sphere. Bauman advocates re-personalization because he equates modernity with some all-encompassing spirit of unemotional, calculating reason that has suppressed human passions and made 'irrational' all that cannot be quantified or allotted obvious utility, including, of course, morality itself. The problem here is one we have encountered a number of times before.

In deploying a wholly fantastical conception of 'instrumental rationality', where what counts as rational is restricted to 'formal' calculations about means to the detriment of 'substantive' goals and commitments, Bauman is inaugurating a split or opposition that simply cannot hold when attention is focused upon the actual forms of conduct developed in modern institutional settings. The formally rational impersonal conduct of the bureaucrat – his or her instituted blindness to inherited differences in status and prestige – also gives rise to 'substantive' ends: namely, democratic equalization and individual liberty. Conversely, the substantively rational pursuit of moral ends is not always a good thing, as the example of Nazi administrative practice indicates. Certainly, the moral zeal that Bauman finds so lacking in 'formally rational' bureaucratic settings is much in evidence here. Decisions based upon the passionate and emotive imperatives of political ideology are allowed to hold sway over the formal rationality produced by a strict adherence to 'positive' bureaucratic technique and procedure.

Because he insists on maintaining such an absolute opposition between 'instrumental' and 'substantive' rationality, and supporting what he considers to be the substantive underdog against the evil instrumental dictator, Bauman ends up in the position of equating 'passion', 'spontaneity' and 'actions without purpose' with morality; and 'reason', 'calculation', 'interest' and 'utility' with immorality. The idea that a manager who allows their own personal moral enthusiasms to override their professional obligations can be described as somehow acting 'morally' is simply daft, yet the logic of Bauman's position requires such an absurd proposition to be taken seriously. Similarly, Bauman (1993: 33) actually seems to believe that 'making a wager on human moral intuition and ability to negotiate the art and uses of living together' constitutes something like profound advice for those charged with governing modern nation states, organizations and individuals.

Concluding comments: persons and contexts (again)

In sum,we can see that what Bauman provides is not a positive sociological or historical account of the bureau – as one of modernity's plural life orders – but rather an abstract theoretical hermeneutic for interpreting it as a symptom of moral failure.

Like MacIntyre before him, Bauman attempts to hold the character of the modern bureaucrat accountable to a particular ideal of the person. For Bauman, it is the inner conviction of the person of conscience that provides the ultimate ethical comportment for human beings.

Unfortunately, it is clear that this figure cannot and should not be made to play the role of an absolute principle to which all personae are to be held accountable. In highly differentiated modern societies, plural spheres of life have given rise to quite different ethical personae that are 'non-reducible'. As Weber (1994b: 357) puts it, 'is it in fact true that any ethic in the world could establish substantively *identical* commandments applicable to all relationships, whether erotic, business, family, or official, to one's relations with one's wife, greengrocer, son, competitor, with a friend or an accused man?' In this world, if not the next, the answer, is of course, No.

Rather than attempting to subordinate the persona of the bureaucrat to that of the inner conviction of the 'man (*sic*) of conscience' by sheer exercise of ethical force, as Bauman insists on doing, surely it would be more productive to learn to describe the different forms of person case by case, each in its own positive terms? For only by so doing can we begin to perceive their limits and to see what it means to conduct ourselves within those limits.

To treat the plurality of modern personae as only partial realizations of an 'ideal' moral self is but a first step on the road to intellectual fundamentalism.

Notes

1. As Rosemary O'Kane (1997: 51–2) has pointed out, this is a very different argument to that advanced by Bauman. The latter suggests that the weakness of the

Weimar Republic was due mainly to the absence of political democracy, rather than professional politicians.

2. For Weber (1994a, 1994b), no administrative institutions are equal to the task of governing a nation when it faces ultimate questions concerning its own survival and identity.

3. In *The Dialectic of Enlightenment* Horkheimer and Adorno proclaimed that having repudiated any substantial goal or telos located in the order of nature, modernity could only offer an instrumental notion of reason that could not rule out the most barbarous ends and that must lead to the bureaucratic domination of men as well as of nature.

4. A second problem arises from the first in that only by so dehistoricizing social and political pluralism can Bauman attempt to project it into the role of intervening factor. The existence of pluralism, he argues, is the best preventive medicine for stopping Nazi-style atrocities. However, by his own admission, the existence of political pluralism turns out not to be wholly independent of the Nazis being in power. Bauman writes: 'The Nazis must first have destroyed the vestiges of political pluralism to set off projects like the Holocaust, in which the expected readiness of ordinary people for immoral and inhuman actions had to be calculated among the necessary – and available – resources' (1989: 165).

The problem here is that if having the Nazis in power proved sufficient to eradicate social and political pluralism, the argument about pluralist political democracy's countervailing powers 'is made redundant' (O'Kane, 1997: 58). If the Nazis could destroy pluralism, political democracy could not be expected to counteract Nazi extremities.

3

The Anti-Bureaucrats: Contemporary Managerial Discourse and Charismatic Authority

I beg each and every one of you to develop a passionate and public hatred of bureaucracy.

Tom Peters

We hope the vision we have laid out will . . . empower you to re-invent your government.

David Osborne and Ted Gaebler

He who yearns for visions should go to the cinema.

Max Weber

Over recent years a particular story about the conduct of organizational life has begun to achieve a somewhat axiomatic status within the fields of organization and management studies, broadly defined. There are many versions of this story and many different storytellers, but they nonetheless appear to work together to constitute a specific discursive formation.

Within this story a chain of equivalences emerges in which the vicissitudes of contemporary 'environmental change' make certain forms of organizational (and, simultaneously, personal) conduct redundant while at the same time bringing novel forms into being. The old and the new can even be named. The former is represented by the impersonal, procedural and hierarchical bureaucracy, the latter by the flexible, decentred, entrepreneurial corporation.

This story is far from historically descriptive for it can be seen to frame

the differences between 'bureaucratic' and 'entrepreneurial' norms of organizational conduct from the perspective of entrepreneurial principles. As
Reed (1992: 229), has argued, the contemporary orthodoxy holds that
bureaucratic organizations are structured 'around a culture of repression
and control' whereas their counterparts are thought to 'generate a culture
of expression and involvement'. In this respect, entrepreneurial organizational forms are represented as facilitating 'the personal development of
individuals' whereas bureaucratic organizations are held to have repressed
and denied people's personal involvement and ideals. Business success
and individual personal fulfilment are therefore held to flow from the dissolution and demise of 'the normative regimes and disciplinary practices
associated with rational bureaucracy' and their replacement by the norms
and ethics of enterprise.

As a number of commentators have indicated, what's on offer from this
litany is less a 'history of the present', in some suitably Foucauldian sense,
than a religious and romantic narrative of collective and individual salvation and emancipation (du Gay, 1994b, 1996; Pattison, 1997; Salaman, 1997).

In this chapter, I seek to problematize this 'just so' story of organizational
and personal transformation. I begin by delineating and analyzing the critique of bureaucratic culture propounded by self-styled 'management
revolutionaries'. In so doing, I indicate the varied ways in which this critique and the new wave management theory and practice its proponents
advocate exhibits many of the characteristics of Christian fundamentalist
sectarianism.

We then make an excursion into the work of the premier theorist of
bureaucratic culture: Max Weber. I argue that, contrary to orthodox inter-
pretations, Weber does not view the impersonal, procedural and
hierarchical character of the bureau as a symptom of moral deficiency.
Instead, he indicates that 'bureaucratic' conduct does indeed possess a
profoundly ethical character. In keeping with earlier chapters of the book,
the aim here is to throw a better ethical light on the practices of bureaucratic administration as these are routinely criticized by purveyors of
other-worldly visions, religious and moral.

'Making up managers'

Throughout the last century a multiplicity of what we might term 'managerial' discourses have appeared each of which has offered a certain way of
drawing the map of the organizational world. All of these discourses – scientific management, human relations, quality of working life, to name but
a few – have offered particular ways of conceptualizing and acting upon
organizational life and have invariably served to construct specific ways
for certain categories of person – most frequently but not exclusively 'managers' – to conceive of and conduct themselves at the workplace.

What it has meant to be a manager, for example, has varied across time and context in relationship to the different ways in which that category of person has been 'made up'. Viewed in this way, the dispositions and attributes constituting management must be approached as a series of historically specific assemblages without any underlying 'essential' or 'natural' form. (du Gay, 1996; Hollway, 1991; Jacques, 1996; Rose, 1990).

During the last two decades the character of the manager has been subject to considerable and ongoing problematization. The dominant discourses of organizational reform throughout this period all placed enormous emphasis on the development of more flexible, responsive and entrepreneurial forms of conduct which would overcome the assumed stasis, rigidity and inefficiency of 'bureaucracy'. In particular, they indicated that the required transformations were in large dependent on the formation of certain attributes and dispositions amongst managerial staff.

The norms and values characterizing the conduct of 'excellent' or 're-engineered' organizations, for example, were articulated in explicit opposition to those deemed to constitute the identity of bureaucratic organizations. Whereas 'bureaucratic culture' was represented as forming and shaping specific capacities and dispositions amongst managerial personae – strict adherence to procedure, abnegation of personal moral enthusiasms and so forth – contemporary organizational discourses stressed the importance of individual managers acquiring more 'proactive' and 'entrepreneurial' attributes. Bureaucratic culture, it was argued, had to give way to 'new approaches that require people to . . . take initiative and assume a much greater responsibility for their own organization' (Morgan, 1991: 56). Similarly, in opposition to the 'personally detached and strictly objective expert' deemed characteristic of bureaucratic management, contemporary organizational discourse represented the manager as a 'charismatic' leader, charged with 'rearranging the quality of people's attachments – to their work and each other' (Champy, 1995: 77).

Contemporary managerial discourse and the critique of bureaucratic culture

The case against bureaucracy and for the sorts of 'organic', flexible organizational forms envisaged in contemporary management discourse begins with changes in what is termed 'the external environment'. While different authors privilege different combinations of phenomena – the dislocatory effects consequent upon an explosion in the deployment of new information and communication technologies; those associated with the competitive pressures resulting from 'global' systems of trade, finance and production – they all agree that the result of these developments is an environment characterized by massive uncertainty in which 'madness is afoot' and 'predictability is a thing of the past' (Peters, 1987: 3, 7, 9; Kanter, 1990; Champy, 1995).

In a world turned upside down, only those organizations which can rapidly and continuously change their conduct and learn to become ever more enterprising will survive. Because bureaucracy is held to constitute a mechanistic system of organization best suited to conditions of relative stability and predictability, it becomes the first casualty of such an uncertain environment (Peters, 1987, 1992, 1994; Kanter, 1990).

> In this environment bureaucratic institutions . . . – public *and* private – increasingly fail us. Today's environment demands institutions that are extremely flexible and adaptable. It demands institutions that deliver high-quality goods and services, squeezing ever-more bang out of every buck. It demands institutions that are responsive to their customers, offering choices of non-standardized services; that lead by persuasion and incentives rather than commands; that give their employees a sense of meaning and control, even ownership. (Osborne and Gaebler, 1992: 15)

If 'bureaucracy' is deemed hopelessly ill-equipped to meet 'the demands of the environment' what then must be done?

The emerging representation of life inside the new 'entrepreneurial corporation' has two distinct but interrelated facets. According to Newfield (1995: 31), the first involves 're-imagining' the corporation as something approximating to a global village. The successful organization will offer its corporate citizens wealth, happiness and 'belonging' in a borderless globalized economy where national and regional governments are little more than obliging brokers (Ohmae, 1990, 1993; Peters, 1992; Reich, 1990). The second component is the transformation of work into pleasure. The two parts are then assembled into a unified 'vision' of corporate and personal regeneration: the power of communitarian governance is synthesized with the pleasure of individual autonomy and responsibility.

Breathing new life into the ideal of the organic – the longing for an all-pervading spirit of community and for the unified moral personality – contemporary management discourse characterizes work not as a painful obligation imposed upon individuals, nor as an activity undertaken for mainly instrumental purposes, but rather as a vital means to individual liberty and self-fulfilment. As Kanter (1990: 281) comments, life in 'new' organizations has a 'romantic quality'. By recasting work as pleasure and business organizations as the foremost spaces in which 'we' can all realize ourselves as autonomous, self-regulating, responsible, liberty-loving individuals, contemporary management discourse seeks to 're-enchant' that which bureaucracy is held to have crassly repressed. As Kanter (1990: 280) argues

> In the traditional bureaucratic corporation, roles were so circumscribed that most relationships tended to be rather formal and impersonal. Narrowly defined jobs constricted by rules and procedures also tended to stifle initiative and creativity, and the atmosphere was emotionally repressive. The post-entrepreneurial corporation ('because it takes entrepreneurship a stage further'), in contrast, with its stress on teamwork and cooperation, with its building the new, brings people closer together, making the personal dimension of relationship more important.

Survival and success in the dislocated environment of the present is there-fore premised on making organizations and persons adopt habits and dispositions that would appear simply 'crazy' to those trapped inside the mindset of 'bureaucractic management' or 'bonkers' as Tom Peters (1994) so elequently puts it. Of crucial import here is an organizational strategy of maximum 'businessing'.

'Businessing' people typically consists in assigning the performance of a function or activity to an individual or group which is then regarded as being accountable for the efficient conduct of that function or activity. By assuming active responsibility for these activities and functions – both for carrying them out and for their outcomes – these individuals or groups are in effect assuming and affirming a certain kind of identity or personality. 'Businessing' represents individuals and groups as 'units of management', and requires they adopt a certain 'entrepreneurial' form of relationship to themselves as a condition of their effectiveness and of the effectiveness of this sort of strategy. As Peters (1994: 73) explains, to be 'businessed' is to be given responsibility and held accountable for running 'one's own show inside the organization'.

Contemporary organizational success is therefore premised upon an engagement by the organization of the 'self-fulfiling impulses' of all its mem-bers. This ambition is to be made practicable by allocating particular enterprising or businessing dispositions and capacities to 'corporate citizens' through the medium of a variety of mutually enhancing techniques. The latter include such devices as mechanisms for reducing dependency and enhancing equality by making management structures 'horizontal' rather than 'vertical'; for encouraging internal competitiveness through small group working; and for eliciting individual responsibility and self-management through peer review and appraisal schemes. In this way, the strategy of 'busi-nessing' plays the role of relay between objectives that are economically desirable and those deemed personally seductive by teaching the arts of self-realization that will enhance employees as individuals as well as workers.

This strategy of 'autonomization' and 'responsibilization' makes paid work (no matter how 'objectively' alienated, deskilled, or degraded it may appear to social scientists) an essential element in the path to self-fulfilment and provides the *a priori* that links together work and non-work, reason and emotion, the public and the private – all that bureaucracy stands accused of fragmenting and splitting. In contemporary organizational dis-course, the 'employee', every bit as much as the 'customer', is represented as an individual in search of meaning and fulfilment. For the businessed subject of this discourse the relations between work life and non-work life, between what is properly inside and and what is properly outside the orbit of the organization, are progresively blurred (du Gay, 1996).

Although both managerial and non-managerial staff are represented as equally amenable to being businessed, the former are held to have a par-ticularly important role in ensuring the latter exhibit suitable responses to the 'challenge of change' by learning to 'run their own shows inside the organization'. As I mentioned earlier, in opposition to the personally detached bureaucrat, 'entrepreneurial' new wave management is represented as calculatingly charismatic in essence. Managers are charged with 'leading' their subordinates to the promised land of individual liberty and self-fulfilment by helping them acquire the status of businessed person. As Champy (1995: 17) argues:

> No more close supervision of workers, no more focus on data irrelevant to running the business, no more energy spent on defending turf. The role of managers becomes one of empowerment – providing workers with the information, training, authority and accountability to excel . . . As workers take on more management tasks, managers must take on more leadership tasks – holding a vision of the business, articulating it to workers and customers, and creating an environment that truly empowers workers.

To sum up: refracted through the gaze of contemporary organizational discourse bureaucratic culture appears inimical to the development of 'entrepreneurial' dispositions and capacities and hence to the production of 'businessed' persons. The bureaucratic commitment to norms of impersonality, adherence to procedure and so on are seen as antithetical to the cultivation of those skills and sensibilities which alone can guarantee a 'manageable' and hence sustainable future in an era of chronic uncertainty.

While contemporary organizational discourse constitutes all forms of bureaucratic conduct as subjects of conscientious objection, it is the perceived failure of bureaucracy to provide a community of meaning and to open up people's personal involvement and ideals which comes in for some of the most severe criticism (Peters and Waterman, 1982: 29–86; Kanter, 1990: 351–65; Peters, 1992, 1994). Because bureaucratic norms are assumed to be founded upon an unhappy separation of reason and emotion, pleasure and duty, and because this is deemed to be inimical to individual liberty, personal responsibility and other 'enterprising' virtues, bureaucracy is represented as fundamentally unethical. For proponents of new wave management, bureaucracy represents a flawed means for the realization of moral personality.

In contrast to the fragmentation characterizing bureaucracy, the entrepreneurial, 'businessed' organization is represented as all of a piece; as an organic entity. It constitutes, in Charles Sabel's (1991) terms, something akin to a *Möbius* strip, where inside and outside imperceptibly blur. In such an organization, work and leisure, reason and emotion, pleasure and duty are conjoined and, as a result, the human being is once again a plenitude – restored to full moral unity.

Critics of management as heirs of religion and romance

It doesn't take too much effort to uncover a distinctly religious and romantic ethos underpinning the forms of critique levelled at bureaucracy by many of its contemporary detractors. Whether the critic in question is Tom Peters or Alasdair MacIntyre a shared assumption is discernible. Self-styled 'management revolutionaries' such as Peters, Kanter and Champy, regard bureaucratic culture as dysfunctional in large part because it is founded upon a disastrous split; it fragments that which should be whole with deleterious economic, emotional and ethical consequences. Similarly, as we saw in Chapter 1, MacIntyre's indictment of the character of the manager is predicated upon the belief that the advent of modern, bureaucratic culture signifies the untimely fragmentation of a previously unified civic moral domain.

What these critics share is a belief that that which does not form an organic whole must be fragmented and anomic. It is this religious and romantic ideal of a whole expressed in each of its parts that shapes their respective visions. In their very different ways, both Peters and MacIntyre, for example, demand that all spheres of existence should be united, and that the individual overcome the alienating distinction between the different roles he or she is forced to inhabit. Neither appears to abide the idea that what is relevant in one domain of existence need not be so in another.

If MacIntyre attempts to hold the bureaucrat accountable to a particular ideal of the person – one deriving many of its characteristics from Christian theology – then contemporary managerial discourse is equally concerned to define the proper role and conduct of management in religious terms. Indeed, one of the most remarkable features of contemporary organizational discourse is the prevalence of religious language and metaphors, especially those derived from apocalyptic, millenarian Christianity (Anthony, 1994; du Gay, 1994b; Pattison, 1997). As Pattison (1997: 68) has commented, it is difficult to think of a recent period in which the religious language of 'visions', 'missions' and the like has enjoyed such widespread currency in the ostensibly banal domain of management. It is important, therefore, to examine some of these concepts and their origins a little more closely in order to discern what sort of organizational reality they seem intent on 'making up'.

As anyone with even the most tangential connection to contemporary discourses of organizational reform would be aware, the construction of 'vision' is deemed to be a crucial feature of senior management activity. Visions are held to provide a clear sense of where an organization is going and what its core activities are. As Pattison (1997: 69) has indicated, contemporary organizational discourse derives its notion of 'vision' from the Judaeo-Christian tradition. Visions come from the creator, God. They are 'given' to specially chosen charismatic figures – such as prophets – who are then seen to have the authority to demand that people learn to change their conduct. Visions are used to challenge habits and established forms of conduct. Those who 'see' them are represented as 'having power from "above"' (Pattison, 1997: 69).

For its contemporary advocates, developing an organizational vision is a crucial device for inspiring people to change the way they relate to their work, each other and themselves by providing them with a sense of both communal and individual purpose ('meaning'). It has connotations of making things better, of not accepting an unsatisfactory present through subverting the powers and arrangements that currently exist (Champy, 1995: 55–8; Peters, 1987: 405–8). As such, the concept of vision appears alluring and motivating.

However, an emphasis on these aspects of vision may serve to downplay other crucial but perhaps more implicit features of its deployment in contemporary organizational settings. These include a new sense of 'arbitrariness' (God does not consult people about the content of visions) and the need for unquestioning obedience in the face of self-authenticating revelation (as non-rational, revealed and mystical things, visions cannot easily be rationally challenged) and a sense of required compliance as mere mortals are expected to radically alter their relationships – to the organization, to customers, to each other, to themselves – to fit in with what is in effect a divinely ordained new order (Pattison, 1997: 70). As Ronald Moe (1994: 111–14) has argued, this 'theological aura' permeates programmes of organizational reform in the public sector as well as the private. Focusing on the Clinton administration's National Performance Review in the USA, Moe indicates that the vision framing this explicitly anti-bureaucratic 'Re-Inventing Government exercise' is not stated in a theoretical manner, as a series of propositions subject to empirical proof or disproof, but rather as a group of statements exhorting people to acceptance and action.

> The report largely rejects the traditional language of administrative discourse which attempts, not always with success, to employ terms with precise meanings. Instead a new highly value-laden lexicon is employed by entrepreneurial management enthusiasts to disarm would be questioners. Thus . . . there is a heavy reliance upon active verbs – reinventing, reengineering, empowering – to maximise the emotive content of what otherwise has been a largely nonemotive subject matter . . . The administrative management paradigm with its emphasis on the Constitution, statutory controls, hierarchical lines of responsibility to the President, distinctive legal character of the governmental and private sectors and the need for a cadre of nonpartisan professional managers ultimately responsible not only to the President but to Congress as well is depicted as the paradigm that failed. This paradigm is the cause of the government being broken in the eyes of the entrepreneurial management promoters. It has not proven flexible enough to permit change to occur at the speed considered necessary in the new, information-driven technological world. The report argues, almost deterministically, that the entrepreneurial management paradigm will prevail in the future. Those who question this paradigm are not merely incorrect, they have no place in the government of the future. (Moe, 1994: 113–14)

If the contemporary managerial metaphor of 'vision' carries with it a host (sic) of charismatic religious connotations and meanings then this is equally true for the associated metaphor of 'mission'. In contemporary organizational discourse, 'mission' is represented as the means through which an overarching vision is operationalized. This can take many forms, but is frequently incarnated in a short 'mission statement'.

As Pattison (1997: 70) indicates, in the Judaeo-Christian tradition one of the primary meanings of 'mission' relates to the activity of carrying the gospel of Christ to all corners of the earth and endeavouring to obtain converts to Christianity. 'Mission' carries connotations that one is commissioned by a higher authority, namely God, to pursue a specific goal, such as making all people believers, and then single-mindedly pursuing this, against all comers, until it is complete. In its contemporary managerial manifestation, 'mission' continues to carry many, if not, all of these connotations: the idea of having a clear and, indeed, 'higher' purpose, of doing what has to be done at almost any cost to realize an unquestionable goal and the idea of converting people to the true (see for example Peters and Waterman, 1982; Peters, 1987). In this way, as Pattison (1997: 71) has commented

> Mission seems to to imply a dualistic world view in which one group of people feel empowered to achieve their own aims at almost any cost to others outside their own particular tribe or group. It is thus unfortunately consonant with many of the other metaphors that inform management, and, indeed, the Christian tradition of war against evil.

Such polarizing functions as a moral and political device for generating dissatisfaction with the present and raising great expectations of quite different futures. It is also, as Weber (1978, II: Chapter XIV) so clearly indicated, a characteristic feature of a charismatic repertoire of conduct.

Indeed, it is not at all difficult to conceive of contemporary managerial discourse as approximating to a system of charismatic authority. The term 'management guru', with its explicit reference to the management consultant as spiritual guide, has been coined in recognition of the quasi-religious ethos pervading much contemporary management theory and practice.

Charismatic conduct and ultimate ethical principles

According to Weber (1978, II: 1115), genuine charismatic domination knows no abstract laws and regulations and no formal adjudication. Its 'objective' law flows from the highly personal experience of divine grace and godlike heroic strength and rejects all external order solely for the sake of glorifying genuine prophetic and heroic ethos. Hence in 'a revolutionary and sovereign manner, charismatic domination transforms all values and breaks all traditional and rational norms . . . From a substantive point of view, every charismatic authority would have to subscribe to the proposition "It has been written . . . but I say unto you"' (Weber, 1978, II: 1115).

Being so 'extra-ordinary', charismatic forms of authority are often sharply opposed to formally rational, and particularly bureaucratic, authority as well as to traditional forms of authority.[1] Bureaucratic authority is 'specifically rational in the sense of being bound to intellectually analysable rules'; while charismatic authority is specifically irrational in the sense of being largely foreign to all such formal, intellectually analysable rules (Weber, 1978, I: 244).

At the same time, while traditional authority is bound to precedents handed down from the past, within the sphere of its claims charismatic authority repudiates the past in favour of the eschatological future time of the 'new man'. In this sense, charismatic authority is a 'specifically revolutionary force'. It recognizes no authority but its own. 'The only basis of legitimacy for it is personal charisma so long as it is proved; that is, as long as it receives recognition and as long as the followers and disciples prove their usefulness charismatically' (Weber, 1978, I: 244).

For Weber (1978, I: 439), the purely individual bearer of charisma functions as a 'prophet', who, 'by virtue of his mission proclaims a religious doctrine or divine commandment'. The 'prophetic revelation', for both prophet and followers, involves predominantly 'a unified view of the world, derived from a consciously integrated meaningful attitude toward life'. To the prophet, both the life of man and the world, both social and cosmic events,

> have a certain systematic and coherent meaning, to which man's conduct must be oriented if it is to bring salvation, and after which it must be patterned in an integrally meaningful manner . . . it always denotes, regardless of any variations in scope and in measure of success, an effort to systematize all the manifestations of life; that is to organize practical behaviour into a direction of life, regardless of the form it may assume in any individual case. Moreover, this meaning always contains the important religious conception of the world as a cosmos which is challenged to produce somehow a 'meaningful', ordered totality, the particular manifestations of which are to be measured and evaluated according to this postulate. (Weber, 1978, I: 45–1)

Charismatic prophecy is therefore aimed in large part at 'organizing life on the basis of ultimate principles' (Weber, 1978, I: 467).

In the light of Weber's comments, it seems quite clear that contemporary managerial discourse approximates to a system of charismatic authority. For proponents of new wave management, bureaucratic forms of conduct are represented as flawed means for the realization of moral personality precisely because they are not regarded as patterning life into an integrated and overarchingly 'meaningful' totality.

The full force of this turn to charisma and its dismissal of bureaucracy is brought into even sharper relief if we focus our attention on the work of one of the most influential of the contemporary 'management revolutionaries' or 'gurus', Tom Peters.

Tom Peters: the anti-bureaucrat as charismatic prophet

A cursory inspection of any of Tom Peters's many tomes or indeed videos quickly reveals the extent to which his work is infused with a religious ethos and style drawn from the Christian tradition.

The basic narrative informing all of Peters's many works is that organizations and their managements are operating in a chaotic environment. This chaos has the capacity to destroy businesses and managers if left unconfronted. The enemy, in the form of global competition, is at the gates and threatens to lay waste the promised land which has been betrayed by inflexible, complacent and immoral 'bureaucracy'. If organizations and managements are to survive and flourish in a world turned upside down, they need to completely alter their modes of conduct. For the old order is passing away, the old ways cannot work and there is a need for radical change and regeneration. However, salvation is at hand if, and only if, the old ways are abandoned and the prophet's commandments are obeyed to the letter and with total commitment – hence the insistent call to develop a passionate and public hatred of bureaucracy. You must receive the spirit whereby you too 'face up to the need for revolution' and 'achieve extraordinary responsiveness' (Peters, 1987: 3–4). Not only must you obey: don't even think about it. Just do it! Do it now or chaos will get you.

If you do all this then the future just might be yours. You, too, will be in tune with ultimate reality and will be able to manipulate the creative/destructive forces of chaos – which are a bottom-line inevitability, don't forget – to your own advantage. You'll be 'liberated', 'emancipated', 'free' because you've learnt to 'thrive on chaos'. The alternative, which doesn't bear thinking about much, is sure-fire death. Not much of a choice, really. So choose life, do 'maximum businessing'!

Using this sort of evangelical rhetorical strategy, Peters sets up a dynamic of fear, anxiety and discontent amongst his would-be followers. An atmosphere of total, but non-specific, threat is evoked; nothing could be more threatening but less specific than chaos. This threat is then blamed on and used to problematize the authority of the present order – the rational 'bureaucratic culture'. Recasting circumstances into polarities that construct polemical comparisons out of non-comparable terms is a favourite 'technique of negation' deployed by Peters. He conjures up an aggressively polarized world in which businesses are either conspicuously successful – entrepreneurial corporations thriving on chaos – or total failures – formal, hierarchical bureaucracies. There is nothing in between. Peters then reveals his simple messages of salvation which people must follow if they are to avoid annihilation and, more positively, become fully developed human beings able to turn the unavoidable chaos to their own advantage. Damnation is not inevitable, but it will be if you don't become that which you have a duty to become: a businessed person.

This constitutes something akin to Peters's basic religious system, within which the underlying metaphor for contemporary managerial reality is that of 'chaos'. This understanding is total and unquestionable, as was the Old Testament prophets' understanding of the nature of God. As Pattison (1997: 137) argues, 'to de-personify the transcendent by getting rid of any overt deity, as Peters does, is not to dispose of its transcendent nature, though it may make it less obvious'. The statement that the world is 'chaotic' is a profoundly religious assertion, one whose veracity cannot be questioned or tested; it can only be accepted or rejected. Acceptance of this basic reality is acceptance of an overarching moral order within which all events, meanings and experiences can be situated and explained. It is the gateway into Peters's 'unified view of the world'.

In *Thriving on Chaos* (1987) Peters appears to derive his own personal authority from an implicit assertion that he is closely in contact with and knowledgeable about the spirit of destructive and creative chaos surrounding us. Indeed, he acts as a channel or voice for the transcendent chaos which communicates its essence through him. Like an exemplary prophet, he issues a number of commandments which will guide his followers to organizational and personal salvation. These culminate in an injunction to intensive and endless effort on the part of every individual member of an organization (Pattison, 1997: 138).

But this wilful and continuous change and transformation on the part of organizations and persons is not represented as a painful burden or tedious obligation, nor is it to be undertaken simply for instrumental purposes. Above all it is a means to self-fulfilment and complete human development. The wholeness that bureaucracy rent assunder is to be recovered, the disenchantment it brought in its wake reversed, through maximum businessing. As Peters (1992: 755) puts it, 'life on the job is looking more like life off the job for a change. ("For a change"? For the first time in a couple of hundred years is more like it.)'

The tone of his commands is direct, didactic and distinctly moral. Peters is definitely trying to organize life, as Weber had it, 'on the basis of ultimate principles'. Indeed, he is quite explicit that adopting his worldview is akin to a 'religious conversion' (1987: 149). In this way, the 'management revolutionary' as charismatic religious prophet has enthroned himself as 'moral judiciary'. His claim is to reunify, through the strategy of 'businessing', that which 'bad old bureaucracy' is held to have set apart as separate spheres of existence: work and leisure, reason and emotion, public and private. For the prophet, this unified view of the world, derived from a consciously integrated meaningful attitude to life, offers the route to salvation.

From Max Weber

The anti-bureaucratic visions conjured up by proponents of new wave management often refer to the work of Max Weber, albeit in passing. They also rely upon a self-consciously Weberian conceptual lexicon when distinguishing between instrumental and value-oriented action and formal and substantive rationality, for example.

However, the Weber that emerges from these visions is a rather contradictory figure. On the one hand, he's viewed as an important, yet ultimately misguided, representative of the 'closed system – rational actor' era in organizational theory (Peters and Waterman, 1982: 92). While this 'school of thought' (of which F. Taylor is also deemed to be a leading member) did some good things, like indicating how organizationally efficient and effective a finite body of rules and techniques that could be learnt and mastered could be, it was ultimately a disaster. Why? Because it was just too formally rational for its own good and soon helped generate a range of dysfunctional effects that far outweighed its initial positivities. It could not ultimately 'make meaning for people'. Weber takes a large portion of the blame because he 'pooh-poohed charismatic leadership and doted on bureaucracy; its rule driven, impersonal form, he said, was the only way to assure long-term survival' (Peters and Waterman, 1982: 5).

On the other hand, Weber is a man racked with anxiety. In this 'take', Weber is a theorist of bureaucratization who can see and articulate this organizational form's tragic downside for 'humanity'. Disenchantment, dehumanization, the 'shell of future servility', 'specialists without soul' and of course, 'the iron cage' are the standard tropes. In this reading, the logic of bureaucracy will lead inexorably to a future devoid of moral substance. Everything human and valuable, all personal, irrational and emotional elements, which escape calculation by the personally detached and strictly objective expert will in the future be regarded as worthless because they are non-instrumental (Osborne and Gaebler, 1992).

What both images of Weber assume is the centrality of 'rationalization' to his work. The former locates Weber as a leading advocate of rational management and displacer of 'morality' from organizational existence. The latter positions him as a critic of instrumental rationalization who views with horror the ethical and emotional disfigurements this process is producing. What both of these Webers share though is the assumption that – for good or ill – rationalism has a ceaseless, singular, logic, meaning and direction.

Now, while this critical discourse on Weber and the bureau relies upon a Weberian theoretical lexicon, its assumptions and conclusions concerning rationalization in general and the ethical and moral vacuity of 'rational bureaucracy' in particular are the very antithesis of Weber's own. Weber, that is to say, is innocent of the so-called Weberianism that adopts a uniform conception of rationalization. Indeed, on more than one occasion as seen in Chapter 2 Weber stated that 'rationalism' means many different things depending on time, place and circumstances (Weber, 1930: 77–8).

One of the crucial conditions for deconstructing the charge – levelled not only by proponents of new wave management, but by communitarian and libertarian intellectuals – that Weberian bureaucratic norms are ethically and emotionally vacuous lies in a different way of approaching Weber's work. Rather than representing Weber as the purveyor of a view of human history as a process of unrelenting rationalization, it is important instead to see him as a historical anthropologist, legal thinker, political economist and activist whose diverse interests are, as Hennis (1988) has so clearly indicated, linked to a specific set of ethico-cultural concerns. Such an approach to Weber's work yields a conception of bureaucratic rationality and culture as consisting in a particular ethos, or *Lebensführung* – not only an ensemble of purposes and ideals within a code of conduct but also ways of conducting oneself within a given life order.

Unpacking bureaucratic rationality

A characteristic feature of the anti-bureaucratic discourse of both charismatic managerialism and contemporary communitarianism is the belief that modern bureaucratic culture signifies the fragmentation of what was, and ideally should again be, a unified civic moral domain. Whether maximum businessing or the reactivated *polis* is the chosen means to closing the 'wound' that bureaucracy opened is neither here nor there. What the various anti-bureaucrats share is a demand that the 'total pattern of life be made subject to an order that is significant and meaningful' (Weber, 1978: 467).

For Weber, only by being not of this world could an ethic claim such universality. He refused to accept that there was a unified moral personality underpinning and unifying human conduct. Instead, he consistently indicated that 'we are placed in various life orders, each of which is subject to different laws' (1994b: 362–3). For Weber, these different life orders do not constitute the anomic fragments of some denied totality nor do they represent different versions of some single homogeneous good or form a ranking or continuum of human cultural development.

As Hennis (1988: 187) makes clear, while Weber recognized the intellectual (and existential) discomfort of living in a culture of particular 'spheres', he attempted to face up to this challenge without 'falling under the influence' of the usual unifying schemes and dreams: the whole personality; the moral-political community; the dialectical synthesis and so on and so forth. This meant breaking with the habit of thinking that one among the several *personae* we may happen to occupy in our passage through social institutions must be or potentially become *the* fundamental form of personhood, the point of unity (Saunders, 1997: 108). It would therefore be a mistake to address bureaucratic or legal personality in the terms – theological or philosophical – used elsewhere to address the unified or 'whole' person. In this way, Weber (1989; 1994a, 1994b) had his readers and listeners take as serious cultural and ethical achievements the modes of conduct – prosaic, reliable, non-prophetic – that come with competence in professional practices.

In his classic account of the persona of the bureaucrat, Weber (1978, II: 978ff.) refuses to treat the impersonal, expert, procedural and hierarchical character of bureaucratic reason and action as morally bankrupt. Instead, he makes it quite clear that the bureau comprises a particular ethos. He insists it be assessed in its own right as a moral institution and that the ethical attributes of the bureaucrat be viewed as the contingent and often fragile achievements of that socially organized sphere of moral existence. According to Weber, the bureau comprises the social conditions of a distinctive and independent organization of the person. Among the most important of these conditions are, first, that access to office is dependent upon lengthy training, usually certified public examination; and second, that the office itself constitutes a 'vocation', a focus of ethical commitment and duty, autonomous of and superior to the bureaucrat's extra-offical ties to class, kin or conscience. In Weber's discussion of the bureau, these conditions mark out the office as a particular sphere of life and provide the office-holder or bureaucrat with a distinctive ethical bearing and mode of conduct.

The ethical attributes of the 'good' bureaucrat – do not therefore represent an incompetent subtraction from a complete, businessed or entrepreneurial conception of personhood. Rather, Weber indicates that they should be viewed as positive ethical achievements. They represent the product of particular ethical techniques and practices through which individuals develop the disposition and capacity to conduct themselves according to the ethos of bureaucratic office.

Contemporary managerial critics are keen to enlist Weber's help (the second of their two Webers', that is) when lambasting the bureau for its (presumed) dysfunctional hyper-rationalism, 'impersonalism' and its general inability to provide meaning. On each of these counts, however, Weber turns out to be no ally at all.

As I indicated in Chapters 1 and 2, Weber's historical, descriptive analysis of 'the ethos of office' just will not lend itself to the sort of general, normative critique of bureaucratic reason deployed by contemporary managerialists. For Weber, the stress on 'impersonality' as a crucial feature of bureaucratic rationality does not equate with a general denial of humanity. It refers to the bureaucratic capacity – hard-won and ultimately fragile – to treat individuals as cases, apart from status and ascription. Similarly, such impersonality does not constitute some blanket negation of the 'affective'. As Weber makes clear, bureaucratic culture engenders no antipathy towards emotional or personal relations within the domain of the office as long as these do not undermine the ethos governing the conduct of that office, through for example, opening the doors to corruption or encouraging inappropriate forms of patronage. Assuming a general (and essential) antagonism between bureaucracy and social relations of friendship, for example, depends upon a historic misreading of Weber as well as a romantic identification of such relations with freedom from normative compulsion, spontaneous attraction, free choice and so on.

When Weber describes bureaucratic conduct as precluding 'personally motivated actions', as operating 'without regard to persons', it is important not to extend his intended reference – as the charismatic managerialists are wont to do – from the exercise of personal patronage to the universal exclusion of the personal or 'private' *per se*.

Weber also indicates that, far from being ethically vacuous, the 'formal rationality' that so upsets contemporary managerialists is itself an ethical capacity. This concept has been consistently misappropriated and made to serve ends that were never Weber's own. It differs from its twin concept of 'substantive rationality' not by being narrowly instrumental and dependent upon arbitrarily given ends but rather by taking account of the heterogeneity of morality. In other words, while the ethos associated with formal rationality is certainly premised upon the cultivation of indifference to certain moral ends, that very indifference is predicated upon an awareness of the irreducible plurality of and frequent incommensurability between passionately held moral ends and thus of the possible costs of pursuing any one of them at the expense of the others. Viewed thus, formal rationality is not consequent with the development of an attitude of amoral instrumentalism, but on the cultivaton of a liberal–pluralist ethics of responsibility which does take account of the consequences of attempting to realize essentially contextable values that frequently come into conflict with other values.

In this sense, as Weber (1978, II: 983ff.) makes clear, the bureau represents an important ethical and indeed political resource because it serves to divorce the administration of public life from private moral absolutisms. Without the historical emergence of the ethical sphere and persona of the bureau and the bureaucrat, the construction of a buffer between civic comportment and personal principles – a crucial feature of contemporary liberal democratic government – would never have been possible. Indeed, without the 'art of separation' (Walzer, 1984) that the public bureau effected and continues to effect, many of the qualitative features of government that are currently taken for granted – such as reliability and procedural fairness in the treatment of cases – would not exist. Instead of heralding the disintegration and fragmentation of a previously integrated political–moral personhood, the emergence of distinct public and private modes of comportment that bureaucracy helps to effect represents a contingent but hard-won positive political and ethical achievement.

If the bureau is seen in this light – as a distinctive life order with its own ethos – then it cannot be open to problematization for its failure to realize ends that it was not designed to meet.

Businessing bureaucracy

The bureaucratic 'ethos of office', with its chief point of honour, the capacity to set aside one's private political, moral, regional and other commitments, should not therefore be regarded as obsolete. The question then remains: what sort of effect is the operationalization of maximum businessing likely to have upon this ethos?

The very identity of new wave management is constituted in opposition to bureaucratic culture. Its advocates tend to represent the bureau in language that leaves very little room for anything but a negative evaluation. Peters's (1987: 459) attempts to incite 'a public and passionate hatred of bureaucracy' amongst his listeners/readers is unlikely to leave them concerned to understand let alone maintain or enhance the bureaucratic ethos. However, it is possible to try and answer the question posed above by once again taking a leaf from Weber's book, as it were. In the *Wissenschaftslehre*, Weber writes:

> Without exception every order of social relations (however constituted) is, if one wishes to *evaluate* it, ultimately to be examined in terms of the human type (*menschlichen Typus*) to which it, by way of external or internal (motivational) selection, provides the optimal chances of becoming the dominant type. (quoted in Hennis, 1988: 60; original emphasis)

As a number of commentators have argued, a defining feature of contemporary programmes of organizational reform in both public and private sectors is their dependence upon a particular understanding of the 'enterprise form' as the privileged model for the conduct of conduct (Miller and Rose, 1990; Burchell, 1993; du Gay, 1996). According to Graham Burchell (1993: 275), for example, strategies such as the maximum businessing advocated by Tom Peters and his ilk involve something like the 'generalization of the "enterprise form" to all forms of conduct – to the conduct of organizations hitherto seen as being non-economic, to the conduct of government, and to the conduct of individuals themselves'. Certainly, the forms of action they make possible for different institutions and persons – schools, general practitioners, housing estates and so forth – do seem to share a general consistency and style.

A crucial technical feature of these programmes is the allocation of a particular function or activity to a distinct unit of management – individual or collective – which is then regarded as being accountable for the efficient (i.e. 'economic') performance of that function or activity. By assuming ongoing responsibility for these activities and functions these units of management are in effect affirming a certain kind of identity or personality that is basically entrepreneurial in character. In other words, maximum businessing requires these units of management to adopt a certain entrepreneurial form of relationship to themselves as a condition of their effectiveness and of the effectiveness of this sort of strategy. As Peters (1992: 235) puts it, maximum businessing both permits and demands that 'each employee be . . . turned into their own little enterprise'.

Thus, a certain 'human type' – what has been termed the 'enterprising self' (du Gay, 1991; Gordon, 1991; Rose, 1990) – is provided with 'the optimal chances of becoming the dominant type'. This *menschlichen Typus* has a complex genealogy but can be characterized, according to Colin Gordon (1991: 43), as both a 'reactivation and radical inversion' of *homo economicus*.

The reactivation consists, he argues, in positing a fundamental human faculty of choice. The great departure from earlier precedents is that, whereas *homo economicus* originally meant that subject the wellsprings of whose activity must remain forever untouchable by government, its contemporary variant is both manipulable man, man who is perpetually responsive to modifications in his environment, and, importantly, man in search of overarching meaning.

As Callon (1998: 51) has pointed out, there is little to be gained from an all too familiar strategy of denunciation of this species of *homo economicus* in the name of a 'sociology of real man, one taken in a bundle of links which constitute his sociality and his humanity'. Such a denunciation has also been, and continues to be, levelled at the persona of the bureaucrat, another form of calculating character deemed to be without soul. Both the persona of the bureaucrat and that of the entrepreneurial self are indeed species of calculating agent. But they are, to use Callon's terms, rather differently 'formatted, framed and equipped' (1998: 51).

And these differences are not unimportant. As Amélie Rorty (1988: 7) has argued, 'some of the apparently intractable debates about persons occur when the concerns of one context are imported into another, in the premature interest of constructing a unified theory, or as a rhetorical move in a political polemic'.[2]

Certainly, contemporary managerialists continually attempt the boundary crossings gently criticized by Rorty. They seem intent on evaluating the persona of the bureaucrat in terms of 'entrepreneurial principles'. Because this persona cannot meet the criteria for existence that these principles set, it is condemned for being a partial or failed version of the complete or full 'entrepreneurial' persona it should ideally be. As Rorty (1988: 7) goes on to say, 'the appearance of forced options' – for example the strategy of 'polarized aggression' beloved of Peters et al. – 'often arises from a misguided attempt to derive decisions from "the" . . . concept of a person'.

Holding separate and distinct personae accountable to one particular ideal of the person is an immodest recipe for confusion, if not disaster. As Weber (1978, I: 1404) argued, the ethos governing the conduct of the politician, the entrepreneur and the bureaucrat, for example, are far from identical. In addressing the different kinds of responsibility that these different personae have for their actions, Weber insists on the irreducibility of different spheres of ethical life and the necessity of applying different ethical protocols to them:

> An official who receives a directive which he considers wrong can and is supposed to object to it. If his superior insists on its execution, it is his duty and even his honor to carry it out as if it corresponded to his innermost conviction, and to demonstrate in this fashion that his sense of duty stands above his personal preference. It does not matter whether the imperative mandate originates from an 'agency', a 'corporate body' or an 'assembly'. This is the ethos of office. A political leader acting in this way would deserve contempt. He will often be

compelled to make compromises, that means, to sacrifice the less to the more important . . . 'To be above parties' – in truth, to remain outside the struggle for power – is the official's role, while this struggle for personal power, and the resulting political responsibility, is the lifeblood of the politician as well as the entrepreneur. (Weber, 1978, I: 1404)

By demanding – in the name of 'globalization', 'the customer' or the 'complete human being' – that the ethos governing the conduct of the public administrator, for example, be evaluated in terms of the ethos governing the conduct of the entrepreneur – in no matter how 'hybridized' or 'inverted' a form – contemporary managerialists are doing exactly what Rorty and Weber argue they should not: subordinating one comportment of the person to another by sheer exercise of ethical force.

As Charles Larmore (1987: 93) has argued, this 'recurrent and hackneyed' demand, so frequently articulated in religious and romantic discourse, has frequently had 'disastrous consequences'. Its manifestation in contemporary management discourse suggests some cause for concern. For example, in seeking to instill a feeling of ownership of particular policies amongst public administrators by inciting them to deploy their personal enthusiasms in their work, proponents of 'entrepreneurial principles' (Osborne and Gaebler, 1992) seem completely unaware that they are coming perilously close to opening the doors to corruption (See Chapters 4 and 6 of this volume).

As Kanter (1990: 355–9) has indicated, the contemporary entrepreneurial corporation harbours its own dangers. According to her, the 'romantic' shift from bureaucratic to entrepreneurial forms of management makes forging a career a more uncertain and political affair. It involves the eradication of various formal rules, regulations and procedures and their replacement by informal networks and an emphasis on individual creativity and deal-making. In other words, the contemporary 'entrepreneurial subjectification' of the workplace places considerable responsibility on the shoulders of individuals for their own advancement. In these circumstances – with the struggle for personal power an increasing feature of entrepreneurial conduct – it should come as no surprise to learn that forms of 'personal patronage' are far from on the wane within such organizations (Minson, 1991: 21–3).[3] This in turn suggests that the global suspicion of formal normative standards of conduct articulated by proponents of maximum businessing is not without its downside.

Concluding remarks

In this chapter I have briefly attempted to indicate that the critique of bureaucratic culture deployed within new wave management discourse should be treated with a healthy dose of scepticism. While it would be ridiculous to suggest that bureaucracy is an unambiguous achievement, the wholesale and largely unreflexive denigration of the ethos of office currently taking place should be cause for not inconsiderable concern.

In popular usage, the term 'bureaucracy' is most strongly associated with the defects of large organizations in both public and private sectors. Nevertheless, it seems obvious that public bureaucracies bear the brunt of popular disdain, associated as they are with a series of images that range from the hilarious (*Yes, Minister*) to the tragic (bureaucratic inertia was blamed for the failure of international governmental bodies to stop the conflict in Bosnia, for example). Such examples are not at all hard to find, but often the reason for their development can be traced to certain qualitative features of government, like the desire to ensure fairness, justice and equality in the treatment of citizens.

If bureaucracy (in its popular sense) is to be reduced and entrepreneurial forms of conduct adopted it has to be accepted that there might well be some costs attached to such a shift in terms of qualitative features of contemporary governance. This may be what some citizens believe that they want, if it also brings lower taxes – and this is indeed what successive administrations in the USA and UK have sought to achieve over the last two decades. However, this raises some important questions about the nature of public bureaux in contemporary liberal-democratic societies. It is to these questions that the second part of this book is addressed.

Notes

1. 'Often' but not always. Weber insists that the 'transition is fluid' between different systems of authority and that mixtures of elements are commonplace. A not insubstantial part of his analysis of 'charismatic authority' in *Economy & Society*, for example, is given over to cases in which charisma combines with something else – discipline, tradition, legal-rational authority and even economic calculation and money-making. Contemporary managerial discourse is perhaps a case in point. Certainly, it is often described as 'creating a marriage' between charismatic leadership and creativity and 'corporate discipline, cooperation and teamwork' (Kanter, 1990: 9–10).
2. To the frequently posed question: How are contexts identified and individuated? (i.e. Callon, 1998: 38–9), Rorty replies simply 'Which contexts?'
3. In a study of the effects of 'entrepreneurial' forms of conduct Martin and Murphy (1988; quoted in Minson, 1991: 22) drew attention to a statistically documented increase in sexual relationships between corporate working colleagues in North America. They attributed this trend to the combination of a growth in the numbers of women in managerial and professional occupations involving teamwork and a significant decrease in leisure time as employees' lives became increasingly work focused. Martin and Murphy implicitly link this sexualization of the workplace to the blurring of personal development and professional achievement that contemporary programmes of work reform engender and explicitly link this to a concomitant exacerbation of the problem of sexual harassment at work.

PART II

4

Office as a Vocation? Entrepreneurial Governance and Bureaucracy Critique

Our governments are in deep trouble today. In government after government and public system after public system, reinvention is the only option left.

David Osborne and Ted Gaebler

If administrative ethical standards are necessarily grounded in specific administrative systems – if they are, so to speak, two sides of the same coin – then it is impossible to change one without changing the other.

John Rohr

There is a heady delight to be derived from perversity and to make a case for the bureaucratic ethos in the public sector is, in today's political climate in the UK, as elsewhere, perverse. Fortunately, despite the speed, scope, scale and direction of recent changes there are also some important reasons – constitutional and ethico-political as well as more mundanely organizational – for mounting such a case and I want to touch on just a few of these in the following three chapters.

In essence, these chapters each explore certain facets of the new norms and techniques of conduct that have been insitituted within the domains of public administration in Britain predominantly, but also in the USA, Australia and other OECD countries, during the last twenty years. In so doing, they seek to delineate some of the constitutional and ethico-political consequences of ongoing alterations in actors' orientations within these domains.

Entrepreneurial governance and the problematization of bureaucratic conduct

As Herbert Kaufman (1981: 1) argued in his famous essay on the 'raging pandemic of anti-bureaucratic sentiment' gripping modern Western societies in the late 1970s and early 1980s, hostility to 'bureaucracy', as a term associated with the defects of large organizations applying rules to cases, is neither new nor a phenomenon peculiar to public sector management. Nonetheless, he continued, anti-bureaucratic sentiment has been expressed most frequently and vociferously in relation to the activities of public sector organizations.

Because public sector organizations have come to epitomize 'bureaucracy' understood as a portmanteau term for the defects of large organizations, it seems hardly surprising that a large degree of agreement has been achieved concerning the perceived need for their reform and modernization. Indeed, not only has the idea that public sector organizations need reforming gained a somewhat axiomatic status, there is also extensive, though by no means complete, agreement on the nature and direction of the required change.

Other forms of bureau critique

By about the mid-1980s tolerably similar problematizations of public bureaux and of the core ingredients for their reform had emerged from a variety of institutional and discursive locales and these – problematizations and prescriptions – have over time come to be known collectively as the new public management, or, more recently, as 'entrepreneurial governance'. According to the authors commonly charged with coining the latter term, entrepreneurial governance consists of ten 'essential principles' which link together to 'reinvent' public sector management. No doubt they seem very familiar (see the Introduction to this volume, p. 5) as they tend to be listed by nearly every commentator writing about contemporary developments in the public sector.

1 Competition between service providers.
2 Empowering citizens through pushing control out of bureaucracies into communities.
3 Focusing on outcomes rather than inputs.

4 Organizations and persons driven by missions and visions, not by rules and regulations.
5 Redefining clients as customers.
6 Preventing problems before they emerge rather than simply treating them once they have arisen.
7 Earning money, not just spending it.
8 Decentralizing authority and encouraging participative management.
9 Using market-type mechanisms rather than bureaucratic techniques and practices.
10 Catalysing partnerships between public, private and voluntary sectors (Osborne and Gaebler, 1992: 19–20).

These ten elements or 'principles' comprise something like a 'shopping list' for those wishing to modernize state bureaux in the OECD countries. Obviously, not every element is present in every case. Characteristic mixtures vary from country to country, as one would expect, with different countries having experienced very different historical trajectories within very different constitutional frameworks and, of course, with administrations of differing political persuasions driving the changes forward. Indeed, some countries – most notably Germany and Japan – appear to have been comparatively little influenced by 'entrepreneurial governance' at all (Pollitt, 1995). Nevertheless, after allowing for these important variations, most modernization efforts do appear to have involved the simultaneous deployment of a number of elements constitutive of entrepreneurial governance. As Osborne and Gaebler (1992: 19) suggest, the various elements can be seen to interact to form something like a systematic programme of reform.

Quite obviously, one key feature of entrepreneurial governance is the crucial role it allocates to 'the commercial enterprise' as the preferred model for any form of institutional organization of goods and services. However, of equal importance is the way in which the term refers to habits of action that display or express 'enterprising qualities on the part of those concerned', whether they be individuals or institutions. Here, 'enterprise' refers to a plethora of characteristics such as initiative, risk-taking, self-reliance, and the ability to accept responsibility for oneself and one's actions (Keat, 1990: 3).

So, a defining feature of entrepreneurial governance is its generalization of an 'enterprise form' to all forms of conduct – 'to the conduct of organizations hitherto seen as being non-economic, to the conduct of government, and to the conduct of individuals themselves' (Burchell, 1993: 275). While the concrete ways in which this entrepreneurial rationality has been operationalized have varied quite considerably within the UK, for example, the forms of action they have made possible for different institutions and persons do seem to share a general consistency and style.

One characteristic feature of this style of governance is the crucial role it accords to 'contract' in redefining organizational and personal relations.

The changes affecting hospitals, government departments and so forth in the UK have often involved the reconstituting of institutional roles in terms of contracts strictly defined, and even more frequently have involved a contract-like way of representing relationships between institutions and between individuals and institutions (Freedland, 1994: 88). An example of the former, for instance, occurred when fund-holding medical practices contracted with hospital trusts for the provision of health care to individual patients when previously that provision was made directly by the National Health Service (NHS). Examples of the latter include the relationships between central government departments and the new executive or Next Steps agencies – where no technical contract exists as such, but where the relationship is governed by a contract-like 'Framework Document' that defines the functions and goals of the agency, and the procedures whereby the department will set and monitor the performance targets for the agency.

Thus, 'contractualization' typically consists in assigning the performance of a function or an activity to a distinct unit of management – individual or collective – which is regarded as being accountable for the efficient (i.e. 'economic') performance of that function or conduct of that activity. These units of management are thereby affirming a certain kind of identity or personality that is basically entrepreneurial in character. Contractualization requires these units of management to adopt a certain entrepreneurial form of relationship to themselves 'as a condition of their effectiveness' and of the effectiveness of this form of governance (Burchell, 1993: 276). To put it another way, contractualization makes these units of management function like little businesses or 'enterprise forms'.

As Colin Gordon (1991: 43) has argued, these entrepreneurial forms of governance involve the reimagination of previously distinct activities and domains of existence as forms of the economic. 'This operation works', he argues, 'by the progressive enlargement of the territory of economic theory by a series of redefinitions of its object'.

One crucial dimension of this process is the reconceptualization of the individual producer/consumer as an economic agent perpetually responsive to modifications in its environment. As Gordon (1991: 43) points out, 'economic government here joins hands with behaviourism'. Entrepreneurial governance doesn't simply make up organizations as 'enterprise forms; it also 'makes up' people as 'entrepreneurs of themselves'.

This conception of the person as an entrepreneur of the self is firmly established at the heart of contemporary programmes of organizational reform in the public sector. In keeping with the entrepreneurial imbrication of economics and behaviourism, such programmes characterize employment not as a painful obligation imposed upon individuals, nor as an activity undertaken to meet purely instrumental needs, but rather as a means to self-development and individual empowerment. Organizational success is therefore premised upon an engagement by the organization of the self-optimizing impulses of all its members no matter what their formal role. This ambition is to be made practicable through a variety of techniques such as the decentralization of management authority within public agencies and by shifting the basis of employment from permanency and standard national pay and conditions towards term contracts, local determination of pay and conditions, and performance-related pay (Marsden and Richardson, 1994).

Performance management and related techniques, for example, involve a characteristically 'contractual' relationship between individual employees and the organization for which they work. This involves 'offering' individuals involvement in activities – such as managing budgets, training staff, delivering services – previously held to be the responsibility of other agents – such as supervisors, personnel departments and so forth. The price of this involvement is that individuals themselves must assume responsibility for carrying out those activities and for their outcomes. In keeping with the rationality of entrepreneurial governance, performance management and related techniques function as forms of responsibilization which are held to be both economically desirable and personally 'empowering'. This requirement that individuals become more personally exposed to the risks and costs of engaging in a particular activity is held to encourage them to build resources in themselves rather than simply to rely on others to take risks and endure uncertainties on their behalf. In this way, entrepreneurial governance makes its own rationality intimately their affair.

Entrepreneurial governance therefore involves the reconstruction of a wide range of institutions and activities along market lines. At the same time, guaranteeing that the optimal benefits accrue from 'marketization' necessitates the production of certain forms of conduct by all members of an organization. In this sense, governing organizational life in an enterprising manner involves 'making up' new ways for people to be; it refers to the importance of individuals acquiring and exhibiting specific entrepreneurial capacities and dispositions.

Refracted through the gaze of enterprise, 'bureaucratic culture' appears inimical to the development of these entrepreneurial capacities and dispositions. The bureaucratic ethos with its commitment to norms of impersonality, adherence to due process, ethos of responsibility, and so forth is seen as antithetical to the cultivation of those entrepreneurial skills and sensibilities now deemed so crucial to securing a 'manageable' and hence sustainable future.

Because advocates of entrepreneurial governance presuppose that no organizational context is immune to what they see as the effects of a rapidly changing, increasingly complex economic and social environment, they assume that ostensibly different organizations – hospitals, charities, banks, government departments – will have to develop similar norms and techniques of conduct, for without doing so they will lack the capacity to pursue their preferred projects. The certainty with which such claims are deployed gives the very definite impression that 'There is no alternative', as Mrs Thatcher once cried. As Kanter (1990: 356) forcefully declares, organizations 'must either move away from bureaucratic guarantees to (post) entrepreneurial flexibility or . . . stagnate, thereby cancelling by default any commitments they have made'. While such insistent singularity has obvious attractions – for one thing it offers the sort of easily graspable and communicable slogan that can act as a catalyst for change – it neglects the fact that the generalization of entrepreneurial 'principles' to all forms of conduct may of itself serve to incapacitate an organization's ability to pursue its preferred projects by redefining its identity and hence what the nature of its project actually is.

While there are obvious similarities between forms of managerial and other non-manual work in public bureaux and private enterprises, for example, there are also significant differences – mainly imposed by the constitutional and political environment within which that work is conducted – which suggest that it might be unwise for public bureaucrats to model their conduct too closely on entrepreneurial lines. It sometimes appears as if advocates of entrepreneurial governance believe that it is possible and desirable to keep politics and public services entirely separate. Because public sector management is conceptualized in terms of the managerially efficient (i.e. 'economic') delivery of services to customers, crucial dimensions of the context within which such management processes occur tend to fall below the horizon of visibility: the political context of representative democracy, for example, in which managers must think not only about their immediate customers, but about their accountability to citizens, and to citizens' representatives – elected legislators.

As advocates of entrepreneurial governance appear incapable of conceptualizing public bureaux in anything other than negative terms, they cannot imagine what sort of positive governmental role the bureau might be performing. Texts such as those by Osborne and Gaebler (1992) tell their readers very little about the technical, political or ethical organization of any actually existing public bureau. Instead their main role appears to be to frame the difference between the vocational ethics of the bureaucrat and those of the entrepreneur from the perspective of entrepreneurial principles. Rather than describing and analysing the ethos of office, the entrepreneurial critique seeks to assess the public bureaucracy in terms of its failure to achieve objectives which enterprise alone has set for it.

If one followed the line adopted by Osborne and Gaebler and others one would have to assume that the processes that evolved in traditional Civil Service systems did so with the perverse aim that money be wasted rather than from a recognition that too much flexibility in allocating money opened the door to corruption. Similarly, the rules, regulations, detailed record-keeping and general 'snaggishness' of the bureau against which Osborne and Gaebler rail were hardly developed with the sole purpose of inhibiting entrepreneurial activity but were seen as a price worth paying to ensure probity and reliability in the treatment of cases (du Gay, 1994a;

Jordan, 1994a). Jettisoning rules and regulations in the pursuit of entrepreneurial innovation seems unlikely to produce the permanent win/win
situation envisioned by advocates of entrepreneurial governance in opposition to the no-win situation they attribute to bureaucratic administration.
The idea, continually propounded by successive British governments, that
the enormous and comparatively sudden changes in administrative culture that have taken place in the UK in recent years have improved
efficiency, effectiveness, economy and public accountability with no
adverse consequences of any kind and without causing any significant
constitutional change simply beggars belief (see, for example, Waldegrave,
1993, but also Cmnd 4310, 1999).

Is it really feasible to assume, for example, that honesty and integrity in
public management will take care of itself while the structures and practices that are generally believed to have help constitute it – common
patterns of recruitment, rules of procedure, permanence of tenure,
restraints on the power of line management – have been reduced, diluted
or removed? Administrative culture is simultaneously a malleable and yet
fragile entity and is affected by many things: changes in institutions or
structures, changes in personnel, changes in codes of behaviour and so
forth. As far as Whitehall is concerned, there have been dramatic changes
in all these areas. A tradition might survive change in one, but hardly in all
of them simultaneously (Greenaway, 1995).

Rather than assuming the innate superiority of new managerial arrangements, perhaps it would be more productive to admit that both
bureaucratic and entrepreneurial forms of conduct exhibit their own particular 'defects' and 'virtues' (Jordan, 1994a). The question is whether, in a
political environment such as that characteristic of Westminster-style
democracies, the virtues and defects associated with an ordered, cautious,
reliable bureaucratic administration are more acceptable than those associated with a more entrepreneurial style. That such a question is still worth
posing despite the scope and speed of the changes that have taken place
can be gauged from a brief examination of some of the ethico-political and
constitutional issues that have arisen in the UK as a result of ongoing radical reforms of the Civil Service.

Reinventing government: the 'long march' through Whitehall

While there were a number of well publicized changes in central government administration in Britain during the years of Conservative rule, by far
and away the most important resulted from the Next Steps programme initiated by the so-called Ibbs Report, subtitled *Improving Management in
Government* (Efficiency Unit, 1988). This report recommended that many
services traditionally provided by government departments directly controlled by ministers should be semi-devolved to executive agencies headed

by chief executives linked to the main departments through a contract-like 'Framework Document' which would set out their tasks and responsibilities and their overall performance targets. The 'Framework Document' would also specify the financial and personnel freedoms judged necessary to the meeting of the agency's performance targets. Thus agencies would be structured to concentrate on what the government conceived to be the crucial feature of public service: value for money, i.e. issues of costs, staffing and quality of service.

The Conservative government's acceptance of the report's recommendations heralded a change in the identity of the Civil Service of quite enormous significance. Following what was conceived to be best current private sector practice the unitary structure of the British Civil Service was replaced by a quasi-autonomous multidivisional structure, where operational responsibilities were separated off from strategic and monitoring responsibilites (Corby, 1993, 1998).

In addition to this commitment to 'contractualization' – in the form of a policy-administration dichotomy – the government's programme for restructuring simultaneously involved a parallel commitment to corporatization. This latter process constituted the service providers as essentially corporate managerial entities capable of being separately accountable for their own budgets (Freedland, 1994, 1998). To this end, the Government Trading Act 1990 made it easier for executive agencies to be assigned and to operate with distinct funding (not all of it granted from parliamentary moneys), while the Civil Service (Management Functions) Act 1992 made it possible for the management of employment within executive agencies to be delegated from central departments to the agencies.

Overall, the government did almost everything possible to foster a sense of corporate responsibility and corporate identity on the part of executive agencies. For example, agencies were encouraged to devise their own corporate plan and mission statement and to elaborate their own organizational arrangements for the pursuit of their particular set of aims and objectives. In order to increase individual civil servants' 'sense of ownership and personal identification' with their own particular product performance-related pay was introduced throughout agencies, while amongst senior staff and an increasing range of other managerial personnel personalized, fixed-term contracts became the norm. Open competition for agency posts, whereby people from outside the Civil Service can be brought into key positions and bring to bear their own managerial competences upon public business, has also played its part in creating this sense of corporate identity – over one third of current agency chief executives are appointed from outside the service.

As a result of these and other changes it is quite obvious that the new executive agencies are affirming a particular type of identity or personality, one that we can instantly recognize as 'entrepreneurial' in orientation, and one that is, it must be said, very different from that traditionally associated with the British Civil Service – where common systems of recruitment, remuneration and organization as well as common standards of conduct contributed to a powerful *esprit de corps* (Chapman, 1991, 1996a).

So how then might the Next Steps initiative be said to have undermined or be undermining the bureaucratic ethos in the British Civil Service? In the rest of the chapter I want to focus on just two aspects of the Next Steps initiative – though I believe there are many more that could be chosen – which have had significant implications for the conduct of bureaucratic office. The first refers to the policy/operations dichotomy that the Next Steps initiative created and the accountability problems it has thrown up. The latter refers to the question of individual enthusiasms among public servants.

The Policy/administration dichotomy and the ethos of office

As O'Toole and Chapman (1994: 119) have argued the doctrine of individual ministerial responsibility to Parliament has always been the working convention that governs the relationship between ministers and their civil servants. This doctrine means that it is the minister and the minister alone who is responsible to Parliament for everything that takes place in her department and for everything that her officials either do or fail to do. It therefore facilitates both the party political impartiality and the anonymity of officials that is a central feature of the British Civil Service. Together these elements of the doctrine give protection to the advice civil servants can give to ministers, thus allowing it to be free, frank and open, and give to the minister the confidence that she has the loyalty of her officials.

Naturally it is impossible for ministers personally to know or control everything that happens in their departments. Only the most politically salient issues or other issues of importance end up on the minister's desk. This has always been so and is recognized to be the case by constitutional and political commentators. All other decisions are handled by civil servants, who have no constitutional personality of their own and who always act in their minister's name. After all, it is up to officials to know what the minister's policy is and it is up to ministers to make known that policy to them. They can then act according to that policy. If the policy leads to political problems then clearly that is a matter for the minister. If the civil servants make a mistake they are subject to internal disciplinary procedures. In all circumstances, however, external accountability is to Parliament (O'Toole and Chapman, 1994: 119).

This is not to say that there have not been problems with the doctrine of ministerial responsibility. Events such as the Westland Affair, the Ponting Affair, the Lewis case and the Arms for Iraq scandal have indicated that, when it suits them, ministers can use constitutional conventions for ambiguous ends and are only too happy to hide behind their officials (O'Toole, 1997, 1998). By and large, though, and despite doubts about the way ministers have discharged their duties to Parliament, it is true to say that the doctrine of ministerial responsibility kept intact: that is, until the onset of the Next Steps initiative. 'Even the introduction of the relatively influential departmental select committee system of the House of Commons did not undermine the doctrine that it was ministers who answered to Parliament and it was ministers who were the public face of their departments. Civil servants remained largely anonymous, ministers took both the credit and the blame for the actions of those civil servants and citizens knew where the buck stopped' (O'Toole and Chapman, 1994: 124). Next Steps has made all of this less clear.

One of the crucial aims of the Next Steps programme, according to its authors, was to separate the spheres of influence and tasks of politicians and bureaucrats, with the latter becoming defined primarily as managers. This meant at central government level excluding ministers from the day-to-day management of services, allowing them to concentrate on the development of sound policy and enabling the bureaucrats to get on with what they should have been doing all along: managing. Once the goals and objectives had been set it was just a matter of 'staying close to the customer' as in any other business context. Service delivery was 'depoliticized', as it should be. The quasi-contractual relationships between ministers and the agencies, which their departments sponsor, allowed the ministers to monitor those agencies to ensure that they were operating within the limits set. Ministers were still formally accountable to Parliament for the policies and the frameworks within which the policies were carried out but not for operational matters, which were the responsibility of the agencies. Such a dichotomy, it was argued, added 'transparency' to the accountability process (Goldsworthy, 1991; Butler, 1994).

This sounds all very sensible but a crucial question remains unanswered. Where does policy end and administration begin, and who decides? One thing is worth noting from the outset. The convention of ministerial responsibility never required that ministers should be the policy-makers and officials merely the advisers and administrators. This is because policy-making and administration are not in practice separable types of activity. There is, for example, considerable historical evidence that throughout the life of the Westminster conventions civil servants, particularly senior ones, have been called upon to make policy decisions, sometimes because their minister was otherwise engaged but also partly by virtue of their unchallengeable experience and judgement. However, there are policy implications in the work of civil servants throughout the organizational chain (Baker, 1971; Chapman, 1988a; Parker, 1993).

As Parker (1993: 70), has argued, 'what we have in legislation are statements of greater or lesser generality, which become meaningful only in application to particular cases'. As only a small portion of such applications can be directly handled by responsible representatives the rest have to be handled by officials. The imprecision of the original statements of purpose inevitably leaves some margin for discretion to ministers and officials – a margin which may permeate to very low levels of the administrative hierarchy. Anyone with discretion helps to determine policy. Furthermore there is the reverse process, equally inevitable, and even more completely beyond the scope of such a simple dichotomy, whereby officials, in the course of their duties, play a part in the deliberate formulation of new purposes – in so far as experience with administering a 'policy' suggests or leads to new ways of improving or modifying it.

If the policy/administration dichotomy can be seen to be a discredited way of conceptualizing the relationship between the work of ministers and that of civil servants under Westminster conventions, what does its concerted operationalization through the agency system mean for the doctrine of ministerial responsibility and the constitutional role of civil servants?

Put somewhat cynically, it means that Next Steps agencies are the ideal organizational innovation for ministers. Because ministers still retain formal accountability to Parliament for the conduct of policy and yet are simultaneously able to decide what is and what is not a policy issue they are now in a position both to have their cake and eat it. This makes the task of parliamentary scrutiny that much harder as ministers are able to sidestep criticism on the floor of the house by redirecting questions to agency chief executives as they see fit. As cases involving the Child Support Agency and the Prison Service have indicated, ministers have played a major role in both the strategic and the operational management of agencies, yet they have had more or less *carte blanche* to refuse to answer parliamentary questions about the work of those agencies if they wish. There can be no doubt that the policy/administration dichotomy has increased the power of ministers but at the expense of weakened parliamentary accountability (O'Toole and Chapman, 1994: 138–9).

The role of civil servants has also been altered by the introduction of the policy/administration dichotomy. Although there has been no formal constitutional change in their position, civil servants have found themselves increasingly taking on the role of politician as well as that of manager as ministers refuse to answer questions on issues they define as 'operational' while still interfering in the day to day running of agencies (Lewis, 1997). This has had implications for public perceptions of their party political impartiality. More pressingly perhaps, civil servants have been used as political scapegoats by ministers who have been unwilling to take responsibility when matters have gone amiss (O'Toole and Chapman, 1994; O'Toole, 1998).

Shining with enthusiasm

Another consequence of the Next Steps initiative in general and the policy/administration dichotomy in particular has been the steady growth of what has been termed a 'can do' attitude amongst civil servants, particularly within the higher echelons of the service. Even before the Next Steps programme was put into effect, evidence was emerging – albeit mainly anecdotal – that top civil servants were increasingly being expected to exhibit an enthusiastic, committed approach to government policy. This style of conduct was described, in a report published in 1987 by the now defunct Royal Institute of Public Administration, as 'characterized by decisiveness and an ability to get things done, rather than the more traditional approach which lays greater emphasis on analysis of options and recommendations for actions based upon that analysis'. However, since the instigation of the Next Steps reforms, the generalization of a 'can do' ethos throughout the senior echelons of the service has continued apace. As a senior civil servant interviewed by a study team from the government's Efficency Unit (1993: 22) argued, 'the drive should be to find people who can show added value, not ask clever questions'.

Because the Next Steps programme is structured to give effect to the view that governments should not have to tolerate obstruction from hidebound bureaucrats and that the latter should be personally committed to the success of government policies, it should come as no surprise to learn that many of the forms of conduct traditionally associated with being a civil servant are represented as largely antiquated products of a bygone era. This is evident, as the above quote also indicates, from what a former head of the Civil Service called the official's obligation to provide 'honest and impartial advice, without fear or favour, [. . .] whether the advice accords with the Minister's view or not' (Armstrong, 1985).

Evidence compiled by the Association of First Division Civil Servants in the 1980s suggested that ministers had been taking a closer interest than in the past in appointments to their own departments at senior levels (Treasury and Civil Service Committee, 1988). Even if this did not constitute politicization in the partisan sense, the effects may be analagous. As one civil servant reported: 'I sometimes think that I see advice going to ministers which is suppressing arguments because it is known that ministers will not want them, and that for me is a betrayal of the Civil Service'. This sort of conduct is an explicit abnegation of what Weber termed the bureaucrat's 'ethos of responsibility' (Weber, 1978, II: 978ff.). Its implications for the concept of an impartial Civil Service able to work effectively with any government regardless of party political persuasion are obvious.

This emphasis on a 'can do' approach to the business of government seems oddly at variance with the sorts of conduct traditionally expected of officials working in a bureaucracy. The representation of bureaucrats as congenital 'snag hunters' is an accurate description of the role of many civil servants; it is also something to be recognized as having positive governmental effects and not something that should be simply seen as a drag on 'efficiency' (narrowly defined). It is or should be the duty of civil servants to hunt out the snags before the machinery is set to work (Jordan, 1994b). This is a very different role from that of ministers, who come and go, and are eager to make their mark and want to implement their ideas as quickly as possible. Civil servants who have to live with the consequences long after the minister has left the scene need to ensure that the new policy can be effectively operationalized and that it will not stall or break down after a few months. Of course, when push comes to shove it is the constitutional right of ministers to overrule any official fears, but at their own risk, as the implementation of the poll tax in Britain in the 1980s so clearly indicated (Dunleavy, 1995).

The dangers that the demand for enthusiasm poses for the bureaucratic ethos of responsibility and for the party political impartiality of the Civil Service also extends to the expectation of procedural fairness and equity in the treatment of cases. The increasing deployment of performance measures and the introduction of performance-related pay, in particular, pose a threat to the spirit of formal impersonality – without hatred or passion and hence without affection or enthusiasm – that Weber described as a constitutive feature of the conduct of office in this regard. Evidence from Parliamentary Select Committee investigations into the workings of the Child Support Agency (CSA), for example, indicated not only that some civil servants appeared to have an unduly passionate commitment to furthering the objectives of their agency – fostered in no small part by the proselytizing example set by the then Chief Executive of the agency – but that this had led them to engage in unacceptable forms of conduct in chasing absent fathers. Not only this, it was also discovered that in order to meet performance and efficency targets set by ministers the agency found it more expedient to try to gain increased sums from absent fathers who were already making a contribution to their children's upbringing than to seek out fathers who were absent and who gave no assistance (Jordan, 1994b). As this case indicates, rather than seeking to moderate the perfectly understandable enthusiasms of officials for particular policies and projects the rationale guiding the conduct of agency staff appears designed to incite them.

It seems then that the Next Steps programme has effected significant changes in the ways that civil servants are expected to conduct themselves. And these changes appear to be to the detriment of the bureaucratic ethos of office. Politicians seem to have undermined the healthy tension between the ethos of the politician and that of the public official that was a constitutive feature of Westminster-style democracies. 'Frank and fearless advice', for example, though often unpalatable to politicians, was thought to be indispensable in a complex society; it could complement political will and make policy more effective in the longer term.

As Parker (1993: 149–50) has argued, 'the trouble is, of course, that there is no objective, unambiguous way of telling when the official response to a ministerial initiative, or the official prompting of the minister, shades over from a legitimate exercise of official independence to an unacceptable frustration or manipulation of the government's purposes. Only governments themselves can make that decision.' Unable to live with these tensions, successive administrations – including the present one – seem intent on recasting the role officials can play in the governmental domain. It is evident that something important may be disappearing in this process of translation.

Concluding remarks

The advocates of the Next Steps and other entrepreneurial reforms, such as market testing, seemed unable to imagine that business management and public administration could not easily be made to be identical in every respect. While there is a sense in which the state and the business concern are both rational 'enterprises', deliberately and explicitly directed towards achieving goals and objectives in an efficient and effective manner (though with rather different meanings attached to these two terms), public administration differs from business management primarily because of the constraints imposed by the political environment within which the management processes are conducted. As Neville Johnson (1983: 193–4), amongst others, has argued:

> Undoubtedly the official in public service is . . . engaged extensively in the use and deployment of resources taken away from the people he or she serves and returned to them as benefits and entitlements legitimated by the system of government. It is clear that in these circumstances he or she bears a responsibility for the efficient use of resources and to this end must be ready and able to use such methods of management as will offer the best prospect of optimal performance. But the function of officials cannot be exhaustively defined in terms of achieving results efficiently. There is also duty to observe the varied limits on action by public bodies and to satisfy the political imperatives of public service – loyalty to those who are politically responsible, responsiveness to parliamentary and public opinion, sensitivity to the complexity of the public interest, honesty in the formulation of advice, and so on. It is out of such commitments that a professional ethic was fashioned in the public services. Even if this has weakened in recent years we cannot afford to dispense with it. This is because a system of representative government does require officials to act as the custodians of the procedural values it embodies. The contemporary concern with efficient management, with performance, and with securing results, should not be allowed to obscure this fact. The pursuit of better management in government, important though it is, has to recognize the political limits to which it is subject.

Simply representing the public bureaucracy in economic terms as an inefficient form of organization fails to take account of the crucial ethical and political role of the bureau that Johnson delineates. If bureaucracy is to be reduced and an entrepreneurial style of management adopted, then it must be recognized that while 'economic efficiency' might be improved in the short term, the longer-term costs associated with this apparent improvement may well include antipathy to corruption, fairness, probity and reliability in the treatment of cases and other forms of conduct that were taken somewhat for granted under traditional arrangements. As Chapman (1991: 17) has argued

> When attention is focused on public sector management as distinct from management in other contexts, a distinctively bureaucratic type of organization, with accountability both hierarchically and to elected representatives, may mean that far from being inefficient it is in fact the most suitable type of organization . . . Consequently, regarding bureaucracy as an inefficient type of organization may reflect a superficial understanding of bureaucracy and, perhaps, a blinkered appreciation of public sector management. Bureaucracy may be more expensive than other types of organization but that is not surprising when democracy is not necessarily the cheapest form of government.

We are in no danger of forgetting the disasters to which bureaucracies are prone if we remind ourselves every now and again of the threats – including those posed by contemporary 'entrepreneurialism' – against which they offer protection. After all, as Dunleavy and Hood (1994: 16) have argued, what's at stake in these reforms are not just 'bread and butter issues of operations, costs and short-term response. Ultimately, the issues involved are constitutional, in that they affect the foundations of political life and capacity.'

5

'Vitalizing' State Bureaux: Some Ethico-political Consequences of Reinventing Government

Sociologically speaking, the modern state is an 'enterprise' (*Betrieb*) just like a factory. This is its historical peculiarity.

Max Weber

We are building for the State, not for any one party.

Peter Kemp

Debates about contemporary administrative reform in the public sector are often hampered by the terms in which they are cast. Simple dichotomies between the 'state' and the 'market', which both reformers and their critics deploy with alarming frequency, are apt to obscure more than they enlighten. After all, as has been pointed out countless times, 'markets' are constructed institutions, and actually existing market societies are in very large part the products of continuous, centrally organized and regulated interventionism, interventionism that is, by states. The 'free' market is an institutional structure which does not emerge spontaneously from an innate proclivity or need to 'trade and truck'. Extra-market sources of social cohesion are necessary in order to sustain market relations (Hirschmann, 1977).

Similarly, the reform of public sector organizations along market lines – the introduction of 'internal markets' and the like – has been largely, if not exclusively, the product of governmental intervention. These organizational markets have not simply appeared out of nowhere. Their emergence has been governmentally induced (Clarke and Newman, 1997; Scott, 1996).

In order to respond to the challenges posed by contemporary

programmes of administrative reform we first need to know what it is we're actually dealing with. This means 'economizing' on moral-political generalizations concerning these reform programmes in order to concentrate on specific differences between established criteria of good public service and the novel criteria these programmes are bringing into being. I begin this task by locating current debates about the proper conduct of public management in the context of changing governmental perceptions concerning the problem of national economic management.

The mobilization of society

The emergence of new ways of governing economic and social life in Western societies, the extension of market and contractual relationships into areas previously governed in alternative ways and the paradoxical appearance in the wealthiest of all modern societies of persistent governmental efforts to restrain public expenditure have been described and analysed under a range of headings: Thatcherism, Reaganism, neo-liberalism, advanced liberalism, contractualism, new managerialism and so on and so forth. The number and variety of such labels suggests that there is no general agreement about the overall significance of the changes they seek to capture and, more importantly perhaps, that they might be more profitably understood as the outcome of several distinct lines of development (Donzelot, 1991; Hindess, 1997).

What I want to suggest here is that these phenomena can be usefully examined in the context of changing governmental perceptions about the problem of national economic management. Certainly, it is a standard move in the literature on the new public management, for example, to seek to explain the emergence of this phenomenon in terms of the logics of fiscal crisis (Foster and Plowden, 1996: 2; Zifcak, 1994: 7–8). However, it hardly needs saying that the ways in which 'fiscal crises' are represented have consequences for the ways they are then acted upon. 'Fiscal crises' do not of themselves possess an innate logic that calls into being their own remedies. They are discursively constituted and as such are understood and acted upon in relation to specific cultural, normative and technical frameworks (du Gay, 1999).

My argument here is that the 'fiscal crises' that are allocated such a crucial causal role in explanations of the development of contemporary programmes of administrative reform in the public sector have themselves to be placed in a wider framework of changing governmental conceptions of national economic management and perceptions of relations between economic and other aspects of the life of a society.

In the name of globalization . . .

If the widespread consensus of the 1950s and 1960s was that the future belonged to a capitalism without losers, securely managed by national

governments acting in concert, then the 1980s and 1990s have been domi-
nated by a consensus based on quite the opposite assumptions: that global
markets are basically uncontrollable and that 'the only way to avoid
becoming a loser – whether as a nation, an organization, or an individual –
is to be as competitive as possible' (Hirst and Thompson, 1996: 6; see also
Krugman, 1996). This zero-sum conception has serious implications for
the ways in which states are encouraged to view their own security. Of
course, security, and security of economic activity in particular, has been
and continues to be a primary concern for any modern state. What this discourse of 'globalization' problematizes is the ways in which security is to
be obtained under conditions of extreme uncertainty. Indeed, this discourse both defines the circumstances in which states find themselves and
advocates particular mechanisms through which security might conceiv-
ably be obtained under those circumstances.

Simply stated, nation-states embedded in (what is represented as) an
increasingly competitive global market and hence exposed to (what are
represented as) supranationally ungovernable economic forces are encouraged to guarantee their survival through devolving responsibility for the
economy to 'the market' – using what remains of their public powers of
intervention to limit, as it were constitutionally, the claims that politics
can make on the economy, and citizens on the polity. Wolfgang Streeck
(1996: 307) testifies to the power of this discourse of globalization when he
writes that 'in many countries today, disengagement of politics from the
economy is defended with reference to constraints of economic interna-
tionalization that would frustrate any other economic strategy'.

In place of a representation of the national economy as a resource, and
therefore as contributing to the well-being of the national community in
other respects – and, of course, in place of technologies designed to make this
practicable – we now find an inversion of that perception, with other aspects
of the life of the national community increasingly perceived in terms of the
contribution they can make to economic efficiency. In this new light, security
can only be obtained, it would appear, through allowing economic problems
to fall back on society, so that society is implicated in resolving them, where
previously the economy was expected to provide for society's needs.

So what are the implications of this new image for governmental perceptions of relations between national economic activity and other aspects
of the life of the national community? Under what we might term the 'old
regime of representation', the national economy could be seen both as a
largely self-regulating system and as a resource for other component parts
or domains of a larger national unity. Since prudential government would
secure the conditions of economic growth, its output, net of depreciation
and replacement costs, could be deployed for investment and for other crucial national purposes, such as defence and social welfare. These latter
expenditures might or might not be seen as 'economic costs' but their net
effect would only be to reduce the rate of growth to rather less than it
might otherwise have been (Hindess, 1997).

Within the discourse of globalization the pursuit of national economic efficiency is the *sine qua non* of national security and well-being. This incessant hunt for economic efficiency appears not only as a foundation of economic growth but of all those other activities that must be financed from growth. As I indicated above, this strategy of economic governance undermines existing divisions between the economy and other spheres of existence within the nation-state. The image of the well-ordered national economy providing resources for the national state and society is now replaced by the image of the extravagant 'big government' state and society undermining efficient national economic performance. This shift helps account for the seemingly paradoxical situation in which governmental discourse in the wealthiest nations on earth contains an assumption that social welfare regimes are no longer affordable in the forms in which we have come to know them. Anything that might seem to have a bearing on economic life (and this includes education, defence and health as well as social welfare) is assessed not only in terms of the availability of resources and the alternative uses to which those resources might be put, but primarily in terms of their consequences for promoting or inhibiting the pursuit of national economic efficiency (Hindess, 1997). The aim here is not simply to save money in the short term but also to induce efficiency-enhancing 'cultural change' in organizational and personal conduct through the introduction of market-type relationships into ever more spheres of existence (Burchell, 1993; du Gay, 1994b).

Building for the state, but not as we know it

Because this governmental discourse paints government itself as a huge drain on national economic efficiency, it hardly comes as a surprise to learn that state sector institutions and activities have found themselves at the cutting edge of efficiency-enhancing initiatives. These have included attempts to reduce government activities, through, for example, ceasing to provide services previously offered or shifting the basis of their provision from the public to the private sector. However, they have also involved wide-ranging administrative reforms which have attempted to change the whole style and conduct – ethos – of public sector management in line with this new understanding of the governmental problem of security.

These contemporary governmental attempts to 'enterprise up' the state (and 'society') to support national economic efficiency do not represent some simple colonization of the state by the market, nor of the 'public' by the 'private'. Such dichotomies cannot be maintained in the face of the hybridizations that are actually taking place. As Clarke and Newman (1997: 29) have argued, analyses of contemporary governmental restructuring which insist on deploying these dichotomies risk missing 'the dynamic relationships which both reconfigure and traverse such boundaries. An emphasis on the transfer of tasks, roles and responsibilities outwards from the state risks neglecting the ways in which the dispersal of power in these processes engages these other agents in the state's field of relationships.' These dispersals – of roles, responsibilities and powers – can and do have the effect of enabling or 'empowering' different agents to provide 'public' services: commercial enterprises, trusts, voluntary organizations and so on. However, they also subject these agents to new constraints and demands through processes of assessment, contracting and evaluation. The capacity of the agents to act or make choices is not their intrinsic property but an effect of their relationship with the state in which they are both empowered and constrained.

Other organizational reforms within the public sector exhibit similarly hybrid logics. One of the most ubiquitous of these reforms, perhaps the single most crucial device in the 'cultural' reconstruction of public sector management, has been the introduction of 'internal markets' or quasi-markets. Once again, simple contrasts between markets and hierarchies prove insufficient in capturing the major innovation in the art of governance that this mechanism represents. As Alan Scott (1996: 99) has indicated, the basic aim of the 'internal market' is neatly captured by Polanyi's description of Bentham's Panopticon as 'not only a "mill to grind rogues honest, and idle men industrious"; it would also pay dividends like those of the Bank of England'. The mechanism has a dual purpose: the reformation of working habits and ethos and the establishment of a system for the provision of public services modelled on a market and thus having the production of profit (no matter how artificial) as its basic organizing principle.

The idea of the internal market as a mechanism for governing organizational and personal conduct is quite simple. A centralized bureaucracy in which commands flow downwards is replaced by 'flatter', less directly controlled organizations. The chief technology deployed to achieve this is the devolved budget. Each section of the organization becomes its own 'budget holder' and 'cost centre'. As such it buys goods/services from other parts of the organization or can go outside the parameters of the organization where comparable goods/services can be found more cheaply. Each unit is also a supplier of goods/services to, as well as a customer of, other parts of the organization and can seek to sell its goods/services on the wider market if this is tenable financially. However, if a cost centre cannot offer its internal (or external) customers competitive rates for its goods/services then it will not be profitable and, all other things being equal, is unlikely to survive. It is thus motivated to try and maximize its efficiency in order to ensure its own reproduction. There is consequently little need for direct command to a unit from above to be more efficient, for unit members themselves will have a personal motive or self-interest in enhancing their own and their unit's overall efficiency.

The flow of commands is thus replaced by the workings of the market's 'hidden hand', or so it would appear. However, appearances are often deceptive and a crucial point to recognize here is that the power of those in the higher echelons is not necessarily diminished by the introduction of internal markets. As Scott (1996: 101), for example, has argued, the power of bureaucratic hierarchy (whether at the local level of a particular organization or at the level of the nation state) is maintained through the mobilization of the remaining regulative authority which is deployed to manipulate opportunity structures by shifting resources and centrally determined pricing. This induces uncertainty and instability into the environment of those released from the kinds of direct bureaucratic domination Weber described. The new autonomy is real but its beneficiaries find themselves in shifting opportunity structures within which they must operate and over which they do not have direct control.

The crucial point here is that these shifting opportunity structures or 'externalities' are not those of the fate-like workings of the market alone but are to a considerable degree the result of political decision-making and governmental intervention. The environment – market – within which organizational actors find themselves is governmentally constituted. Those at the centre do not relinquish their overall powers by constituting newly autonomous subjects as long as they retain control over the environment in which actors act autonomously.

What we have here then is neither a traditional bureaucracy nor a free market but a governmentally constituted quasi-market. It is the formation of opportunity structures and environmental parameters rather than routine daily decisions that is the object of organizational manipulation. In the public sector, particularly, there is nothing very subtle about this form of governing at a distance. For example, in the provision of health care and educational services, where the state is still paymaster, the price of 'units of resource' is set centrally. By altering these nominal prices the state retains enormous power over those very agencies to which it has also granted a degree of real autonomy (Scott, 1996: 101).

The newly freed actors, whether organizations or individuals, find themselves responding to centrally determined decisions but not as they once knew them. It is perhaps questionable whether subordinates in traditional bureaucratic structures – those exhibiting a greater degree of fit to Max Weber's characterization – had any more influence over the formulation of strategy than they do in the new quasi-market organizations, but what is certain is that they now have a much greater direct responsibility for the success or failure of 'outcomes' (Scott, 1996). With the introduction of quasi-markets and the decoupling of policy and operations, actors are no longer servants of, but rather entrepreneurs for, an institution. Freed from the necessity of constant participation in the flow of commands on a routine basis, senior managers are encouraged to focus on the development of goals and strategies whose day-to-day implementation they are not expected to supervize directly. This is deemed more efficient and businesslike than a traditional bureaucracy because extensive supervision of day-to-day operations is made redundant, replaced by market mechanisms whose very operation has the effect of making people 'entrepreneurs' of their own conduct (du Gay, 1994a, 1996).

The restructuring of state institutions and activities along 'market' lines does not therefore involve the diminution of state capacity *per se* but transforms it in keeping with a revised problematization of the role and responsibilities of government. As Peter Kemp's comments, quoted on page 196, suggest, those engaged in reform have not seen themselves as party political ideologues out to dismantle the state but as architects of a 'vitalized' state formation equipped to secure its goals and objectives in a world in which 'the only way to avoid becoming a loser . . . as a nation . . . is to be as competitive as possible' (Hirst and Thompson, 1996: 6).

New administrative cultures

Through the introduction of 'contractorization', internal markets and the like, contemporary programmes of administrative reform in the public sector have sought to establish organizational and personal forms of conduct that promote and sustain national economic efficiency. However, there is a danger that the demands of national economic efficiency have assumed the status of a 'nodal point' through which all other aspects of the conduct of public administration – political, legal, constitutional – are interpreted and allotted weight.

That this is more than just a possibility is demonstrated by the almost complete disregard for the complex juridico-political context within which the management of public services takes place; this is evident within much of the 'new managerialist' literature – including 'official' governmental publications (Barzelay, 1992; Cmnd 4310, 1999; Efficiency Unit, 1988; Gore, 1993; Osborne and Gaebler, 1992). Where such issues are considered, it is normally assumed that contemporary programmes of administrative reform are just making things work better. They may well be significant (they must be if they are to live up to the 'reinventing' or 'modernizing' hyperbole) but they are also inherently uncontroversial, and regarded as common sense (Waldegrave, 1993).

What I want to suggest in the rest of this chapter is that these programmes of reform in fact create new criteria of public service which do not sit comfortably with existing understandings. This is in large part, I argue, because they transform the practices through which these existing criteria are produced. Protagonists of the Next Steps reforms in the British Civil Service, for example, could indeed claim that they had no wish directly to alter existing constitutional practice. For they have really operated in another dimension, namely that of restructuring the financial management of public administration. The Next Steps programme, unlike previous exercises in internal restructuring and agency separation, was in essence designed to set up agencies which would be separately accountable in a *financial* rather than a *political* sense. The targets and criteria of assessment for the agencies were intended to be, and have been, financial ones; the emphasis has been on 'efficiency' and 'value for money'; and the implicit comparison, made explicit by the market testing programme, was with the efficiency of the management of private sector organizations (Freedland, 1996). Considerable importance has been invested in the appointment of the agency Chief Executive as accounting officer of the agency in question. This 'empowerment' of the agency chief executive represents both philosophically and practically, his or her elevation to the position of managing director of a distinct quasi-commercial or business enterprise which operates as a dependency (or wholly owned subsidiary) of a government department. What this clearly indicates is that the culture and conduct which the Next Steps programme is designed to inculcate in executive agencies is one of financial or commercial accountability (Doig and Wilson, 1998).

How, then, does this prioritizing of financial and commercial accountability impact upon established constitutional practice and criteria for good public service? According to Mark Freedland (1996: 28) one of its main effects is to undermine the doctrine of political ministerial responsibility for departmental decision-making through transmuting and fragmenting it into two distinct accountabilities, each of which is primarily financial.

On the one hand, executive agencies have a primary decision-making role and responsibility for the decisons they make. But this responsibility in the sense of answerability 'is conceived of and expressed in terms primarily of financial accountability, that is to say in terms of a liability to show that there has been efficient financial management and adherence to targets and budgets' (Freedland, 1996: 28).

On the other hand, the parent department retains a kind of responsibility for the decision-making which occurs at agency level. But the separation of the agency as a distinct centre of decision-making means that departmental responsibility has become secondary and essentially supervisory. The parent department has become in effect accountable for its supervision of the agency.

> Moreover, that departmental accountability is, in a way which mirrors that of the agency, increasingly conceived of in financial terms – the primary role of the parent department tends to become that of accounting to the Cabinet and Parliament for the efficiency and good financial management of the departmental operation as conducted through the subsidiary agencies. As if by a conjuring trick, the spell of financial accountability has enabled ministerial responsibility not only to be sawn in half but actually to be spirited off the stage. (Freedland, 1996: 28)

The enthusiastic promulgation of, dare I say it, narrowly financial criteria of accountability and efficiency thus creates a situation in which, if the relationship between the agency and the parent department is working in the way it is meant and intended to work, the decision-makers and decision-making at agency level cannot be seen as part of an integrated (bureaucratic) departmental structure, a departmental unity, such as the doctrine of political ministerial responsibility essentially demands.

As the example of the Next Steps initiative indicates, rather than lying within the boundaries of constitutional orthodoxy contemporary programmes of administrative reform have some startling constitutional implications. The 'see no problems' perspective of many reform enthusiasts fails to acknowledge that 'the design of government involves choosing between different packages of costs and benefits. If one chooses to remedy a certain defect one has to face up to the adverse consequences in other areas' (Jordan, 1994: 278). Instead, enthusiasts continually stress that it is now possible to 'make government work better and cost less' (Gore, 1993; Osborne and Gaebler, 1992). That this position is both untenable and potentially dangerous can be adduced from a closer examination of two of the main tenets of the contemporary orthodoxy in administrative reform. First, that if you look after 'economic efficiency', effectiveness will take care of itself. Secondly, that it is possible and desirable to keep politics out of public services.

Efficiency, effectiveness and economy: cake and eating it

That a concept of efficiency should occupy a privileged place in contemporary programmes of administrative reform in the public sector is far from surprising. These programmes are themselves part of a wider governmental imperative: the pursuit of economic efficiency as the *sine qua non* of national security and well-being in an environment of chronic uncertainty. The first question that comes to mind, however, is what is meant by 'efficiency' in contemporary programmes of administrative reform? This is more difficult than it might appear because the term is so often deployed without any real precision (Chapman, 1976b). Instead, it seems to function as something of a 'hurrah' word exhorting change in the direction of some future state in which things will be better for everyone. In this loose sense, efficient government is government which works better but costs less.

Disaggregating this vague statement we can say that 'efficiency' seems to mean the provision of the same or greater outputs with reduced inputs. It thus subsumes within itself two other attributes, economy (less cost) and effectiveness (the achievement of specified objectives). The assumption here is that efficient government is also economic and effective government. This seems a somewhat immodest, one could even say simplistic, assumption. Nonetheless it appears to be taken seriously by many of those at the forefront of recent administrative reform, as this striking exchange between Sir Peter Levene, the then British Prime Minister's Efficiency Adviser (brought into government from the private sector), and a member of the House of Commons Treasury and Civil Service Select Committee indicates:

Q: Sir Peter, your role is to be the Prime Minister's Adviser on Efficiency and Effectiveness. What have you ever done for effectiveness?

A: I think the two are virtually synonymous.

Q: Surely not?

A: Let us say that one should follow from the other. (House of Commons Treasury and Civil Service Committee, 1993: 94)

If only things were quite so easy. As Conrad Russell (1993: 91) commented in relation to the ceaseless pursuit of 'efficiency' savings in higher education, 'if we take in more undergraduates without increasing the supply of books, the number of undergraduates who come to me and report that they cannot do their essays, because they cannot find the books, goes up. This appears to me to be inefficiency rather than efficiency.'

Russell's comments suggest a rather more complex relationship between economy, efficiency and effectiveness than many contemporary administrative reformers allow for. In this instance, demanding greater outputs from the same inputs may well be more economical, in the short term at least, but efficiency and effectiveness appear to be reduced. As this example indicates, it is not useful to assume that economy, efficiency and effectiveness all work in a unitary direction or follow on from each other. Each is non-reducible, having its own particular rationale within any given organizational context.

So what might those particular rationales be in the context of public sector management? According to Richard Chapman (1982: 60–61) discussion of economy, efficiency and effectiveness in this context needs to start with an appreciation of the differences between *goals* and *objectives*. The former refers to a higher level of activity, which is often general in nature and the responsibility of the most senior management levels within an organization – for example, the elimination of substandard public housing or the provision of a self-assessment taxation system. *Objectives* refers to more specific and measurable activities, the responsibility of lower levels in the management hierarchy – for example, the processing of clearance schemes or of self-assessment submissions. *Effectiveness* may be reserved for the achievement of specific, measurable, desired ends (i.e. objectives). *Efficiency* may be reserved for the achievement of the ends set by the higher level of management – goals: 'some of which may involve numerical targets and may therefore include quantifiable elements; however, because it will include human factors and take into account the unintended consequences of management activity, it will be mainly concerned with unquantifiable elements' (Chapman, 1982: 61). For example, the achievement of management objectives might be at the cost of unacceptable working conditions, or in a manner inconsistent with other – perhaps procedural – standards expected of those working within a certain context. Consequently, when the terms are used in this way, it becomes apparent that it is more than possible for effective management to be inefficient or for effective management that is efficient in one context or at one time to be inefficient in another context or another time. *Economy* can then be introduced to refer to the cost elements and the relationship of inputs to outputs.

By arguing that economy, efficiency and effectiveness are basically synonymous, advocates of contemporary administrative reform seem unable or unwilling to acknowledge the very different rationale that each of these terms can possess and the necessarily contingent or haphazard relationships between them in any given organizational context. What's worse, in not recognizing that efficiency, economy and effectiveness are plural and frequently conflicting values, reformers may unconsciously encourage public sector managers to assume that there are no real costs associated with the single-minded pursuit of any one of these because it will not be at the expense of any of the others. This constitutes a serious abnegation of what Weber referred to as the bureaucrats' 'ethos of responsibility' – the trained capacity to take account of the potential consequences of attempting to realize essentially contestable values that frequently come into conflict with other values.

Of course, undermining the bureaucratic ethos is an avowed intention of contemporary reformers, as we saw in the last chapter, but their understanding of 'bureaucracy', like their conception of 'efficiency', leaves a lot to be desired (Osborne and Gaebler, 1992; Peters, 1987). Rather than referring to a form of organization exhibiting many if not most of the characteristics of Max Weber's (1978, II: 978ff.) classic 'bureau', contemporary reformers use 'bureaucracy' as a composite term for the defects of large organizations. In their minds it is a synonym for waste, inertia, excessive red tape and other dysfunctions. Bureaucracy then is something to be against. Its replacement by more efficient, businesslike methods can only be to everyone's advantage.

Because bureaucracy is so negatively coded and yet so under-described it is impossible to see what positive role any actually existing bureaucracies might be performing in any specific context. Examples of 'bureaucratic' defects – in this populist sense – in public sector organizations are not difficult to find and yet often the reasons for their development can be traced to qualitative features of government that many people take for granted, such as the desire to ensure fairness, justice and equity in the treatment of cases (Rhodes, 1994). As Chapman (1991: 16–17) has argued, these factors are not always as necessary in the conduct of business, though this shouldn't be taken to mean that they are always absent, but they are quite crucial in modern government, especially for democratic governments. He continues: 'if bureaucracy (in the popular sense) is to be reduced and a business style of management is to be adopted it should be recognized that the cost may well be less equality and rougher justice'. Such a shift may well be an intentional reflection of altered national priorities and the installation of a novel governmental perception of national economic management based upon the ceaseless pursuit of economic efficiency suggests that this is indeed the case. However, such a shift should not go unexamined or be allowed to be represented as basically uncontroversial. Certainly, it raises some important questions about the nature of bureaucracy in a public administration context and its relationship to efficiency, effectiveness and economy.

When attention is focused on public sector management rather than management in another context, a distinctively bureaucratic type of organization, with accountability both hierarchically and to elected representatives, might well be the most appropriate and efficient vehicle for the achievement of overall management purposes and goals, bearing in mind their qualitative as well as quantitative dimensions. Regarding bureaucracy as simply an 'inefficient' form of organization in this context might well be regarded as somewhat short-sighted. It certainly seems to indicate both a superficial understanding of 'efficiency' and 'bureaucracy' and an underdeveloped appreciation of public administration. Bureaucracy may be more expensive than other forms of government (though Weber had a few choice words to say about this: 1978, II: 983–4) but that's not too surprising when democracy is not necessarily the cheapest form of government.

If public sector managers were not trying to manage their services in a democracy or if – as contemporary administrative reformers so often do – we conveniently ignore the norms and requirements of democratic politics and concentrate on the straightforward task of 'managing' (whatever that might mean), the question of how to run education, transport and welfare in ways that satisfied their 'customers' might (and that's a very big 'might') be relatively simple – in the short term. But, in the long term, as Francis Plowden (1994: 306) argues, attention has to be paid to the claims of democratic politics:

> because with all its imperfections it is the best process we know for allocating scarce resources, adjudicating between competing claims on resources . . . allowing for appeals by those aggrieved at the outcomes and ensuring that the outcomes are generally seen as legitimate even if not always popular.

This suggests that there are and should continue to be distinct limits to the ambitions of contemporary administrative reformers to break through bureaucracy (Barzelay, 1992) and to keep politics out of the management of public services.

The bureaucratic ethos and democratic politics

As exemplified by the *Next Steps* initiative in Britain, the 'Re-Inventing Government' exercise in the USA and any number of similar developments in locations as diverse as Australia, Canada and New Zealand, one of the central objectives of contemporary programmes of administrative reform has been 'depoliticization': separating out the spheres of influence and the tasks of politicians and managers (Doig, 1995; Moe, 1994; Minson, 1997; Peters, 1993; Peters and Savoie, 1995).

That bureaucrats and politicians had got their respective roles a little too blurred, with negative effects for 'efficiency', 'customers' being taken for granted by reform enthusiasts from across the political spectrum (O'Toole and Chapman, 1994; Rhodes, 1994). Thus a clear separation of role, status and responsibility between politician and bureaucrat was absolutely necessary in order to ensure more economical and 'better' government. This meant, at central government level, excluding elected representatives from the day-to-day management of public services. In Britain, for example, it was argued that if managers in central government were to have the 'freedom to manage' (in itself a good thing because it would lead to greater economic efficiency and more customer satisfaction), then the 'myth' of individual ministerial responsibility – with its 'fiction' that the minister could in practice be 'truly' responsible for everything that happened in her or his department – must be abandoned. The Next Steps initiative attempted to make this assumption practicable through instituting an organizational distinction between 'policy' and 'operations', with politicians responsible for the former and managers for the latter. Freed from the constraints of political (and hence 'bureaucratic') overlay on their activities civil servants could then concentrate on the proper tasks of management: improving efficiency – getting more for less – and serving customers.

Somehow, this reorganization was also meant to result in greater accountability. The accountability in question though was rather different from its traditional 'political' variant. Accountability was now conceptualized as the provision of responsive and cost-effective services to customers. As Ronald Moe (1994: 114) argued in his discussion of the 'Re-Inventing Government' exercise in the USA:

> While political accountability may once have been properly the highest value for government executives, this is no longer true. The highest value in the entrepreneurial paradigm, to all accounts, is customer satisfaction ('We will . . . measure our success by customer satisfaction') . . . This precedence of economically based values over legally based values is evident throughout the report's recommendations.

Many of the 'virtues' of professional public service simply do not register in the dominant governmental language of economic efficiency. This is equally true, and with similarly deleterious consequences, when the language of 'customer satisfaction' is deployed.

Close to the 'customer'

When thinking about the provision and administration of public services in a democracy it is worth remembering that such services are provided with the authority and resources of the state. They are provided first and foremost for 'citizens'. It is citizens, or their elected representatives, who originally decide that some needs will be met by state provision (whether directly or through the use of private contractors). Naturally, citizens, whose tax revenues finance these services, have a keen interest in various features of these services, including economy, efficiency and effectiveness. They express these views, and views about the relative quantity of resources that should go into each service, in no matter how ramified a sense, through the ballot-box and thus through their elected representatives. Even when they are not themselves direct 'customers' of some services, they are likely to have and express views about those services in some way, shape or form. Their elected representatives are thus bound to be involved on their behalf (Plowden, 1994).

Indeed, they should be involved. A key feature of representative democracy, as Weber (1994b: 230–1) argued long ago, is its ability to accommodate and modify potentially disruptive forces of raw public opinion by interposing a buffer between citizens and policy-making. It does this in two ways. The first is institutional: the views of citizens are transmitted, through electoral machinery and legislatures, to ministers and bureaucrats. The second is chronological: this process takes time, thus allowing opportunities for reflection on and possible modification of initial points of view.

The focus on 'customer satisfaction' may be an important value for those keen to promote entrepreneurial forms of organizational governance but in the context of public sector management it seems constitutionally surprising, hierarchically anomalous and, furthermore, potentially dangerous.[1]

It is constitutionally surprising because the operative functions of government can be fairly distinguished from private manufacturing and service functions in that they are regulatory and based on legal powers over the citizen. Hence, in Britain, they are usually subject to the detailed political accountability of ministers to Parliament – even though they are in large part routine and uncontroversial – at least until something goes wrong. The focus on 'customer satisfaction' as a primary value of public sector management therefore downplays the political context within which management processes take place. The demand for economic efficiency, for customer orientation and for giving greater discretion to managers cannot be the main values governing organizational conduct in the public sector. The constitutional demands of the bureaucratic role, including *inter alia* loyalty to those who are politically responsible, responsiveness to parliamentary opinion and sensitivity to the complexity of the 'public interest', indicates that public sector management is bound to remain a highly political activity. Managers will still need the crucial skill of knowing how to operate in this context (very different from the private sector). They will also need to respect democratic political processes and their outcomes, no matter how individually uncongenial.

Likewise, the focus on customer satisfaction is hierarchically anomalous because the political and legal context within which public sector managers have to operate demands a coherent institutional framework approximating to classic models of bureaucracy. A distinctly bureaucratic type of organization, with accountability both hierarchically and to elected representatives, puts certain limits on the operational discretion available to individual managers. It means that public sector managers cannot and should not enjoy the freedom available to their private sector counterparts to expand investment and levels of service provision in response to customer demand, let alone if such investment is speculative and there is an element of risk involved (Doig, 1995; Jordan, 1994a).

Finally, the focus on customer satisfaction may be dangerous in the sense in which officials in the famous Crichel Down case were criticized (Chapman, 1991; Chester, 1954). In that case Sir Andrew Clark's inquiry, in 1954, found that the Lands Service and the Land Commission had become 'infatuated with the idea of creating a new model farm'. Mr Melford Stevenson, one of the lawyers appearing at the inquiry, asserted that, while officials concerned in the case had no corrupt motive, 'they derive(d) great satisfaction from the exercise of personal power' and that 'there is a time when the public administrator can become, if not drunk, unfit to be in charge of his personal power' (quoted in Chapman, 1991: 15). The danger, it seems, may be from the sorts of enthusiasms developed by officials for particular policies, the sort of enthusiasms currently encouraged without much attention being paid to ensuring the introduction of appropriate safeguards to protect the interests of citizens in a liberal democracy.

In keeping with their prioritization of economically based values over and above constitutionally and legally based values, reform enthusiasts regard questions of political accountability as neither particularly interesting nor important (Plowden, 1994: 310). In answer to complaints about the diminishing political accountability of many public services in Britain, William Waldegrave (1993: 3) famously argued that opinion surveys conducted amongst sections of the public indicated that only 28 per cent of those canvassed mentioned political accountability as one of their criteria for assessing public services, compared to 54 per cent mentioning 'cost and quality of service'.

This assumption is, of course, totally in tune with a view of the purpose of government as the economically efficient provision of services to customers. However, it is completely at variance with established constitutional values – including, inter alia, the doctine of individual ministerial responsibility to Parliament. The fact is, still, that government is not simply about delivering services to 'customers'. Strange as it may seem, it is about governing. And governing in a liberal, representative democracy requires a precise and coherent framework of political accountability. Citizens might not set much store by such accountability in the abstract, but as a means to other ends – as a connecting device, for example, ensuring them some, suitably ramified, influence over the totality of public services – they can certainly sense its absence. So long as competing and mutually incompatible accountabilities – between the requirements of traditional forms of political accountability and the newer forms of 'customer' responsiveness – continue to be fostered, confusion concerning the location of authority and responsibility in government is likely to persist.

Because operative functions of government departments and agencies are first and foremost regulatory and based on legal powers over the citizen, accountability in government should be primarily to citizens and not to customers. How is that accountability to be guaranteed if substantive decisions in government are to be taken by managers at their level, for which ministers can disclaim responsibility? If ministers do accept the restrictions on their powers which new forms of contractorization imply, then what channels are to be available for the redress of grievances by individual citizens?

Some have suggested that serious thought will have to be given to a system of judicial review linked to some definitions of citizens' rights (Plowden, 1994). However, frequent resort to judicial review is likely to prove politically controversial (why should judges make administrative choices?), as well as costly and time-consuming (Chapman, 1988a: 298; Freedland, 1994: 104). In the world of practical rather than ideal administration, government business has to carry on and there is – as we are continually told – a limit to the resources that can be deployed, including those allocated to safeguards and appeals procedures.

Whatever its defects, which are clear and manifold, the traditional system of parliamentary accountability based upon hierarchical systems of unified authority at least provides some of the benefits which more fragmented modes of accountability manifestly do not provide (Scott, 1996). Not only this, such a system may also turn out to be less expensive than the pluralistic modes of delegated management responsibility that are meant to supersede it. The transaction costs of devolved and fragmented management are apt to be very high, and it often turns out to be necessary to reintroduce new mechanisms of standardization and control – witness the contemporary 'audit' explosion – which are more elaborate and less 'economically efficient' than the centralized bureaucracies that they were intended to eliminate (Freedland, 1994; Pollitt, 1995; Power, 1997; Doig and Wilson, 1998).

Concluding comments

There may well be a compelling case for making public bureaux operate more economically. It may also be that some of the approaches favoured by contemporary administrative reformers are not without merit in achieving this objective. For example, many government controls and inspections at all levels are now subject to constant review and some have been scaled down or stopped altogether. While the potential disadvantages of such 'controlled de-control' may include an increase in arbitrary judgements and more mistakes within the bureaucracy, this is not a foregone conclusion and commentators have indicated that a reduction in the frequency with which senior officials check the work of junior officials may lead to more rather than less accuracy in the work of juniors (Chapman, 1982: 66; Cooper, 1995; Foster and Hoggett, 1999).

Similarly, arguing that there are distinct limits to the efficacy of deploying 'entrepreneurial' norms and techniques of conduct within public bureaux does not amount to saying that such forms of governance are uniformly a bad thing. If nothing else, entrepreneurial strategies for reducing the cost and scale of central government activity have forced citizens to consider fundamental questions about the scope and management of public services in which they may have been able to avoid taking an interest in the past. Making citizens aware of the economic dimensions of public service activities can hardly be considered a bad thing, though, equally, informing citizens that economic questions are the only ones that need to be asked concerning the management of public services certainly can be.

It is this latter point that is really the issue. The central discourse of many contemporary programmes of administrative reform – the 'Re-Inventing Government' exercise in the USA and the Next Steps initiative in the UK, for example – is a financial and commercial one rather than a political or constitutional one. It's not so much that this discourse deliberately ignores the complex juridico-political context within which the management of public services takes place; rather it redefines that context in its own terms. It does so, as I argued in the previous chapter, by progressively expanding the domain of economic theory by a series of redefinitions of its objects. So when these programmes claim, as they so often do, to bring about an increase in accountability for public service provision, the accountability in question turns out to be strongly, if not exclusively, led by considerations of financial efficiency, and by cost-related numerical performance targets. Political accountability is thus transmuted into a liability to prove that there has been 'efficient' (i.e. 'economic') financial management and adherence to targets and budgets, and little more. In the case of the Next Steps initiative in the UK, this spell of financial accountability has enabled the constitutional convention of individual ministerial responsibility to Parliament literally to be 'spirited off the stage' (Freedland, 1996: 28).

This form of 'discursive reimagination' serves to incapacitate an institution's ability to pursue its ongoing projects by effectively redefining its identity and hence what the nature of its projects actually are. After all, if a particular discourse is jettisoned or marginalized in favour of another, the world that discourse brings into being will no longer be available. As reform enthusiasts and legislators become ever more ambitious in their project of reinventing and modernizing public management it is worth remembering that if the principles of 'entrepreneurial governance' are allowed to set the terms by which the public bureau is understood and judged, then we should expect the job the bureau has performed and continues to perform for us to gradually disappear.

Note

1. Even the first Next Steps Project Manager, the otherwise fulsomely 'entrepreneurial' Sir Peter Kemp, had certain reservations about the applicability of the term 'customer' to the public sector management context. He told the Public Accounts Committee of the House of Commons in 1989: 'The customer can be the immediate member of the public you are dealing with, the customer can be seen as being the Minister who is in charge of the organization, the customer can be seen as Parliament representing the public as a whole. The word "customer" is a very dangerous and difficult word to use in the context of public service' (quoted in Chapman, 1997: 150).

6

Separate and Distinct Personae: Bureaucrats and Politicians

We are placed in various orders of life, each of which is subject to different laws.

Max Weber

The drive should be to find people who can show added value, not ask clever questions.

Grade 2 civil servant quoted in the Oughton Report (1993)

Contemporary discourses of administrative reform in the public sector have a lot to say about the respective role and duties of politicians and bureaucrats in government. Underpinning many of the contemporary criticisms of public administration they articulate is an assumption that these two crucial participants in the practice of government had got their roles a little too blurred, with negative consequences for, amongst many other things, the achievement of policy objectives, efficient and effective management and democratic accountability. Some critics have framed the problem as one of political 'control' and have sought measures through which elected representatives might tame the power of 'officials' and enhance their own position within government. Others have focused attention on the need to exclude elected representatives from the day-to-day management of public services, thus enabling public sector managers to get on with their 'core' business of delivering services to customers with maximum efficiency. Interestingly, these two approaches have often fed off of one another. Proponents of increased political control have frequently advocated managerialist measures to achieve their desired ends, while managerialist critics have themselves cited control axioms – concerning, for example, the budget-maximizing propensities of officials – in the course of demanding that public bureaux should be structured more like private enterprises (Campbell, 1993: 123).

The outcome of these and other lines of criticism has been the reappearance – suitably formulated in the language of the moment – of an old dichotomy between politicians as policy creators and officials as administrators or, more fashionably, managers, of their policies (Moe, 1994; O'Toole and Chapman, 1994; Plowden, 1994; Pollitt, 1995). In practical terms this separation asserts that in democratic societies policy-making is the province of duly elected governments. If policy-making were conducted by unelected career officials we would have rule by a non-responsible bureaucracy. As this would obviously be a bad thing, officials should be kept in their place and not allowed to interfere in policy-making.

On the other hand, public sector management is or should be the expert implementation of policy and delivery of government-sanctioned services in an economic, efficient and effective manner. Politicians should keep out of this because they are not trained or experienced managers. They will make a mess of things if they unduly constrain public sector managers in the conduct of their business by, for example, 'politicizing' their basically 'technical' work. There is a core of wisdom in this approach to the relationship between politicians and officials, not least in the recognition that they possess distinct and non-reducible personae in the domain of democratic government. However, while it is undeniable that there is a proper role for politicians and another for officials in democratic systems of government, these roles are not satisfactorily distinguished by a dichotomy between 'policy' and 'management'. In searching for a better understanding of these two personae we might begin by attempting to understand how the above dichotomy arose and why it has proven so problematic.

Machine reasoning

The idea that political and bureaucratic roles in modern democratic government can and should be instrumentally differentiated in terms of a dichotomy between policy and administration is generally traced to Woodrow Wilson's (1887) influential article, 'The study of administration'.

In this piece Wilson noted the failure of the classic doctrine of the 'separation of powers' to protect American public life from the effects of corruption in the years after the civil war and argued for a separation of politics from administration within the executive arm of government. The political part of the executive was to use its discretion within the law to develop policy, which Wilson saw primarily as rules which it was then up to the career bureaucrat to execute as far as possible without discretion. Policy was to be the realm of politicians, who were to be expected to have their 'political' and other interests. The administration and execution of policy were to be left to a career civil service which as far as possible should be immune to corruption and the influence of party political influence. If politicians within the executive were limited to the role of rule-making and policy development, Wilson believed, it would be possible to dissociate administration from the dysfunctional consequences of the 'spoils system' (See Rohr, 1986: Chapter 5).

It is important not to underestimate the historical embeddedness of Wilson's arguments when seeking to problematize his division between 'policy' and 'administration'. The rationale for this dichotomy was, of course, an extremely important one: the desire to insulate public administration from political favouritism or corruption and thereby ensure that laws or public policies were applied impartially and effectively by properly qualified and trained persons who had no 'personal' – in Weber's sense – stake in their outcome.

The problem arises with the language deployed to conceptualize the relationship between politicians and bureaucrats. Perhaps the most popular analogy in the earliest days of administrative study was that between the governmental process and a machine (Parker, 1993: 69; Self, 1997: 9). The responsible politician was conceived of as the operator of the machine. Officials were compared (consciously or unconsciously) to the cogs and other mechanisms. The operator alone makes judgements, conceives purposes, makes decisions. The machine is simply a vehicle for implementing the operator's will. It has no discretion. It can do nothing except by the direction of the operator. Such machine reasoning was a central element of the so-called 'scientific management' school which emerged gradually as the dominant paradigm of efficient administration in the early twentieth century. Because public administration in this period, as Wilson noted, was still infused with pre-bureaucratic forms of patronage and personally motivated favour, scientific management offered the prospect of more rational and systematic procedures and forms of conduct that would help eliminate these features. Its achievements in delivering on this promise should not be underestimated (Pollitt, 1990).

However, that said, prescriptions for administrative practice based upon the machine analogy, with its absolute oppositions between 'conception' and 'execution', 'policy' and 'operations', have often proven ill-suited to the practicalities of the political environments within which they must operate. As I argued in Chapter 4, p. 90, historical evidence from throughout the life of the Westminster conventions indicates that officials are actively involved in formulating as well as implementing policy. Nor is there anything controversial or suspect about this. The rationale for the conventions (namely to secure broad answerability to Parliament for policy/administration) never required that ministers should be policy-makers and officials merely the administrators, but only that the minister should have the final word and be publicly accountable. As Sir Edward Bridges (1971) indicated in his famous Rede Lecture 'Portrait of a profession: the Civil Service tradition', it has been a 'cardinal feature of British administration that no attempt be made to formulate a new policy in any matter without the fullest consultation with those who have practical experience in that field, and with those who will be called upon to carry it out'.

There appear to be two very good reasons for this practice. First, as Bridges pointed out, 'the constitutional responsibility of Ministers to Parliament covers every action of the Department, whether done with their specific authority or by delegation, expressed or implied. Ministers cannot therefore escape responsibility for administrative matters.' What may appear to be a mere matter of administration – such as the provision of an unsuitable computer system for a passport agency – can quickly and easily become politically and electorally important when things go wrong. This being the case it is the duty of civil servants to make sure that ministers receive 'the fullest benefit of the storehouse of departmental experience; and to let the waves of the practical philosophy wash against the ideas put forward by . . . ministerial masters'. Officials play a crucial role in policy-making by contributing 'practical knowledge such as no Minister could be expected to possess'. Ministers are, of course, ultimately free to ignore such advice but at their own risk, as a number of well-publicized 'policy disasters' in recent years has testified (Dunleavy, 1995).

There is a second, and related, way in which the operative functions of government and those of creation or adaptation prove difficult to separate in this context. Adaptation and creation of new policy often arise through the way old policy has worked out – or has failed to work out – and the people responsible for making it work are involved, in all sorts of ways, in reporting difficulties, making suggestions, consulting and advising. The involvement of officials – at all levels – in the formulation of new purposes, in so far as experience with administering a policy suggests or leads to ways of improving or modifying it, demonstrates the limits of the machine analogy and its dichotomy between 'policy' and 'administration'.[1]

What we find under the 'Westminster conventions', then, is a division of administrative labour, widely diffused amongst both ministers and officials and not based on a distinction between two different levels or even kinds of decision, nor on a distinction between the processes of decision and action, but on what Parker (1993: 71) describes as 'a gradual narrowing down from broader statements of purpose to increasingly specific decisions and actions'. In this complex hierarchy of decisions and action there is no obvious dividing line between policy decisions, on the one hand, and operational decisions, on the other, nor between decision-making and decision-applying. The application of decisions itself involves further decision-making.

This is not to deny that key distinctions between the role and duty of ministers and that of officials cannot be drawn but rather to point out that these do not obviously fit on to some neat division between 'policy' and 'administration'. For example, the administrative 'values' of efficiency, effectiveness and economy and so forth should not be inconsistent with, or defeat, the purposes expressed by more authoritative persons on the same subject. In this sense, it is important to distinguish between decisions of broader generality and 'subordinate' decisions giving effect to the broader ones. Once again, though, this relationship of subordinate to superior decisions occurs at many levels, not only at two (Parker, 1993: 71).

Similarly, there is a distinction between the role of officials and that of ministers and other elected representatives in the sense that the decisions and actions of the former are always subject to reversal or approval by the latter (Rohr, 1979). However, this doesn't mean that the decisions of ministers are dramatically different *in kind* from those of officials. Nor does this significant difference in 'role' mean that the responsibility and authority of the minister correspond solely with a concern with the very highest level of the hierarchy of decisions, that which approximates to something called 'policy'. The constitutional and organizational position of ministers allows them to reverse or review any decision at any level or of any degree of generality, so that there can be no grounds for distinguishing a category of decision appropriate only to ministers as 'policy' (Chipperfield, 1994; Parker, 1993). As Chipperfield (1994: 11) has pointed out, while ministers are interested in that which is politically important, there is, unfortunately, 'no notable convergence between the politically important and policy, on the one hand, and the politically unimportant and administration, on the other'. To sum up, then, we can say that under the political framework established by the so-called 'Westminster conventions', ministers have a constitutional right and duty to make decisions or pursue actions within the domain of their department or portfolio at every level of generality or particularity.

As a matter of convenience, ministers can delegate the power of decision and action, at any level permitted by law, to public servants. Ministers may also obtain the advice of these officials in arriving at decisions, whether or not they are decisions upon particular actions or about a new line of activity. Not only this; public servants themselves may initiate suggestions for new lines of decision and action. This means that no level of subject-matter is forbidden, as such, to either ministers or officials. At every level, the minister has the constitutional right and duty to know of impending decisions and actions and to have the last word in determining them. This follows from the constitutional position of officials as mere extensions of the minister's own 'personality' because ministers are constitutionally responsible to Parliament for all their acts as holders of an office (including the acts of their departments). Overall, because no real dividing line can be established between policy and administrative decisions or acts, such a dichotomy provides no basis for distinguishing the roles of ministers and officials (see Parker, 1993, esp. Chapters 6 and 10).

'Orderings of life' and types of responsibility

If the mechanistic division between policy and administration contains 'a core of important principle' concerning the relationship between politicians and officials it nonetheless signally fails to offer 'a satisfactory description of reality nor a guide to action' (Parker, 1993: 68). Where, then, are we to look for a more realistic statement of the respective roles of these key participants in the process of government which might also serve as a guide to action? One useful starting point is provided by the work of Max Weber. Given the frequency with which Weber's work is located by his critics at the 'mechanistic' pole of organizational studies, this may seem somewhat surprising. After all, doesn't Weber's focus on the formal specification of organizational structure, rather than on the ways in which 'bureaucrats' (and 'politicians') *really* behave, simply replicate, rather than challenge, the policy/administration dichotomy?

This might be the case if we were talking about the Weber of general theories of modernity, rationality and domination. But instead, we are talking of the Weber 'reconstructed' by Wilhelm Hennis (1988), whose 'central theme' is the formation of 'personalities' fitted to existence in definite life orders. Of crucial import here is the match between the properties of personae and the properties of specific cultural settings. Investigation of a persona in a specific 'life order' entails attending to the practical techniques for living a given 'conduct of life'. This requirement foregrounds 'description'. As Weber (quoted in Hennis, 1988: 102–4) indicates, given their 'regional' character, personae and their definite but limited settings must not be left underdescribed. If they are, we risk failing to see that each has its own history and distribution, possesses its own ethos and is directed towards its own ends. Conversely, it is only through underdescription, through regarding 'the stream of events from the heights of reflective thought', that superficial dichotomies, such as that between politicians as policy creators and officials as implementers of their policies, are enabled to flourish.

There are no theoretical fireworks in evidence here. As Hennis (1988: 24) argues: 'It is not so much the complexity, but rather the *simplicity* of Weber's problematic – confronting us in our modernity, poised upon our intellectual heights – that is an obstacle to its comprehension.' Weber (1978, 1989, 1994b) approaches the task of investigating the formation of the personae of the 'Bureaucrat' (in *Economy & Society* Vol.II) and the 'Politician' (in 'The profession and vocation of politic') in their definite 'orderings of life' in just such a descriptive mode. As Hennis (1988: 71–2) points out, Weber begins each of these studies by outlining the 'external given conditions' of these life orders in the 'material sense of the term' before going on to describe the demands they make on individuals in terms of 'inner personality'.[2]

For example, Weber (1978: Chapter XI) describes how the bureau functions as an administrative centre that detaches decision-making as far as possible from personal loyalties. Chief amongst the organizational features that produce this effect are a formal division of jurisdictional areas; an office hierarchy, a system of 'files' (i.e. information inscription and processing); expert personnel; strict procedural management of office routines; tenure and pensions. These features of the bureau comprise the social and

what Weber describes as 'spiritual' conditions of a distinctive and independent organization of the person. Among the most important of these are,
first, that access to office is dependent upon lengthy training 'in a field of
specialization', usually certified by public examination; and secondly, that
the office itself constitutes a vocation, a focus of ethical commitment and
duty autonomous of and superior to the holder's extra-official ties to kin,
class, community or conscience. In Weber's account, these conditions mark
out the bureau as a distinctive life order, and they provide the bureaucrat
with a distinctive ethical bearing and status conduct.

The ethical attributes of the good bureaucrat can therefore be seen as a
positive moral achievement requiring mastery of a difficult ethical milieu
and practice. They are the product of definite ethical techniques and routines – 'declaring' one's personal interest, developing professional relations
with one's colleagues, subordinating one's ego to procedural decision-
making – through which individuals develop the disposition and ability to
conduct themselves according to the ethos of bureaucratic office (to
become officials with 'personality', in Weber's terms). 'Without this
supremely ethical discipline and self-denial', Weber (1994b: 331) states,
'the whole apparatus would disintegrate'.

By contrast, the honour of 'the political leader, that is, the leading states-
man' consists, for Weber (1994b: 331; original emphasis), 'precisely in
taking exclusive, *personal* responsibility for what he does, responsibility
which he cannot and may not refuse or unload onto others. Precisely those
who are officials by nature and who, in this regard, are of high moral
stature, are bad and, particularly in the political meaning of the word, irre-
sponsible politicians, and thus of low moral stature . . .'

While it might appear at first sight that Weber is reintroducing a somewhat mechanistic contrast between the work of politicians and that of
officials in terms of a policy/administration split, nothing could be further
from the truth. Commenting upon the popular belief that differences
between the personae of politicians and bureaucrats approximated to such
a distinction, Weber (1994a: 160; original emphasis) argued that officials,
every bit as much as politicians or indeed, entrepreneurs

> are expected to make independent decisions and show organizational ability and
> initiative, not only in countless individual cases but also on larger issues. It is
> typical of littérateurs and of a country lacking any insight into the conduct of its
> own affairs or into the achievements of its officials, even to *imagine* that the
> work of an official amounts to no more than a subaltern performance of routine
> duties, while the leader alone is expected to carry out the 'interesting' tasks
> which make special intellectual demands. This is not so. The difference lies,
> rather, in the kind of *responsibility* borne by each of them, and this is largely
> what determines the demands made on their particular abilities.[3]

Weber is referring to 'responsibility' in a very particular sense. The term as
he uses it does not pertain to a simple 'division of organizational labour',
in which officials are allocated the responsibility for administration, and

politicians the responsibility for policy. Rather 'responsibility' refers to a division of ethical labour in which official and politician are subject to specific and quite different imperatives and points of honour and develop quite different personal capacities and comportments as a result of being placed in different life orders. This plurality of obligation and comportment also occurs *within* as well as between institutional milieux – such as that characterizing modern government – where life orders intersect (Minson, 1997). Weber gives us a broad idea of the respective kinds of responsibility governing the conduct of 'offical' and 'politician' when he writes:

> An official who receives an order which, in his view, is wrong can – and should – raise objections. If his superior then insists on the instruction it is not merely the duty of the official it is also a point of *honour* for him to carry out that instruction as if it corresponded to his own innermost conviction, thereby demonstrating that his sense of duty to his office overrides his individual wilfulness . . . This is what is demanded by the spirit of *office*. A political *leader* who behaved like this would deserve our *contempt*. He will often be obliged to make compromises, which means sacrificing something of less importance to something of greater importance . . . The official should stand 'above the parties', which in truth means that he must remain outside the struggle for power of his own. The *struggle* for personal power and the acceptance of *full personal responsibility for one's cause (Sache)* which is the consequence of such power – this is the very element in which the politician and the entrepreneur live and breathe. (1994a: 160–1; original emphasis)

In addressing the different kinds of responsibility that politicians and bureaucrats have for their actions, Weber is insisting on the irreducibility of different orders of life and on the consequent necessity of applying different ethical protocols to them. Forged in the party system and tempered by the organized adversarialism of the Parliament, the politician belongs to an order of life quite unlike that of the bureaucrat. The party leader possesses the political abilities and ethical demeanour required by the unremitting struggle to win and regain power. As Weber (1994a, 1994b) makes clear, it is this, and not the trained expertise and impersonal dedication of the official, that equips the politician to pursue the worldly interests of the state in the face of a hostile and unpredictable economic and political environment.

Seen in this light, modern systems of government appear as irrevocably hybrid milieux housing quite different and distinct personae. Officials *are* or should be very different animals from politicians, not because they 'administer' and elected politicians 'make policy', but because both are subject to quite distinct ethical demands as a result of their positioning within different life orders. As Weber (1994b; see also Chapter 4 of this volume) indicated, 'responsible government' requires that neither ethic be rejected, that we learn to live with both and with the inevitable tensions that exist between them.

Challenges to the 'ethos of office'

As I indicated in the introduction to this chapter, recent and ongoing changes in the machinery of government, whether framed by the problematic of 'political control' or that of 'managerialism' (or more often than not, by a combination of both), have given a new lease of life to the dichotomy between politicians as policy-makers and officials as policy implementers. Given that a wealth of literature, going back over three quarters of a century and drawn from both sides of the Atlantic, has effectively discredited this hygienic dichotomy as a useful means of organizing the business of government, what are the consequences of its re-emergence for the conduct of both officials and politicians, for their relationship with one another, and for the concrete workings of responsible government?

The problematic of control

The discretion and latitude for legitimate advocacy exercised by unelected officals has been a recurring source of anxiety for politicians and commentators on all parts of the political spectrum throughout the last century. In Britain, for example, Labour thinkers in the 1930s were much concerned with the possibility that a future Labour government would be effectively sabotaged by the Civil Service, whose senior echelons were populated by individuals from a class background that could be expected to have imbued them with an innate hostility to the policies of a socialist administration. Although it appears that ministers in the 1945–51 Labour administration were entirely satisfied with the quality of advice they received from their officials, and the loyalty of those officials to them, it did not stop the next generation of Labour thinkers and politicians expressing almost identical concerns (Campbell and Wilson, 1995: 45).

At the opposite end of the political spectrum, Conservative thinkers and politicians of New Right persuasions, have viewed bureaucrats with as much antipathy as their Left Labour counterparts and for equally political reasons. The New Right regarded the Civil Service as having 'captured' a role for itself in the machinery of government that was inappropriate for it to aspire to, let alone to play. The idea of the Civil Service as something akin to as a 'gyroscope of state' (Hennessy, 1995: 127) fitted, through its slow accretion of practical experience in the business of government, to advise governments on the potential problems and pitfalls of their own political enthusiasms, was anathema to a party driven by a desire to make a radical and permanent political impact on the country. Sir John Hoskyns, one-time head of Margaret Thatcher's Downing Street Policy Unit, argued that key aspects of the ethos of 'office' such as detachment and engaged scepticism towards policy proposals, were completely antithetical to the 'revolutionary' zeal and total commitment demanded by the Thatcher government (Campbell and Wilson, 1995: 51; Fry, 1995: Chapter 3; Ridley, 1996).

It was this determination to forcefully reassert the primacy of elected politicians, combined, of course, with a remarkably long tenure in office, which distinguished the Thatcher government from its immediate predecessors and enabled it to effect important changes in the ethos governing the conduct of officials. One crucial aspect of these changes was the attempt to make officials more personally responsive to the needs of the government. For Thatcher and her supporters, officials were from the beginning objects of suspicion. Armed with the simplistic views of the public choice approach to the study of politics and government, Thatcherites believed that bureaucrats were predominantly, if not exclusively, motivated by material self-interest (masquerading as an ethos of public service). For a party committed to shrinking the size and cost of government in the interests of the economic security of the state, bureaucrats motivated by an unerring quest for larger staffs and bigger budgets were, in effect, a political opposition *manqué* which would have to be brought to heel (Campbell, 1993: 120–2; Peters and Savoie, 1995).

This representation of permanent officials as illegitimate participants in the political process led to a number of attempts to constrict their 'official independence'. The Rayner Efficiency scrutinies, the introduction of MINIS (Management Information Systems for Managers) and then of the Financial Management Initiative were all aimed, as Thatcher herself was quick to admit, at changing the culture of the Civil Service. This was also the objective of the Prime Minister's interventions in high-level promotions in the service. Thatcher took a close interest in senior appointments in the Civil Service from the first as she believed that the quality of leadership affected the ethos of an entire department (Thatcher, 1993: 46). This gave rise to immediate accusations of 'politicization', as it was assumed that preference was being given to officials who shared her political outlook. While Thatcher always denied taking political allegiance into account when making promotion decisions – and there is no evidence to refute her claim – she did admit that 'drive and enthusiasm were what mattered' (1993: 46).

This admission that preference was indeed given to individuals who possessed certain capacities and predispositions, known popularly as 'can do' types, should alert us to another, less party political, facet of the term 'politicization'. This term can, for example, refer to the ability and willingness of officals to implement politicians' ideas enthusiastically (Ståhlberg, 1987; Chapman, 1988b). Put simply, politicization can refer to a civil service that reacts over-favourably to political signals without the officials personally and necessarily having a commitment to a specific political party. When this interpretation is used, allegations of politicization may be more easily substantiated.

Even before the end of Thatcher's first term, the former civil servant Ian (Lord) Bancroft, noted that the 'grovel count' amongst senior civil servants 'was much higher than normal'. There was, he argued, a 'subtle' and 'insidious' problem developing that could be described as politicization in our latter sense of the term. 'The dangers', he explained, 'are of the younger people, seeing that advice which ministers want to hear falls with a joyous note on their ears, and advice which they need to hear falls on their ears with a rather dismal note, will tend to . . . make their advice what ministers want to hear rather than what they need to know' (quoted in Hennessy, 1995: 130).

As Campbell and Wilson (1995: 60) argue, continuous political demands for a 'responsive' style amongst officials, one characterized by decisiveness and the ability to get results, appears to have led to a shift in the persona of the senior civil servant in terms of inner motivation. Their wide-ranging interviews with senior officials in the 1990s suggest that civil servants are redefining the nature of their role, self-consciously moving away from a style of conduct which laid great emphasis on the provision of full, frank and fearless policy advice to ministers, towards a more implementational style, characterized by providing ministers with what they say they want.[4]

As the comments of the Grade 2 civil servant noted in the Efficiency Unit's 1993 report on career management and succession planning indicate (see p. 114, the drive was most definitely towards finding 'people who can show added value, not ask clever questions'. Such an approach flies directly in the face of the idea of the civil servant's duty outlined by Lord Armstrong (and with distinct echoes of Weber). He described the provision of 'honest and impartial advice, without fear or favour . . . whether the advice accords with the minister's view or not' as a key facet of the ethos of bureaucratic office (quoted in Chipperfield, 1994: 3). While it is easy to see how this critical role could be viewed by politicians as a licence to obstruct, it was, until relatively recently, generally considered indispensable to the achievement of 'responsible' (rather than purely 'responsive') government because it was seen to balance and complement political will, making it more effective in the longer run.

The problem is, once again, that there is no 'objective' way of judging when the official response to ministerial initiative, or an official prompting of the minister, crosses over from a legitimate exercise of 'official independence' into an unacceptable frustration or manipulation of the government's purposes. Only governments themselves are empowered to make that judgement and many of them throughout the world appear to have decided that any form of official independence is unacceptable. Instead, they seem set on demanding that officials act as enthusiastic, committed champions of their policies. As Parker (1993: 173) has indicated:

> A superficial analogy with private business is visible in all these moves, along with the archaic assumption that 'policy' can be wholly dictated by ministers and then applied by . . . 'managers' with no further questions asked.

It is somewhat ironic that governments which have sought forcefully to depoliticize the activities of state bureaux by curtailing the policy responsibilities conceded to officials, have ended up by politicizing (in our quite specific sense of the term) the conduct of those very same officials in the process of making them only responsible for implementation. While such an outcome is ironic it is not very surprising. The will to depoliticize the bureau exhibited by these governments has been based on the unproven assumption that bureaucrats challenge the right of elected politicians to ultimate power. In their search for an increased level of control that they really did not need to exercise politicians have helped to weaken the legitimate and extremely important role of officials in government, by undermining crucial aspects of their bureaucratic 'ethos of office'.

The managerial imperative

At the same time as public-choice-style assaults on the discretion and latitude for independent advocacy exercised by officials within government became the order of the day in the USA, the UK and elsewhere, the political leaders of the very same countries were also seeking ways of making officials more 'responsive' in managerial terms. Using currently fashionable models of private sector management, these approaches have attempted to make government bureaux function more like business corporations operating in a competitive market environment (Corby, 1993; du Gay, 1994b, 1995; Pollitt, 1990). Of crucial importance here has been the assumption that as individual officials are made more personally aware of and responsible for achieving results in an economic (and hence, in the understandings of the moment), efficient manner they will be more committed to the projects they are involved in and will obtain greater value for money from using the resources at their disposal.

Underpinning the 'managerialist imperative' is a supposition that politicians and officials have separate and distinct personae corresponding to a division of labour between policy/strategy on the one hand and management/implementation on the other. Efficient and effective government will only come about, according to advocates of this approach, when both parties learn to 'stick to the knitting' and concentrate on their 'core competencies' rather than needlessly and unproductively blurring the boundaries between their respective roles. Thus, politicians should remove themselves from any involvement in day-to-day operations of government bureaux to concentrate their attention on the development of policy, whilst officials should give up on the 'clever questions', rejoice in their new-found freedom to manage and focus on 'adding value' through delivering the required results.

As any number of commentators have indicated, this managerialist imperative for sharper definition of costs and outputs, and of personal responsibility for achieving them, has brought massive changes of organization, of approach and of ethos within contemporary public administrations throughout the world (Boston et al., 1991; Campbell, 1993; Hood, 1995; Moe, 1994; Pollitt, 1995).

In Britain, the *locus classicus* of the managerialist imperative within the machinery of government is represented by the Next Steps programme of 'agencification'. The Next Steps intiative recommended that the vast bulk of government work, traditionally undertaken by hierarchically co-ordinated departments directly controlled by ministers, be hived off to semi-autonomous executive agencies. Each of these was to be headed by a chief executive linked to the main departments through a contract-like 'Framework Document' which would set out an agency's specific tasks and responsibilities and their overall performance targets. As the original Ibbs Report made clear, each agency was to enjoy considerable latitude in determining its organization and staffing arrangements:

> the main strategic control must lie with the Minister . . . [B]ut once the policy objectives and budgets are set, the management of the agency should then have as much independence as possible in deciding how those objectives are met . . . .The presumption must be that [management] must be left as free as possible to manage within that framework. To strengthen operational effectiveness there must be freedom to recruit, pay, grade, and structure in the most effective way as the framework becomes sufficiently robust and there is confidence in the capacity of management to handle the task. (Efficiency Unit, 1988: para. 21)

The development of these agencies and the 'managerialist imperative' they embody has had a profound influence on the ethos of office in several ways. At a structural level, there is no longer in any meaningful sense a unified state bureaucracy. A bewildering host of agencies now exist, each with its own conditions of service, grading, pay and recruitment procedures. While this 'pluralization of the centre' is assumed by its advocates to have unleashed sorely needed managerial dynamism in the public sector it is felt by critics to have erased traditional features of public administration such as the restraint of political and official patronage, a unified and consistent wage policy in public employment, service-wide career opportunities, uniform fair employment and promotion standards, innovative central leadership in staff training, counselling and techniques of management, and, most importantly for this discussion, the inculcation of a common ethic of public service. As Richard Chapman (1992: 3–4) has argued, staff working in these agencies tend now to think of themselves as belonging to a particular organization,

> not to a wider civil service. They work in units that, far from displaying a team spirit with a common ethos, compete with each other, issue contracts to each other, and in so doing charge what are considered business-like rates for their services. In some respects, the agencies are not completely independent entities, especially as they have been created by executive decisions and no legislation has been required, but conscious efforts are now made to stimulate feelings of enterprise and initiative in them and there can be no doubt that these have resulted in a fundamental change from an ethos that was previously admired and which contributed to the identity of the Civil Service.

As Chapman (1992, 1996a) has indicated, little serious attention has been given to the question of how traditional high standards of conduct are to be maintained or adapted – or how potential conflicts of interest, corruption or fraud are to be guarded against – in this emerging environment.

Unfortunately, despite the plethora of customer service charters, codes of conduct for civil servants and ministers, and new commissioners for administration and Parliament which have appeared in recent years there is still much to be concerned about in this regard. As Doig and Wilson (1998: 271) have observed, current research is indicating that ongoing structural and cultural change within the machinery of government has, for example, inculcated a commercial ethos in Next Steps agencies, with chief executives adopting more entrepreneurial attitudes to the conduct of public business and other senior public sector managers wanting more discretionary powers as well as independence from political considerations and constraints. These commercial attitudes have percolated downwards within public organizations and have also affected those organizations' perceptions of external accountability and the public interest (see, for example, Horton and Jones, 1996). Doig and Wilson conclude that it is

> hardly surprising that the impact and direction of change . . . [has] led to the development of a management culture within a public service context which is not only embraced by officials as the route to managerial independence and rewards commensurate with the size and complexity of the public services being provided but has also brought with it the development of other private practices and expectations . . . that have led to a conflict between private sector values and the enterprise culture on the one hand, and the roles, responsibilities and standards of the public sector on the other. (1998: 271–2)

One area in which such a conflict between the ethos of office and what we might term the 'entrepreneurial vocation' is evident is in relation to the appointment of senior managers from outside of the Civil Service to chief executive positions within Next Steps agencies. The move to open competition for senior appointments to the service was, of course, part and parcel of the managerial imperative in that an influx of outside expertise – particularly from persons with a commercial bent – was deemed essential to fostering within state bureaux 'the same commitment to performance and achievement found in the best outside organizations' (Cmnd 2627, 1994: para. 5.2); the assumption being not only that private sector management was in and of itself superior to anything to be found in the public sector, but that public and private sector management contexts were so fundamentally alike that practices suitable to one could be unilaterally grafted on to the other without too much of a problem.[5]

This was not an assumption shared by either Robert Sheldon of the Public Accounts Committee or Sir John Bourn, the Comptroller and Auditor General, both of whom made the point that in searching for outside talent for Whitehall the emphasis has been excessively on what skills and competencies the incomers will bring at the expense of what they will have to learn about the particular – and 'political' – nature of the public service (see Greenaway, 1995: 362).

Sheldon and Bourn's concerns seem justified when one considers what some of those appointed to chief executive posts within Next Steps agencies from outside of the Civil Service have understood by the 'ethos of office'. For example, John Ford, appointed to the post of Chief Executive in the Driving Standards Agency from the private sector, described his role in the following terms:

> I don't actually understand the phrase 'public service ethos' because really we're paid to do a job for the benefit of the people who produce the money; and in principle that's no different from what one tries to do in the private sector. We try to satisfy the people who in the end give us the money that we can put into our pay packets and take home. So, in that sense, the private sector is in the business of public service because if the public don't like the service, they vote with their feet and go somewhere else. (BBC, 1994: 7 January)

Ford went on to say that he had 'joined specifically in order to be Chief Executive of the agency and I feel committed to the agency, I'm not really looking for moves within the Civil Service and don't expect to become a "civil servant"' (BBC, 1994: 20 January). Quite what benefits are meant to accrue from having someone occupying a senior position within the Civil Service who doesn't want to be a civil servant are not at all clear. Nor is it entirely obvious why someone should be appointed to a position in which they are expected to play an important leadership role in inculcating a 'common ethic of public service' among their staff when the person in question does not believe that there is such a thing as a 'public service ethos' in the first place. However, as Mark Freedland (1995: 22) has commented in relation to Next Steps and other mechanisms of public sector reform in Britain, 'the sense of irony does seem to have become blunted of late'.

Ford himself was not unaware of this irony when he commented that he had been appointed to the job because he was a 'doer' from the private sector but that the political and regulatory environment in which he was now expected to work limited – in a personally frustrating but, he acknowledged, 'absolutely understandable' manner – his scope to act as he would have done in the private sector.

> I think that coming in from the outside the first thing you notice is in trying to take a simple, common-sense solution to a problem you are often completely fenced in by regulatory frameworks. To give a very simple example, we're market testing at the moment some of our booking-office services. What we would do in the private sector is simply call in a few prospective contractors that one happened to know from the past and say 'Well, how do you think we should do this, how should we write the specification to enable you to save money and us to save money? How can we quickly get to a solution?'

That is not possible in the public sector because for a start it would be against EEC law and I would be deep in trouble. I have to put an advert out in EEC journals and wait thirty-seven days for a reply. I have to have very good reasons if I only call in some of the prospective contractors and not others. And that makes a simple, common-sense solution to a problem really quite difficult to implement. (BBC, 1994: 20 January)

Ford's evident frustration at not being able to conduct himself as a private sector manager in a public sector context indicates once again that while managers in public services have a responsibility for the efficient use of resources, and to this end must be ready and able to use such methods of management as will offer the best prospect of optimal performance, this is never their only role. There is also a duty to observe the varied limits on their ability to act autonomously imposed, for example, by public bodies of various sorts as well as by the political imperatives of public service – loyalty to those who are politically responsible, responsiveness to parliamentary opinion and so on and so forth.

As Ford's Permanent Secretary at the Department of Transport, Patrick Brown, acknowledged:

I think he's finding it, I was going to say 'difficult'. I think he's finding it a little bit difficult to come to grips with these checks and balances that there are. But once he's looked at the requirements for probity, and impartiality, and fair dealing and all the rest of it, I think he will find a way of managing within those constraints. (BBC, 1994: 20 January)

One is left wondering exactly what senior civil servants have been doing all their working lives if not managing within the constraints imposed by the political environment within which they have to operate. Moreover, if this is the case, what exactly is the use of, let alone the need for, recruiting executives from the private sector to undertake this work? As Ford's testimony suggests, private sector managers can find the constraints of the public sector environment extremely frustrating. In different times this might have been seen as a good reason for not encouraging them to apply for public service management positions.

Another example of the 'entrepreneurial vocation' finding itself somewhat out of kilter with the requirements of the public service environment is provided by the case of Ros Hepplewhite, former Chief Executive of the Child Support Agency. From the beginning of her tenure, Hepplewhite, who was appointed from outside the Civil Service to become first head of the CSA, adopted an extremely 'enthusiastic' approach to the work of her organization quite at odds with the forms of conduct hitherto expected of a senior civil servant. In contrast to the disinterestedness – very different from uninterestedness – traditionally deemed to be a constitutive element of the ethos of office, in which officials are expected to pursue a policy with energy but to withhold commitment, Hepplewhite was keen to ensure that her staff were infused with a discernible sense of 'mission'.

There has been a very real shift in making civil servants more accountable for what they do and recognizing that part of that accountability is identifying with the policy they are actually implementing . . . I was recruited from outside the Civil Service to do this job. I do feel that the child maintenance system needs changing, I do feel that the new arrangements are an improvement on the previous arrangements, and I want my staff to feel that as well. And I feel quite comfortable about going out to my staff and saying it is important that we make these changes work. For reasons other than security of our own jobs, but also because we believe in what we do, but it is . . . a very real cultural shift from the Civil Service of ten years ago . . . in general terms, I think that . . . all civil servants in these agencies do need to have not only an understanding of policy, but a sense of driving a policy forward. (BBC, 1994: 20 January)

Such zeal is completely at odds with the formalistic impersonality traditionally associated with the ethos of office but totally in tune with the forms of conduct being encouraged by 'the new culture into which civil servants are being increasingly socialized, which is in turn associated with the new methods of recruitment, training and management which the recent reforms have introduced' (Chapman and O'Toole, 1995: 17). The preference is for 'can do' types – including 'change agents' from outside the Civil Service – who are capable of generating commitment to particular policies and programmes.

Part of Hepplewhite's commitment to 'driving policy forward' involved appearing regularly in public to answer questions about the CSA's work. As a result of this stance, when the shortcomings of the CSA legislation began to manifest themselves much of the public criticism of the agency was directed at Hepplewhite rather than at the relevant minister, Peter Lilley (Barberis, 1998: 456–7). So personally associated had Hepplewhite become with the CSA that it was she and not her minister who was in effect held politically responsible for the failings of the agency and who resigned from post (to be replaced by a career civil servant, Ann Chant).[6]

Doesn't such an outcome appear odd in a system of government which still proclaims itself to be based upon the accountability of ministers to Parliament? Surely, conventions of ministerial responsibility, according to which democratically accountable politicians are the representatives of the public in departments of state, cannot easily accommodate a managerial view of government in which individual civil servants become non-partisan political actors in their own right? At one level – in terms of constitutional theory – this is true, but in practical terms the Next Steps programme creates a situation in which such an outcome is altogether likely.

Agencification involves the delegation of responsibility for management or operational matters to individual chief executives. Such delegation marks a significant shift in the official position of civil servants within the system of government. Under the doctrine of ministerial responsibility to Parliament, ministers, and only ministers, as politicians and representatives of the public in departments, are responsible and answerable for all the activities of their department. Civil servants possess no constitutional personality of their own. They are officially anonymous because they always act in the name of their minister.

So what is the position of civil servants under the agency system? Officially, nothing has changed. In principle, individual ministers are still responsible for all the activities taking place within their department. Civil servants are still that: servants of ministers and hence without personality in the constitutional sense. However, in practice the demand for greater individual managerial responsibility has led to agency chief executives – especially those working in politically sensitive areas – becoming public figures in their own right.

Because these civil servants are now regarded as directly responsible for operational matters they are expected to answer questions about these matters in public, whether in the form of giving evidence to parliamentary select committees independently of their ministers or appearing on television and in other media to explain aspects of the work of their organization. But how can questions of operation be divorced from questions of policy? If someone is denied a benefit, or a child is denied admission to a school of first choice, is that a question of policy or management? While the official position is that chief executives should explain policy if necessary but not defend it, how is it practically possible to draw such a distinction? The answer must be that it is not in fact possible. In practical terms, as the case of Ros Hepplewhite makes clear, the result has been Chief Executives adopting stances in public more akin to those expected of politicians than of bureaucrats and becoming publicly associated with the success or failure of the policies they are charged with implementing. Such a situation does seem remarkably at odds with an ethos in which officials are expected to be the disinterested and anonymous servants of democratically accountable ministers.

Once again, attempts by political leaders to make officials more responsive have resulted in an insidious form of non-partisan politicization. At the heart of the managerialist imperative – as with the problematic of political control – lies the dichotomy between policy and operations. Ministers are accountable to Parliament for their policies and for the frameworks within which those policies are conducted; 'operational' matters are the responsibility of the agencies and in particular of their chief executives. The question is, as ever, where does policy end and operations begin? It is a question which only ministers can decide and it provides them with considerable scope for 'cherrypicking' what they are prepared to be accountable for, yet at the same time enables them to maintain the overall control they desire.

By making chief executives directly responsible for operational matters and expecting them to answer publicly for the performance of their agencies, while maintaining their own ability to intervene in and effectively control the activities of those agencies under the doctrine of individual ministerial responsibility to Parliament, ministers are able to have their cake and eat it. As the case of Ros Hepplewhite and the CSA, and the more recent case of Derek Lewis and the Prison Service, indicate, the agency system and the policy/operations dichotomy it creates is a perfect vehicle for allowing ministers to absolve themselves of their responsibilities to Parliament by defining any problems as 'operational matters' and hence deferring responsibility to chief executives. In the process, chief executives find themselves in the position of politicians *manqué*, increasingly exposed to scrutiny as public figures in their own right with their reputations and indeed their careers dependent upon their public performance and upon the perceived success or failure of the policies they are charged with implementing.

Once again, it is ironic that governments which forcefully claimed to be making political accountability more 'transparent' by returning responsibility for policy to politicians and responsibility for management to officials have ended up allowing ministers to avoid political responsibility as and when they wish and turning senior civil servants into something akin to politicians. Under the banner of depoliticization, the 'managerial imperative', like the 'problematic of control', has ended up politicizing – in our quite specific sense of that term – the conduct of officials. In large part this has been due to an over-enthusiastic attempt to import private sector management ethics and techniques into a public sector management context without appreciating the fundamental differences in regime values between these two contexts.

Concluding comments

In Britain, as in many other countries, the state service has evolved as a career bureaucracy, with limited interchange of personnel with the worlds of either business or politics. As exemplified by its 'mandarin' elite, the state service was to be both anonymous and neutral, in the party political sense. Public service neutrality, a much misconstrued notion, meant not being committed, by conviction guiding one's official actions, to the creed, spirit or platform of a current political party, while being able without a crisis of conscience to further the policies of any current party. Hence the forms of conduct that were most prized included honesty, detachment, flexibility, ability to clarify competing policy options, capacity to work in a team, integrity and disinterestedness. Indeed, candidates for selection who exhibited too much enthusiasm, passionate commitment, excessive cynicism or over-ambition risked being classified as unsuitable for a career in state service.

The crucial role of proffering policy advice to ministers also entailed a duty to influence, hence the relationship between politician and bureaucrat was represented as one of partnership.[7] Members of the mandarin elite prided themselves on their role as experts in managing the political environment and hence on their political and administrative sensitivities. They were, in a sense, political administrators engaged on terms of intimacy and mutual respect, tempered by occasional creative tension, with whoever happened to be their political masters at the time. Nevertheless, this symbiotic relationship was one in which both participants had, and recognized each other as having, separate and distinct personae: the politician visible, committed, publicly accountable and temporary; the official anonymous, disinterested, internally accountable and permanent (O'Toole, 1993; Greenaway, 1995).

Under the rubrics of 'political control' and the 'managerial imperative' political executives have sought to decouple this policy partnership of ministers and officials and to recast the personae of politicians and bureaucrats in terms of a policy/operations dichotomy, with the former as policy creators and the latter as managers of their policies. The idea of bureaucrats as partners in government, if ultimately subordinate ones, is no longer to be tolerated. This agenda is promoted as more in keeping with democratic principles of public accountability than earlier forms of bureaucratic power.

On this as on so many other counts profound scepticism should be the order of the day. Attempts at reconfiguring the role and responsibilities of politicians and bureaucrats to obtain a clearer, purer distinction between them has blurred rather than added transparency to processes of democratic accountability. The doctrine of ministerial responsibility lies in tatters with no effective alternative safeguards in place. Likewise, the 'ethos of office' has been undermined by political demands for 'responsive' management. The political administrator providing frank and fearless advice is being replaced by the 'can do' type whose style of conduct is characterized by decisiveness and an ability to get results. This more businesslike category of person is charged less with pointing out the administrative and political difficulties with policy proposals than with enthusiastically, energetically and even zealously removing those difficulties. In a democracy, however, as we know to our cost, too much enthusiasm is not always a good thing.

Notes

1. This argument is not restricted to political environments of the Westminster variety. In the United States, for example, 'street-level bureaucrats' also regularly make decisions that can have constitutional significance. The police officer who asks demonstrators to move along must interpret concretely the meaning of the First Amendment's guarantee of the 'right of the people peaceably to assemble to petition the government for a redress of grievances'. The welfare officer who removes a client in the interests of her or his welfare, or a public school principal who suspends an unruly teenager, is taking 'property' from an individual and, under the Fifth and Fourteenth Amendments, may do so only with 'due process of law' (Rohr, 1979).
2. Weber's use of 'personality' is diametrically opposed to contemporary 'personalist' psychological and moral philosophical understandings of this term. While

values might well be 'personal' in the sense of deriving from processes of moral reflection which individuals identify – rightly or wrongly – with their own inner conscience, they can also be 'personal' in the sense of simply providing a focus for individual moral commitment and ethical action. Clearly, the two senses are not identical. Individuals can and do find a (personal) focus for moral life in ethoses that derive from impersonal ethical institutions, rather than their own individual moral reflections. It is in this sense that 'bureaucrats', for example, can and should be 'personally' committed to the ethos of their office even though that ethos lies outside of their personal moral predilections or principles. For Weber, it is just such commitment that confers 'personality' upon the official (see also Hunter and Minson, 1992).

3. As I indicated in Chapter 2, Weber regarded the election and cultivation of professional politicians of sufficient calibre as the key to controlling the inescapable 'official power' of state bureaux. This did not mean that he thought those politicians should have the same kinds of qualities as those possessed by the official – quite the contrary: only that they should have the same or greater strength of character.

4. They also indicate that such a shift is not exclusive to the British system of government. They point to the United States, where similar trends are evident. In particular, they note that power in the executive branch of government has increasingly passed from politically impartial career bureaucrats to political appointees whose main qualification is their party political allegiance to the President (see also Moe, 1994). As in Britain, this has raised fears that much-needed 'institutionalized scepticism' in government is being abandoned.

5. Both these assumptions were at best questionable and at worst erroneous. As the former Permanent Secretary at the Department of the Environment, Sir Terry Heiser (1994: 23) argued, it was 'nonsense' to think that senior civil servants only discovered 'management' as a result of Next Steps and other such initiatives. He argued that, 'Like M. Jourdain in "Le Bourgeois Gentilhomme", who was surprised to find he had been talking prose all his life, so civil servants have been "managing" for most of their professional lives.' Similarly, another former Permanent Secretary, Sir Michael Quinlan (1994: 30) pointed out that the management changes that had taken place in state bureaux did not constitute 'a hugely overdue replacement of vagueness by precision'. Rather, he argued, 'there was much precision before but usually along different structural lines'. He concluded that traditional forms of management had 'conferred dividends which' under the new organizational arrangements 'we must now be ready to forgo'.

John Garrett, MP, in evidence to the Treasury and Civil Service Select Committee of the House of Commons in 1994, argued that the British Civil Service was more efficient and effective than many if not most of its private sector counterparts:

> The civil service is remarkably efficient at running large transaction processing operations and has a long record of innovation in office automation. It is often forgotten that the Scientific and Technical Civil Service has an outstanding record of discovery and innovation in, for example, aviation, environmental protection and agriculture, from which private industry has benefited immeasurably. The idea that the Government simply consumes wealth and is a burden on the public and on industry is also a fallacy. (Quoted in Fry, 1995: 146)

6. An exactly analogous situation seems to have prevailed in the controversial appointment (and then dismissal) of Derek Lewis, a former private sector executive with no experience in prison management, to head the Prison Service. Originally, Lewis was chosen, in preference to the career civil servant who had previously run the service, on account of his sympathy for opening up the Prison Service to private contractors (see, for example, Cooper, 1995).

7. The contemporary disavowal of this sort of 'partnership' (very different from the sort currently being touted by the British 'New Labour' government, see Cmnd 4310, 1999) between ministers and officials in the policy process has achieved such axiomatic status that it is sometimes hard to remember that it has not always been with us. *The Times* has never been a friend of bureaucracy but this is what it said in a leading article in 1953:

> The whole theory of the Civil Service is that it should meet the half-formed, sometimes ephemeral, schemes of politicians with a 'wall of experienced opinion' . . . Once one accepts the conception of a Civil Service which is both independent and permanent, one accepts also that it will exert some independent influence. (*The Times*, 23 November 1953, quoted in Parker, 1993: 58)

It is indicative of how far we've travelled that one can hardly imagine a leading article in *The Times* or indeed any other broadsheet newspaper today endorsing the legitimate influence of state officials on public policy.

Conclusion: The Ethos of Office and State Interest

Precisely those views which most strongly glorify the 'creative' discretion of the official accept, as the ultimate and highest lodestar for his behaviour in public administration, the specifically modern and strictly 'objective' idea of *raison d'état*.

Max Weber

Enthusiasm being founded on strong spirits, and a presumptuous boldness of character, it naturally begets the most extreme resolutions . . .

David Hume

'Change', in today's management terminology, is often represented as an unalloyed good. Indeed, it has become a matter of serious criticism to accuse an institution or individual of being incapable of adjusting to 'change' or of failing to grasp its multifarious 'opportunities'. Transformation is the order of the day and those that cannot or will not accede to and thrive on its demands are history (Clarke and Newman, 1997; du Gay, 1996).

In the public sector, as Ronald Moe (1994: 113) has argued, 'change' has 'acquired a theological aura'. Contemporary discourses of administrative reform in government, he points out, are characterized by dramatic, epochal assertions that set up their co-ordinates in advance and leave no 'way out' from their terms of reference. Focusing on the Clinton administration's National Performance Review report *From Red Tape to Results*, Moe highlights the ways in which this text constructs a caesural distinction between a 'failed' bureaucratic governmental past and a 'reinvented' entrepreneurial governmental future in such an emotive manner as to make criticism almost unthinkable.

In contrast to the traditional language of administrative discourse which attempted, not always with success, to employ terms with precise meanings, Moe describes the ways in which the entrepreneurial management enthusiasts employ a highly value-laden lexicon to disarm would-be questioners. Thus, 'the term "customer" largely replaces "citizen" and there is a heavy reliance upon active verbs – reinventing, reengineering, empowering – to maximize the emotive content of what otherwise has been a largely nonemotive subject matter' (1994: 114).[1]

In the report, as we saw in Chapter 5, the 'administrative management paradigm' with its emphasis on the Constitution, statutory controls, hierarchical lines of responsibility to the President, the distinctive legal character of the governmental and private sectors, and the need for a cadre of nonpartisan bureaucrats ultimately responsible not only to the President but to Congress as well, is depicted as the 'system' that failed.

> This paradigm is the cause of the government being broken in the eyes of the entrepreneurial management promoters. It has not proven flexible enough to permit change to occur at the speed considered necessary in the new, information-driven technological world . . . The report argues, almost deterministically, that the entrepreneurial management paradigm will prevail in the future. Those who question this paradigm are not merely incorrect, they have no place in the government of the future. (Moe, 1994: 114)

Whilst recognizing that the 'entrepreneurial paradigm' has been presented as something akin to a *fait accompli* for those working within state service, Moe (1994: 116) is nonetheless disturbed by the fact that 'much of the public administration community leadership early-on joined in celebrating this unshackling from the allegedly outdated bureaucratic paradigm' and in welcoming the opportunities provided by entrepreneurial 'change'.[2] Questions about 'reinventing government', he suggests, may well be intellectually challenging and personally exciting to public administrators but the latter need to be careful that this does not lead them to act with degrees of enthusiasm and personal involvement not consistent with the detachment normally expected of bureaucrats working within government. In particular, they should respect the fine, if often unclear, lines separating their own responsibilities from the responsibilities of politicians. Responsible public servants, he insists, should still be advocating evidence first – decision afterwards.

The enthusiasm with which senior bureaucrats in a variety of institutional domains have sought to 'own' the transformative vocabulary of managerialism offers cause for concern in just this regard. For a century or more, what senior bureaucrats did was called 'administration'. This term contained two distinguishable elements, 'policy-advising' on the one hand and 'management' on the other. Management usually meant 'mobilising and co-ordinating resources to carry out accepted policy' (Parker, 1993: 170). However, a crucial feature of contemporary programmes of organizational reform within the public sectors of many OECD countries is the supersession of 'administration' and 'administrator' by the terms 'management' and 'manager'. Does this matter?

The argument of this book has been that it matters very much indeed. First, in the commercial and industrial domains 'management' has long existed as the inclusive term for the role of administrative leadership. That alone would account for the political conversion to the term in the present climate of opinion. But, secondly, maybe management functions in business are not identical with administrative functions in government? Perhaps in business and industry most managers spend their time in 'mobilising and co-ordinating resources to carry out accepted policy' (Parker, 1993: 170) made by senior directors, and business lacks any real equivalent to advising on policy, which in government includes framing legislation, dealing with other governments, regulating aspects of the economic system, administering justice and distributing all sorts of social services? Perhaps there is a good reason for the broader term 'administration' prevailing in government? If this is indeed the case, do recent shifts in terminology assume that members of the administrative cadre should now approximate their role to this, dare I say it, more 'modest' business management model? The logics of both public choice and managerialist critiques of the bureaucratic ethos of office point inexorably in this direction.

Gyroscopes of state

While it may well be true that the proportion of modern governmental activity resembling that of the private sector is now vastly greater than it was in the past, and that as a result there is a clear need for specific sets of management skills that may have been neglected in more traditional public service training, this should not blind us to the vital importance of continuing aspects of public service which are unknown in private enterprises. Indeed, one inescapable part of the ethical role of the public bureaucrat, as a bureaucrat, is to serve the interests of the state, as a state (Chapman, 1993; Minson, 1997; Rohr, 1979). In this sense, as Rohr (1979: 40) has put it, the public bureau should not be seen, or see itself, simply as a 'neutral instrument of management', but rather as 'a mighty institution of government'. Only by being recognized and appreciated as an 'instrument of state power' (Hennessy, 1995: 121) can the public bureaucracy develop a self-image that is directly connected to the public interest that it inevitably affects.

In an era of reinventing or modernizing government such *étatiste* sentiments have become virtually unutterable in polite democratic society. As we have seen, a central tenet informing new managerialist programmes of reform is the democratic-political imperative of 'responsive government' (Parker, 1993). Because popular election is increasingly represented as the sole constitutionally legitimate entitlement to govern, the idea of state or public interest is equated exclusively with the interests of the duly elected government of the day. Consequently, the public interest role of state bureaucrats is held to consist exclusively in the 'managerial' tasks of delivering results efficiently, economically and effectively for their political masters (and with maximum enthusiasm and commitment to boot).

There is a certain logic to this position, but it assumes a supremacy for popular election that it simply does not possess. In the USA, for instance, elections – congressional or presidential – are not viewed as exclusively an expression of the will of the people. Elections do, of course, albeit in a ramified sense, express the will of the people but they do so only in fulfilling the design of the American Constitution, which is 'the object of the primordial expression of the will of the people' (Rohr, 1995: 65). Elections express this 'will' only because the Constitution indicates when, where and how they may do so. The Congress or President elected is itself a creature of the Constitution and has no meaning whatsoever outside that Constitution. Therefore, constitutional supremacy overrides electoral supremacy. 'In American constitutional theory, elections do not confer power on anyone. They merely determine who will occupy a particular office that the Constitution has already endowed with certain powers' (Rohr, 1995: 66). In this sense, the public bureaucracy as an institution of government derives its legitimacy from its constitutional role, from the fact that it 'is part of the constitutional order that was chosen by the people in the great ratification debate of 1787/88. The fact that administrators, like judges, are not elected in no way diminishes their constitutional stature. Popular election is simply one of at least twenty-two ways that have been or still are approved for holding office under the Constitution' (Rohr, 1986: 185).

Although the constitutional context is very different, a similar argument can be made for the Civil Service in Britain. British civil servants are 'servants of the Crown . . . employed in a civil capacity' (Chapman, 1988a: 295). At the most basic level of analysis this definition may be uncontroversial, but beyond this difficulties soon arise from the largely unwritten nature of the British Constitution. Formally, the Crown means the Queen, but for all practical purposes the Crown is the government: not a particular administration with a constitutionally limited period of office, but the executive branch of the state which is ultimately controlled by the Cabinet.

This aspect of the British Constitution makes it very different from that of almost every other modern nation state. Unlike most other countries, Britain has no Civil Service Act. There is therefore no fundamental legal document to which officials can refer which contains a statement of their organization and their responsibilities. Individual government departments may similarly lack such basic documents. Indeed, departments and other forms of governmental organization can be created or abolished almost overnight by Order in Council (as the development of Next Steps agencies testifies). Acts of Parliament are not necessary (Chapman, 1988a: 295).

One of the practical implications of this constitutional arrangement is that there can, quite legitimately, be a variety of opinions about what is constitutionally correct in particular circumstances. This applies to the administrative sphere of government as well as the political sphere. For all day-to-day purposes, however, loyalty and duty to the Crown has meant loyalty and duty to the Queen's ministers who act in her name and are accountable to the Queen's Parliament. A civil servant's primary professional duty therefore is to his or her minister, not to the people who are ministers, but only to people in so far as they are holding the office of minister. This duty, though, is *prima facie* not absolute, and it cannot override all other considerations (Jay, 1996: 141; O'Toole, 1990).

So why is this the case? First, it is important to recognize that ministers are political animals. As professional politicians, this is their vocation. However, if the idea of 'state' or public interest is to possess any meaning it cannot be registered solely in terms of the political interests of any duly elected government. Political acts are not necessarily acts geared towards 'the public interest'. Perhaps the question could be settled by simply asserting that there is an acceptable area of political controversy and political debate that is itself bounded by a perimeter of propriety entitled 'the public interest'. But who, in a state without a written Constitution, where convention and precedent are all, sets this perimeter and who possesses the authority to say when it has been breached?

In Britain, as O'Toole (1990) has argued, the Civil Service has traditionally played a crucial role in providing one of the bases for the stability of the state in just this regard. It has done so by dint of its constitutive characteristics – its permanence, party political neutrality, impartiality, provision of frank and fearless advice and its expert knowledge of the business of government. As Trollope put it in *Phineas Finn*: 'every question so handled by [the Prime Minister] has been decided rightly according to his own party, and wrongly according to the party opposite. A political leader is so sure of support and so sure of attack that it is hardly necessary for him to be right. For the country's sake, he should have officials under him who know the routine of business'. Cue the Civil Service – that 'gyroscope of state', in Peter Hennessy's words – whose function is precisely 'to act as a permanent piece of ballast in the Constitution', providing a degree of balance and permanence in what can be 'a very volatile legislature and an equally volatile ministerial executive' (Lord Bancroft, quoted in Hennessy, 1995: 127).

This is not simply a managerial role. It is a crucial constitutional and hence ethico-political one. As Graham Wallas (1908, quoted in Chapman, 1993: 108) argued long ago, 'The real "Second Chamber", the real "constitutional check" in England, is provided, not by the House of Lords and the Monarchy, but by the existence of a permanent Civil Service appointed on a system independent of the opinion or desires of any politician and holding office during good behaviour.' Whether they be an administrative assistant using their discretion in assessing a case across the counter from 'a customer' in the Benefits Agency, or a Permanent Secretary offering advice on constitutional practice to, or interpreting constitutional

conventions for, their minister, civil servants in the British system of government do not simply execute policy, they play a significant role in
governing the country.

In this sense there is an obvious political dimension to their work. As I
have argued throughout this book, the so-called 'Westminster syndrome'
has never required civil servants to be apolitical, in large part because the
nexus of responsibility that defines that syndrome presupposes the inter-
twining of policy and management.[3] How, then, is this political role to be
squared with a 'reason of state' or 'public interest' vocation?

The answer lies, once again, in distinguishing between different uses of
the term 'politics' (Wheare, 1955: 26–7). Public bureaucrats work within a
political environment: that is their fate. Most of what they do has potential
political implications, even activities of an apparently routine nature. Their
mistakes may lead to political embarassment for the government of the
day and even, in extreme cases, to its downfall. Awareness of the political
nature of their work, and expertise in the dynamics of the political environment within which they have to operate, is a crucial competence they
have to master. However, this political dimension does not make them
partisan political actors in their own right. It does not establish them as an
independent political force vying with government and opposition for
ultimate power.

The public bureaucrat may be a political beast but she is not a *party*
political beast. This is a crucial difference. The doctrine of public service
neutrality requires her not to be. This doctrine means not being committed,
by convictions guiding one's official actions, to the creed and platform of
a current political party, while being able without a crisis of conscience to
further the policies of any given party. The fact that public bureaucrats do
work in an inherently political environment and perform work with political content and implications does not make a nonsense of the notions of
objectivity and neutrality as defined in the orthodox view of the public servant's role under the Westminster conventions. As Weber (1994b: 331), for
example, argued, the idea that the political content of public administration makes public servants incapable of minimizing the influence *of their
own political opinions* on their daily work is nonsense. Without this
'supreme ethical discipline' that they bring to their duties, he stressed, 'the
whole [governmental] apparatus would disintegrate'.

Civil servants have been trained to conduct themselves in such a
manner. Indeed, in Britain, as elsewhere, people with strong party political
views have – at least until recently – been unlikely to be appointed to
senior Civil Service positions, or to present themselves for consideration in
the first place (Chapman, 1988a). As a result, civil servants have been likely
to greet the panaceas of all political parties with caution if not scepticism.
Inevitably this leads them to embrace party political programmes with
less fervour than party enthusiasts would like. But that is part of their job,
and in that way they may be seen as *servants of the public interest*. As
Richard Wilding (quoted in Chapman, 1993: 109) wrote some time ago, it

is necessary for civil servants 'to pursue today's policy with energy; it is equally necessary, in order to survive, to withhold from it the last ounce of commitment'.

It is the Civil Service's *étatiste* role as a governmental/constitutional 'gyroscope', as evidenced in the ethical discipline required by the doctrine of party political neutrality, that is perhaps most threatened by contemporary programmes of management reform in the public sector.

Successive governments have made no secret of their wish to divert Civil Service attention from a presumed concentration upon policy advice to ministers towards better management of their departments/agencies. The current favourites amongst ministers may well be those who genuinely espouse managerialism. In principle, this need not be reprehensible, even if it is distasteful to the doubters, as long as it does not lead to a significant diminution of the bureaucracy's 'state interest' obligations. However, as Richard Chapman (1988b: 16–17) has argued, recent reforms in the British context

> seem to represent such a significant change of emphasis and ultimately of direction, that even if welcomed on the grounds of cost-cutting and rolling back the frontiers of the state, they seem out of character with the highly regarded traditions, standards and expectations of public sector management in this country. It may appear premature to issue dire warnings of the dangers of corruption, but if the sorts of safeguards that worked so well in the past are removed – safeguards involving the regular posting of staff, recruitment on the basis of open competition with the objective assessment of applicants, and socialisation which encourages the highest standards of integrity and public service as the most desirable qualities in public sector management – if these safeguards no longer exist, then it may be necessary to ask if alternative measures should be introduced to ensure that high standards of public sector management are still achievable . . . Quite simply, to move at great speed in the apparent direction of improved value for money, while disregarding other values, may not be what most citizens would wish to experience if they were better educated about the British system of government and better informed about the probable and possible consequences of fashionable new management techniques.

The issues at stake in the enthusiastic 'reinvention' of state administration in Britain, as elsewhere, are not simply issues of operations, costs and responsiveness, they are ethico-political and constitutional in that 'they affect the foundations of political life and capacity' (Dunleavy and Hood, 1994: 16). Dramatic, epochal representations of the 'bad' old 'public service ethic' being replaced by a 'good' public sector adaptation of market-oriented managerial ethics signally fail to pay attention to these very issues. In no small part this is due to the way reformers imagine the environment they seek to reinvent.

As I argued in Chapters 4 and 5, protagonists of the Next Steps reforms in the British Civil Service claimed, without any sense of irony, that they had no wish to alter directly existing constitutional practice because they saw themselves as operating in a completely different dimension, namely that of restructuring the financial management of public administration. They were concerned with issues of financial rather than political accountability. Because government/Civil Service relations were understood in quasi-commercial terms, it was no surprise to find the unitary structure of the state administration being replaced by a quasi-autonomous multidivisional structure, in the manner of presumed best private sector practice.

Indeed, once the discursive map informing the Next Steps initiative is recognized, much that happens in relations between executive agencies and their parent departments becomes readily explicable. It is not uncommon in the private sector for a group managing director and a subsidiary managing director, 'each under huge pressure to make a success of the enterprise at the level for which each is responsible, to come into conflict about the management of the subsidiary, and to argue whether the sphere of autonomy of the subsidiary management, often conceptualized as a split between policy and operations, has been sufficiently respected by the group management. On occasion these quarrels can even result in the dismissal of the subsidiary managing director' (Freedland, 1996: 27).[4]

As a number of commentators have pointed out, the financial/organizational innovation of Next Steps has profound consequences for a key constitutional principle – the doctrine of ministerial responsibility (Bogdanor, 1996; O' Toole and Chapman, 1994). The executive agencies created under the Next Steps programme constitute groupings with interests which are distinguished from those of their parent department by the structures of separate financial accountability which it is the very aim of the Next Steps programme to produce. Through this process ministerial responsibility for departmental decision-making is transmuted and fragmented into two distinct accountabilities each of which is primarily financial. If the relationship between the parent department and the agency is working in the manner it is intended to, the decision-makers and decision-making at agency level cannot be seen as a part of an integrated (bureaucratic) departmental structure, a departmental unity, such as the doctrine of political ministerial responsibility demands and requires (Freedland, 1996).

As this example indicates, rather than lying within the boundaries of constitutional orthodoxy, contemporary programmes of organizational reform have some startling constitutional implications. That senior civil servants, and not simply politicians, enthusiastically embraced the Next Steps programme without, perhaps, adequate prior consideration of its constitutional implications, once again highlights the dangers such enthusiasm poses for the proper conduct of bureaucratic office and, in particular, for what Weber termed the bureaucrat's 'ethos of responsibility'. Not only this, it also indicates the problems with imagining that business management and public administration are identical in all regards.

There can be no doubt that state bureaucrats bear a real responsibility for the efficient and economic use and deployment of the resources at their disposal – taken as these are from the people they serve and returned to them in the form of benefits and entitlements sanctioned by the system of government. It would, as Sir Frank Tribe (1971: 159) argued in 1949, be quite improper for the many Departments of the public service to believe that mundane questions of cutting out unnecessary expenditure were issues beneath the dignity of those charged with proffering policy advice to ministers: 'every officer . . . should take an active interest in the cost of the particular service he administers, and should ask himself at frequent intervals whether the service is giving the State and his fellow tax-payers full value for what it costs'. In these circumstances, every civil servant bears a responsibility for the economic use of resources and to this end must be ready and willing to use such methods of management as will offer the best prospect of optimum performance.

But, and this is the crucial point, this does not exhaust the civil servant's responsibilities. State officials are subject to competing and often incommensurable demands. In negotiating these competing value claims they are required to exercise discretion and make ethical judgements. Efficiency, economy and effectiveness, for example, are plural and often competing values within the public administration context. An exclusive emphasis on one can have serious implications for the degree to which the others will be secured. Anxieties arise when the pressures for change and an emphatic emphasis on financial economies pay inadequate attention to the governmental/constitutional context within which public services are administered.

Bluntly stated, the function of officials in the British system of government cannot be exhaustively defined in terms of achieving results with maximum 'economic efficiency', 'value for money' or 'best value'. There is a host of other obligations and responsibilities imposed on state officials, be it the varied limits imposed on action by public bodies or the political imperatives of public service – loyalty to those who are politically responsible, sensitivity to the complexity of the public interest, honesty and fearlessness in the formulation and provision of advice to government and so on. Administrative responsibility focuses on governmental/constitutional capacity, process and structure, not simply on 'outcomes'. Public administrators are responsible for doing all they can to maintain what Parker (1993: 38) calls 'the integrity and independence of representative government'. This in turn suggests, once again, that they have ethical responsibilities of a 'state interest' or 'public interest' kind that are more complex and onerous than those required simply to meet the bottom lines of management. The contemporary concern with financial economies, 'efficient' management and the obtaining of results should not be allowed to obscure these crucial 'state interest' responsibilities. The pursuit of better management – different from the pursuit of better bureaucratic public administration – has to recognize the political and governmental limits to which it is – or should be – subject. As John Rohr (1998: 104) has argued, this does not require a complete renunciation of contemporary managerialism but rather involves an attempt to 'tame its excesses by subjecting it to the discipline of constitutional scrutiny'.[5]

Concluding comments

Without trying to excuse its shortcomings of argument and scholarship, this book has been intended as a sustained attempt to find some thought-provoking things to say in praise of bureaucracy and bureaucrats. By focussing on bureaucrats' capacities and character *as* bureaucrats, rather than as critical intellectuals or entrepreneurs, and through locating their working environment at the intersection of distinct orders of governmental and political life, I have sought to amplify the Weberian perspective on the ethos of office as an extension of the repertoire of human possibilities (rather than as a dehumanizing subtraction).

Such an enterprise is at odds with the conventional wisdom of many analysts within the social and human sciences, as well as with many contemporary reform exercises in the field of public administration. Both the philosophical-critical and contemporary managerial/political reformist agendas regard the 'ethos of office' as an anachronism and represent those who would defend it as suffering from an unworldly nostalgia. It has been my contention, however, that on both counts the critics are mistaken. Charges of unworldliness are best levelled at the anti-bureaucrats themselves, because it is they who have most vociferously sought to establish commandments of identical content across what are plural life orders.

In their different ways, both philosophical and managerial forms of bureau critique evaluate the ethos of office in relation to its failure to register a certain sort of morality. For the philosophical critical variant, this failure is registered in terms of a distinction between personal and collective morality. Because the ethos of office is antithetical to the consistency and interactive unity of heart and mind which this form of critique expects of an 'authentic' moral personality, it is interpreted as a symptom of moral failure.

For the managerialists the demands are rather different. Here the (public service) bureau 'fails' because it is seen to be incapable of fostering the forms of conduct and habits of action that are deemed essential for organizational survival and flourishing in the dislocated environments of the present. Unless public bureaux are 'modernized' and learn to become more 'enterprising', it is argued, they will lack the capacity to pursue their goals and objectives. The problem here is that in taking up this entrepreneurial challenge and 'modernizing' or 'reinventing' themselves in the manner suggested, the ability of public bureaux to continue carrying out certain of their governmental/constitutional responsibilities has been somewhat incapacitated.

My criticisms of the managerialist and various politicized or self-styled 'radical reformist' agendas for the reshaping of the public service have been registered with precisely this concern in mind – that they are playing a crucial role, whether consciously or unconsciously, in evacuating public administration of its determinate content by making it into something else. Within the managerialist critique, for example, the public bureaucracy is represented as an inefficient form of organization without due regard to its ethico-political role in contemporary liberal democracies. In the context of public administration under the so-called Westminster conventions, as distinct from management in other contexts, a distinctively bureaucratic type of organization, with accountability both hierarchically and to elected officials – such as the doctrine of ministerial responsibility requires – may be an extremely appropriate form of organization. To subject that form of organization to critique for its failure to operate more like a business is, perhaps, to misunderstand its role. 'Bureaucratic rationality' may seem inefficient viewed through the concerns of the new public management, but it might also be seen as crucial to the securing of effective parliamentary democracy.

In sum, it is both misguided and remarkably premature to announce the death of the ethos of bureaucratic office. Many of its key features as they came into existence a century or so ago remain as or more essential to the provision of good government today as they did then – as a number of recent well-publicized cases of improper conduct in government, at both national and supranational level, indicate all too clearly. These features include the possession of enough skill, status and independence to offer frank and fearless advice about the formulation and implementation of distinctive public purposes and to try to achieve purposes impartially, responsibly and with energy if not enthusiasm. Representative democracy still needs the bureaucratic ethos.

Notes

1. Anyone wishing to see a paradigm instance of 'irrefutable metaphysics' functioning as government policy need look no further than the current British government's *Modernising Government* (Cmnd 4310, 1999).
2. The leadership of the National Academy of Public Administration in the USA, for instance, aligned itself with the supporters of this new paradigm to the extent that it created an Alliance for Redesigning Government chaired by David Osborne within its own walls. Such enthusiastic grasping of the 'opportunities' provided by 'change' was also exhibited by public bureaucrats in other contexts. See, for example, the 1994 article 'Re-inventing British government' by the then head of the British Civil Service, Sir (now Lord) Robin Butler.
3. Under Westminster conventions, legislative and executive powers are united and between them there are none of the formal 'checks and balances' present in the American context.
4. Comparisons with the Derek Lewis case immediately come to mind! Lewis was appointed as Chief Executive of the Prison Service after a career as a television executive in the private sector. In his autobiography, Lewis (1997) raises a number of interesting questions about the nature of public sector management and draws attention to what he considers to be certain crucial weaknesses in the British context. However, his book is also revealing in that it indicates Lewis's lack of familiarity with Civil Service ways of working and, in particular, of the political environment within which that work inevitably occurs and which affected the activities for which he was responsible.

Perhaps the key issue arising out of all this is that attempts to 'reinvent' public administration so that it will function according to 'regime values' quite extrinsic to it risk undermining the crucial ethico-political role the public administration plays in liberal-democratic societies such as Britain. Attempting to make public administration embody some goal (e.g. commercial enterprise, consumer sovereignty, wealth maximization, liberty, community) that can be specified apart from public administration and that can serve as the standard by which public administration is to be assessed, is a sure-fire way of losing the determinate content of public administration by making it into something else entirely.

When a legal practitioner listens to a client's story, for example, she listens with *legal* ears and what she hears is quite different in its emphases from what the client hears when he tells her his sad story. The client may stress a moment or action that appears to him to be defining of his cause only to hear the lawyer say that it is not something that can be brought under categories with which and within which the law thinks (Fish, 1995: 21). A similar point can be made in relation to the different frameworks within which public administrators and their private sector counterparts operate. The 'regime values' that shape the respective endeavours of public administration and commercial enterprise are not identical. Attempts to view one through the lens of the other's complex of concerns are likely to generate more heat than light. 'Public administrative phenomena' come into view only under the pressure of a public administrative analysis; otherwise they would not be public administrative phenomena but something quite different. As we saw in Chapter 6, unfortunate consequences can flow from attempts to think the political environment of public administration from the standpoint of private sector management regime values.

5. Maybe such an exercise would conclude that enhanced representative democracy requires neither more democracy nor less administration? It might even challenge the popular supposition that 'big' government is bad government and that 'lean' or 'entrepreneurial' government is better government. While it would undoubtedly be suspicious of ministerial attempts to vest more control over the public policy process it might not lead to an enthusiastic demand for radical parliamentary reform. Most importantly, perhaps, for our current concerns, it might also reveal the continuing constitutional and ethico-political importance of the kind of worldly professional conscience associated with the ethos of bureaucratic office.

References

Anthony, P. (1986)*The Foundation of Management*. London: Tavistock.

Anthony, P. (1994) *Managing Culture*. Milton Keynes: Open University Press.

Armstrong, Sir R. (1985) 'Note by the head of the Civil Service', in *The Duties and Responsibilities of Civil Servants in Relation to Ministers*. London: Cabinet Office.

BBC (1994) *Inside the New Civil Service*, Radio 4 series in three parts, January.

Baker, R. (1971) 'Organization theory and the public sector', in R.A. Chapman and A. Dunsire (eds) *Style in Administration*. London: Allen & Unwin. pp. 137–45.

Barberis, P. (1998) 'The new public management and a new accountability', *Public Administration*, 76: 451–70.

Barker, A. (1998) 'Political responsibility for UK prision security – ministers escape again', *Public Administration*, 76:1–23.

Barzelay, M. (1992) *Breaking through Bureaucracy*. Berkeley: University of California Press.

Bauman, Z. (1989) *Modernity and the Holocaust*. Cambridge: Polity Press.

Bauman, Z. (1993) *Postmodern Ethics*. Oxford: Basil Blackwell.

Blau, P. (1956) *Bureaucracy in Modern Society*. New York: Random House.

Bogdanor, V. (1996) 'A threat to democracy?' in P. Barberis (ed.) *The Whitehall Reader* Milton Keynes: Open University Press. pp. 195–7.

Boston, J., Martin, J., Pallott, J. and Walsh, P. (1991) *Re-Shaping the State: New Zealand's Bureaucratic Revolution*. Auckland: Oxford University Press.

Bridges, E. (1971) 'Portrait of a profession: the Civil Service tradition' (1950), in R. A. Chapman and A. Dunsire (eds) *Style in Administration*. London: Allen & Unwin.

Burchell, G. (1993) 'Liberal government and techniques of the self', *Economy & Society*, 22 (3): 266–82.

Burrell, G. (1997) *Pandemonium*.London: Sage.

Butler, R. (1994) 'Reinventing British government', *Public Administration*, 72: 263–70.

Burchell, G., Gordon, C., and Miller, P. (eds) (1991) *The Foucault Effect: Studies in Governmentality*. Brighton: Harvester Wheatsheaf.

Callon, M. (1998) 'Introduction: the embeddedness of economic markets in economics', in M. Callon (ed.) *The Laws of the Markets*. Oxford: Blackwell.

Campbell, C. (1993) 'Public service and democratic accountability', in R.A. Chapman (ed.) *Ethics in Public Service*. Edinburgh: Edinburgh University Press.

Campbell, C. and Wilson, G. (1995) *The End of Whitehall*. Oxford: Blackwell.

Caplan, J. (1988) *Government without Administration: State and Civil Service in Weimar and Nazi Germany*. Oxford: Clarendon Press.

Champy, J. (1995) *Reengineering Management*. London: Harper Collins.

Chapman, R.A. (1982) 'Strategies for reducing government activities', in G.E.

Caiden and H. Siedentopf (eds) *Strategies for Administrative Reform*. Lexington, MA: Lexington Books. pp. 59–69.

Chapman, R.A. (1988a) *Ethics in the British Civil Service*. London: Routledge.

Chapman, R.A. (1988b) 'The art of darkness', an inaugural lecture, University of Durham.

Chapman, R.A. (1991) 'Concepts and issues in public sector reform: the experience of the United Kingdom in the 1980s', *Public Policy & Administration*, 6 (2):, 1–19.

Chapman, R.A. (1992) 'The end of the British Civil Service?' *Teaching Public Administration*, 12 (2): 1–5.

Chapman, R.A. (1993) 'Reasons of state and the public interest', in R.A. Chapman (ed.) *Ethics in Public Service*. Edinburgh: Edinburgh University Press. pp. 93–110.

Chapman, R.A. (1994) 'Change in the Civil Service', *Public Administration*, 72: 599–610.

Chapman, R.A. (1996a) 'Standards in public life', *Teaching Public Administration*, 16 (1): 1–19.

Chapman, R.A. (1996b) 'From croquet mallets to flamingos: perspectives on change', *Public Policy and Administration*, 11 (4): 1–17.

Chapman, R.A. (1997) *The Treasury in Public-Policy Making*. London: Routledge.

Chapman, R.A. and O'Toole, B. (1995) 'The role of the Civil Service: a traditional view in a period of change', *Public Policy and Administration*, 10 (2): 3–20.

Chester, D. N. (1954) 'The Crichel Down affair', *Public Administration*, 32: 389–401.

Chipperfield, G. (1994) *The Civil Servant's Duty*, Essex Papers in Politics and Government. Colchester: University of Essex.

Clarke, J. and Newman, J. (1997) *The Managerial State*. London: Sage.

Cmnd 2627 (1994) *The Civil Service: Continuity and Change*. London: HMSO.

Cmnd 4310 (1999) *Modernising Government*. London: HMSO.

Cooper, P. (1995) 'Separating policy from operations in the Prison Service: a case study', *Public Policy and Administration*, 10 (4): 4–19.

Corby, S. (1993) 'How big a step is Next Steps? Industrial relations developments in the Civil Service executive agencies', *Human Resource Management Journal*, 4 (2): 52–69.

Corby, S. (1998) 'Industrial relations in Civil Service agencies: transition or transformation', *Industrial Relations Journal*, 29 (3): 194–206.

Deetz, S. (1995) 'Character, corporate responsibility and the dialogic in the postmodern context: a commentary on Mangham', *Organization*, 2 (2): 217–25.

Doig, A. (1995) 'Mixed signals? Public sector change and the proper conduct of public business', *Public Administration*, 73: 191–212.

Doig, A. and Wilson, J. (1998) 'What price New Public Management?, *The Political Quarterly*, 69 (3): 267–276.

Donzelot, J. (1991) 'The Mobilization of Society', in G. Burchell, C. Gordon and P. Miller (eds) *The Foucault Effect*. Brighton: Harvester Wheatsheaf. pp. 169–79.

Du Gay, P. (1991) 'Enterprise culture and the ideology of excellence', *New Formations*, 13: 45–61.

Du Gay, P. (1994a) 'Making up managers: bureaucracy, enterprise and the liberal art of separation', *British Journal of Sociology*, 45 (4): 655–74.

Du Gay, P. (1994b) 'Colossal immodesties and hopeful monsters: pluralism and organizational conduct', *Organization*, 1 (1): 125–48.

Du Gay, P. (1996) *Consumption and Identity at Work*. London: Sage.

Du Gay, P. (1999) '"In the name of globalization . . .": enterprising-up nations, organizations and individuals', in P. Leisink (ed.) *Globalization and Labour Relations*. London: Edward Arnold. pp. 78–93.

Dunleavy, P. (1995) 'Policy disasters: explaining the UK's record', *Public Policy & Administration*, 10 (2): 52–70.

Dunleavy, P. and Hood, C. (1994) 'From old public administration to new public management', *Public Money and Management*, 14 (3): 9–16.

Dwivedi, O.P. and Olowu, D. (1988) 'Bureaucratic morality: an introduction', *International Political Science Review*, 9 (3): 163–5.

Efficiency Unit (1988) *Improving Management in Government: The Next Steps*. London: HMSO.

Efficiency Unit (1993) *Career Management and Succession Planning Study (Oughton Report)*. London: HMSO.

Elcock, H. (1995) 'The fallacies of management', *Public Policy & Administration*, 10 (1): 34–48.

Executive Office of the President, National Performance Review (1993) *From Red Tape to Results: Creating a Government that Works Better and Costs Less*. Washington DC: US Government Printing Office.

Ferguson, K. (1984) *The Feminist Case against Bureaucracy*. London: Sage.

Fish, S. (1994) *There's No Such Thing as Free Speech . . . and It's a Good Thing Too*. Oxford: Oxford University Press.

Fish, S. (1995) *Professional Correctness*. Oxford: Clarendon Press.

Foster, D. and Hoggett, P. (1999) 'Working for the Benefits Agency: "empowerment" and the exhausted employee', *Work, Employment & Society*, 13 (1): 19–39.

Foster, C. and Plowden, F. (1996) *The State under Stress*. Milton Keynes: Open University Press.

Freedland, M. (1994) 'Government by contract and public law', *Public Law*, Spring: 86–104.

Freedland, M. (1995) 'Privatising Carltona: Part II of the Deregulation and Contracting Out Act 1994', *Public Law*, Spring: 21–27.

Freedland, M. (1996) 'The rule against delegation and the Carltona doctrine in an agency context', *Public Law*, Summer: 19–30.

Freedland, M. (1998) 'Public law and private finance – placing the Private Finance Initiative in a public law frame', *Public Law*, Winter: 288–307.

Friedrich, C.J. and Brzezinski, Z.K. (1965) *Totalitarian Dictatorship and Autocracy*. Cambridge, MA: Harvard University Press.

Fry, G. (1995) *Policy and Management in the British Civil Service*. London: Prentice-Hall.

Gaukroger, S. (1986) 'Romanticism and de-commodification: Marx's conception of socialism', *Economy and Society*, 15 (3): 287–333.

Goldsworthy, D. (1991) *Setting Up Next Steps*. London: HMSO.

Goodsell, C. (1985) *The Case for Bureaucracy*, 2nd edn. Chatham, NJ: Chatham House Publishers.

Gordon, C. (1991) 'Governmental rationality: an introduction', in G. Burchell, C. Gordon and P. Miller (eds) *The Foucault Effect*. Brighton: Harvester Wheatsheaf, pp. 1–51.

Gore, A. (1993) *Creating a Government That Works Better and Costs Less: the Report of the National Performance Review*. Executive Summary, Washington, DC.

Greenaway, J. (1995) 'Having the bun and the halfpenny: can old public service survive in the new Whitehall?' *Public Administration*, 73: 357–74.

Hassard, J. and Parker, M. (eds) (1993) *Postmodernism and Organizations*. London: Sage.

Heiser, T. (1994) 'The Civil Service at a crossroads', *Public Policy & Administration*, 9 (1): 14–26.

Hennessy, P. (1995) *The Hidden Wiring*. London: Victor Gollancz.

Hennis, W. (1988) *Max Weber: Essays in Reconstruction*. London: Allen & Unwin.

Hennis, W. (1996) *Max Weber's Wissenschaft vom Menschen: neue studien zur Biographie des Werkes*. Tübingen: Mohr.

Hindess, B. (1997) 'Neo-Liberalism and national economy', in B. Hindess and M. Dean (eds) *Governing Australia*. Sydney: Cambridge University Press.

Hirschmann, A. (1977) *The Passions and the Interests*. Princeton, NJ: Princeton University Press.

Hirst, P. and Thompson, G. (1996) *Globalization in Question*. Cambridge: Polity Press.

Hollway, W. (1991) *Work Psychology and Organizational Behaviour*. London: Sage.

Holmes, S. (1993) *The Anatomy of Anti-Liberalism*. Cambridge, MA: Harvard. University Press.

Holmes, S. and Larmore, C. (1980) 'Translators' introduction', in N. Luhmann, *The Differentiation of Society*. New York: Columbia University Press. pp. xiii–xxxvii.

Hood, C. (1995) 'Contemporary public management: a new global paradigm?'. *Public Policy & Administration*, 10 (2): 104–17.

Horkheimer, M. and Adorno, T. (1974) *Dialectic of Enlightenment*. London: Verso.

Horton, S. and Jones, J. (1996) 'Who are the new public managers? An initial analysis of "Next Steps" chief executives and their managerial role', *Public Policy & Administration*, 11 (4): 18–44.

House of Commons Treasury and Civil Service Committee (1988–89) *Fifth Report. Developments in the Next Steps Programme* (HC348). London: HMSO.

House of Commons Treasury and Civil Service Committee (1993–94) *Fifth Report. The Role of the Civil Service, Vol. I: Report, Vol. II: Minutes of Evidence, Vol. III: Appendices to Minutes of Evidence* (HC27). London: HMSO.

Hunter, I. (1987) 'Setting limits to culture', *New Formations*, 4: 103–23.

Hunter, I. (1991) 'Personality as a vocation: the political rationality of the humanities', *Economy & Society*, 19 (4): 391–430.

Hunter, I. (1992) 'Subjectivity and government', *Economy & Society*: 123–34.

Hunter, I. (1994) *Re-thinking the School*. Sydney: Allen & Unwin.

Hunter, I. and Minson, J. (1992) 'The Good Bureaucrat', *Australian Left Review*, May, 26–30.

Jacques, R. (1996) *Manufacturing the Employee*. London: Sage.

Jay, P. (1996) 'Public duty and public interest', in P. Barberis (ed.) *The Whitehall Reader*. Milton Keynes: Open University Press. pp. 137–43.

Jennings, I. (1971) 'The achievement of British bureaucracy', in M. Dalby and M. Werthman (eds) *Bureaucracy in Historical Perspective*. Glenview, IL and London: Scott, Foresman. pp. 22–27.

Johnson, N. (1983) 'Management in government', in M.J. Earl (ed.) *Perspectives on Management*. Oxford: Oxford University Press. pp. 170–98.

Jordan, G. (1994a) 'Re-inventing government: but will it work?' *Public Administration*, 72: 21–35.

Jordan, G. (1994b) 'From Next Steps to market testing: administrative reform as improvisation', *Public Policy and Administration*, 9 (2): 21–35.

Kanter, R. (1990) *When Giants Learn to Dance*. London: Unwin Hyman.

Kaufman, H. (1981) 'Fear of bureaucracy: a raging pandemic?' *Public Administration Review*, 41 (1): 1–9.

Keat, R. (1990) 'Introduction', in R. Keat and N. Abercrombie (eds) *Enterprise Culture*. London: Routledge.

Krugman, P. (1996) *Pop Internationalism*, Cambridge, MA: MIT Press.

Larmore, C. (1987) *Patterns of Moral Complexity*. Cambridge: Cambridge University Press.

Lassman, P. and Speirs, R. (eds) (1994) *Weber Political Writings*. Cambridge: Cambridge University Press.

Lewis, D. (1997) *Hidden Agendas: politics, law and disorder*. London: Hamish Hamilton.

Luhmann, N. (1980) *The Differentiation of Society*, trans. S. Holmes and C. Larmore. New York: Columbia University Press.

MacIntyre, A. (1981) *After Virtue*. London: Duckworth.

McMylor, P. (1994) *Alasdair MacIntyre: Critic of Modernity*. London: Routledge.

Mangham, I. (1995) 'MacIntyre and the manager', *Organization*, 2 (2): 181–204.

Marsden, D. and Richardson, R. (1994) 'Performing for pay? The effects of "merit pay" on motivation in a public service', *British Journal of Industrial Relations*, 32 (2): 243–261.

Miller, P. and Rose, N. (1990) 'Governing economic life', *Economy & Society*, 19 (1): 1–31.

Minson, J. (1991) *Bureaucratic Culture and the Management of Sexual Harassment*, Institute for Cultural Policy Studies, Occasional Paper 12. Brisbane: Griffith University.

Minson, J. (1993) *Questions of Conduct*. Basingstoke: Macmillan.

Minson, J. (1997) 'Ethics in state service', in B. Hindess and M. Dean (eds) *Governing Australia*. Sydney: Cambridge University Press.

Moe, R. (1994) '"The Re-Inventing Government" exercise: misinterpreting the problem, misjudging the consequences', *Public Administration Review*, 54 (2): 111–22.

Morgan, G. (1991) *Riding the Waves of Change*. San Francisco: Jossey-Bass.

Mulhall, D. and Swift, A. (1992) *Liberals and Communitarians*. Oxford: Basil Blackwell.

Nash, L. (1995) 'Whose character? A response to Mangham's "MacIntyre and the Manager"', *Organization*, 2 (2): 226–32.

Newfield, C. (1995) 'Corporate pleasures for a corporate planet', *Social Text*, 13 (3): 31–44.

Ohmae, K. (1990) *The Borderless World*. London: Collins.

Ohmae, K. (1993) 'The rise of the region state', *Foreign Affairs*, 72 (2): 78–87.

O'Kane, R. (1997) 'Modernity, the Holocaust and politics', *Economy & Society*, 26 (1): 43–61.

Osborne, D. and Gaebler, T. (1992) *Re-Inventing Government*. Reading, MA: Addison-Wesley.

O'Toole, B. (1990) 'T.H. Green and the ethics of senior officials in British central government', *Public Administration*, 68: 337–352.

O' Toole, B. (1993) 'The loss of purity: the corruption of public service in Britain', *Public Policy and Administration*, 8 (2): 1–6.

O'Toole, B. (1997) 'Ethics in government', in B. Thompson and F. Ridley (eds) *Under the Scott-light: British Government seen through the Scott Report*. Oxford: Oxford University Press. pp. 130–42.

O'Toole, B. (1998) '"We walk by faith not by sight": the ethic of public service', in M. Hunt and B. O'Toole (eds) *Reform, Ethics and Leadership in Public Service*. Aldershot: Ashgate.

O'Toole, B. and Chapman, R.A. (1994) 'Parliamentary accountability', in B. O'Toole and G. Jordan (eds) *Next Steps: Improving Management in Government*. Aldershot: Dartmouth.

Pattison, S. (1997) *The Faith of the Managers*. London: Cassell.

Parker, R. (1993) *The Administrative Vocation*. Sydney: Hale & Iremonger.

Peters, B.G. (1993) 'Managing the hollow state', in K. Eliassen and J.C. Kooiman (eds) *Managing Public Organizations*. London: Sage. pp. 46–57.

Peters, B.G. and Savoie, D. (1995) 'Civil Service reform: misdiagnosing the patient', *Public Administration Review*, 54 (5): 418–25.

Peters, T. (1987) *Thriving on Chaos*. Basingstoke: Macmillan.

Peters, T. (1992) *Liberation Management*. Basingstoke: Macmillan.

Peters, T. (1994) *The Pursuit of Wow! Every Person's Guide to Topsy-Turvy Times*. New York: Random House.

Peters, T. and Waterman, R.H. (1982) *In Search of Excellence*. New York: Harper & Row.

Plowden, F. (1994) 'Public interests the public services serve: efficiency and other values', *Australian Journal of Public Administration*, 53 (3): 304–12.

Pollitt, C. (1990) *Managerialism and the Public Services: the Anglo-American Experience*. Oxford: Blackwell.

Pollitt, C. (1995) 'Justification by works or by faith? Evaluating the new public management', *Evaluation: the International Journal of Theory, Research & Practice*, 1 (2):133–54.

Power, M. (1997) *The Audit Society*. Oxford: Oxford University Press.

Pringle, R. (1989) *Secretaries Talk*. London: Verso.

Quinlan, M. (1994) 'Changing patterns in government business', *Public Policy & Administration*, 9 (1): 27–34.

Reed, M. (1992) *The Sociology of Organizations*. Hemel Hempstead: Harvester Wheatsheaf.

Reich, R. (1990) 'Who is us?' *Harvard Business Review*, Jan.-Feb.: 53–64.

Rhodes, R. (1994) 'The hollowing out of the state: the changing nature of public service in Britain', *Political Quarterly*, 65 (2): 138–51.

Ridley, F. (1996) 'Reinventing British government', *Parliamentary Affairs*, 387–400.

Rohr, J. (1979) *Ethics for Bureaucrats*. New York: Marcel Dekker.

Rohr, J. (1986) *To Run a Constitution: the Legitimacy of the Administrative State*. Lawrence, KS: University of Kansas Press.

Rohr, J. (1988) 'Bureaucratic morality in the United States', *International Political Science Review*, 9 (3): 167–78.

Rohr, J. (1989) 'Reason of state as political morality: a benign view', in N. Dale Wright (ed.) *Papers on the Ethics of Administration*. Provo, UT: Brigham Young University.

Rohr, J. (1995) *Founding Republics in France and America: a Study in Constitutional Governance*. Lawrence, KS: University of Kansas Press.

Rorty, A.-O. (1988) *Mind in Action*. Boston: Beacon Press.

Rose, N. (1990) *Governing the Soul*. London: Routledge.

Royal Institute of Public Administration Working Group (1987) *Top Jobs in Whitehall: Appointments and Promotions in the Senior Civil Service*. London: RIPA.

Russell, C. (1993) *Academic Freedom*. London: Routledge.

Sabel, C. (1991) 'Moebius strip organizations and open labour markets: some consequences of the reintegration of conception and execution in a volatile economy', in P. Bourdieu and J. Coleman (eds) *Social Theory for a Changing Society*. Boulder, CO: Westview Press. pp. 23–54.

Salaman, G. (1997) 'Culturing production', in P. du Gay (ed.) *Production of Culture/Cultures of Production*. London: Sage.

Saunders, D. (1991) *Authorship and Copyright*. London: Routledge.

Saunders, D. (1997) *The Anti-Lawyers: Religion and the Critics of Law and State*. London: Routledge.

Savage, M. and Witz, A. (eds) (1994) *Gender and Bureaucracy*. Oxford: Basil Blackwell.

Schmitt, C. (1986) *Political Romanticism*. Cambridge, MA: MIT Press.

Scott, A. (1996) 'Bureaucratic revolutions and free market utopias', *Economy and Society*, 25 (1): 89–110.

Scott, R. (1996) 'Ministerial accountability', *Public Law*, Autumn: 410–426.

Self, P. (1993) *Government by the Market? The Politics of Public Choice*. Basingstoke: Macmillan.

Self, P. (1997) 'What's happened to administrative theories?' *Public Policy & Administration*, 12 (1): 8–20.

Ståhlberg, K. (1987) 'The politicization of public administration: notes on the concept, causes and consequences of politicization', *International Review of Administrative Sciences*, 53: 364–82.

Streeck, W. (1996) 'Public power beyond the nation-state: the case of the European Community', in R. Boyer and D. Drache (eds) *States against Markets*. London: Routledge. pp. 299–315.

Thatcher, M. (1993) *The Downing Street Years*. London: HarperCollins.

Tribe, F. (1971) 'Efficiency in the public services' (1949) in R.A. Chapman and A. Dunsire (eds) *Style in Administration*. London: Allen & Unwin. pp. 146–160.

Trollope, A. (1982) *Phineas Finn*. Oxford: Oxford University Press.

Turner, C. (1992) *Modernity and Politics in the Work of Max Weber*. London: Routledge.

Waldegrave, W. (1993) 'The reality of reform and accountability in today's public service', Public Finance Foundation/BDO Consulting inaugural lecture, 5 July.

Walzer, M. (1984) 'Liberalism and the art of separation', *Political Theory*, 12 (3): 315–30.

Weber, M. (1930) *The Protestant Ethic and the Spirit of Capitalism*. Oxford: Basil Blackwell.

Weber, M. (1978) *Economy & Society*, 2 vols. Los Angeles: University of California Press.

Weber, M. (1989) 'Science as a vocation', in P. Lassman, I. Velody and H. Martins (eds) *Max Weber's 'Science as a Vocation'*. London: Unwin Hyman.

Weber, M. (1994a) 'Parliament and government in Germany under a new political order', in P. Lassman and R. Speirs (eds) *Weber: Political Writings*. Cambridge: Cambridge University Press.

Weber, M. (1994b) 'The profession and vocation of politics', in P. Lassman and R. Speirs (eds) *Weber: Political Writings*. Cambridge: Cambridge University Press.

Weinrib, E. (1988) 'Legal formalism: on the immanent rationality of law', *Yale Law Journal*, 97 (6): 949–1016.

Wheare, K. (1955) *Government by Committee*. Oxford: Clarendon Press.

Willmott, H. (1993) 'Ignorance is strength; slavery is freedom: managing culture in modern organizations', *Journal of Management Studies*, 30 (4): 512–52.

Wilson, W. (1887) 'The study of administration', *Political Science Quarterly*, 2: 197–222.

Zifcak, S. (1994) *New Managerialism*. Milton Keynes: Open University Press.

Index